Christians and the Future of Social Democracy

Christians and the Future of Social Democracy

edited by
Michael H. Taylor

G.W. & A. Hesketh, Ormskirk and Northridge

First published 1982 by G.W. & A. Hesketh, P.O. Box 8, Aughton Street, Ormskirk, Lancashire L39 5HH, Great Britain, and of 18765 Tuba Street, Northridge, California 91324, U.S.A.

Design by G.W. & A. Hesketh, Ormskirk, L39 5HH.
Photosetting & Origination by Lloyd Williams, 22 Union Street, Southport.
Printed and bound in Great Britain by A. Wheaton & Co. Ltd., Hennock Road, Exeter EX2 8RP.

ISBN 0 905777 32 8 Hardback

Contents

Acknowledgements

Thanks are due to all who shared in the consultation held in Manchester in March 1980 out of which this volume arose, especially to John Elford who helped to organise it and acted as *rapporteur* and Jack Keiser the secretary, to the contributors for their patience and co-operation, and to Brenda Peck and Rhoda Smith for typing various manuscripts.

Michael H. Taylor
Northern Baptist College, Manchester, January 1981

Contributors

Paul Abrecht. Director of the Department on Church and Society, World Council of Churches since 1954.

John R. Atherton. Joint Director of the William Temple Foundation, Manchester, since 1979 and chairman of the Board for Social Responsibility of the Diocese of Manchester since 1980.

Edwin Barker. Secretary of the Church of England Board for Social Responsibility 1961-73 and the Bishop of Coventry's Council for Social Responsibility since 1973.

Duncan B. Forrester. Professor of Christian Ethics and Practical Theology at New College in the University of Edinburgh since 1978.

Gerard J. Hughes, S.J. Lecturer in Ethics since 1970 and Head of the Department of Philosophy at Heythrop College in the University of London since 1973.

Kenneth Medhurst. Senior Lecturer in Government since 1974 and Reader since 1980 in the University of Manchester; appointed Professor of Political Studies in the University of Stirling in 1981.

Ronald H. Preston. Samuel Ferguson Professor of Social and Pastoral Theology in the University of Manchester from 1970 until 1980.

Michael H. Taylor. Principal of the Northern Baptist College, Manchester and Lecturer in Ethics and Theology in the University of Manchester since 1969.

M.M. Thomas. Director of the Christian Institute for the Study of Religion and Society, Bangalore, India, from 1960 until 1975 and chairman of the Central Committee of the World Council of Churches from 1968 until 1975.

1

Introduction

Michael H. Taylor

Writing in the early weeks of 1981 in the North West of England there seems little need to justify a discussion of the future of social democracy. Democracy in our society is closely tied up with capitalism and both appear to be in trouble at the present time, to put the matter no more strongly than that. Some would see a real crisis looming not far ahead heralded by record post-war unemployment figures, workers being left with little choice but to participate in wage restraint and the loss of jobs under threat of even more closures and redundancies, revived talk of 'two nations' and new political alignments, and the continuing apparent inability of government to solve our long-term economic problems, to mention only some features of the contemporary scene. All of these issues and some of the intractable underlying problems are discussed in this book by Christians who firmly believe that they are required by their faith to get to grips with them as creatively as they can along with everyone else.

Acting on the same conviction, the Department of Social and Pastoral Theology of the University of Manchester has organised a number of consultations since 1974 bringing the insights of the Christian tradition to bear on issues of public concern and attempting a contribution to the formation of public opinion especially where it was divided and confused. *Perspectives on Strikes* edited by Ronald Preston, London SCM Press, 1975 arose out of the consultation held in 1974 and *The Coming Penal Crisis* edited by A.E. Bottoms (Professor of Criminology and Director of the Centre for Criminological Studies, University of Sheffield) and Ronald Preston, Edinburgh, Scottish Academic Press 1980, out of one held in 1978. A consultation on 'leisure' was held in 1976 but no publication followed.

When it came to making arrangements for a fourth consultation (held in Manchester in March 1980) there seemed to be good reasons for departing at certain points from what were becoming established procedures. On previous occasions the basic position paper, to which all other contributors were asked to refer, had been written by someone not belonging to the Department and not professionally engaged in the study and teaching of theology. On this occasion, the then Head of the Department, Professor R.H. Preston, had just published his Maurice Lectures for 1977 on "Religion and the Persistence of

Capitalism" in a volume with that title (London, SCM Press 1979) and it looked to his colleagues like a good point of departure for a timely discussion on the future of social democracy, especially as he himself is persuaded that many of the economic issues of the day require of us political decisions.

Ronald Preston was also due to retire from his professorship at the end of the academic year in which the consultation was due to be held. His colleagues wished to honour him in some suitable way, not least in a way which he himself would enjoy. The result was the second departure from normal procedures. The Department has always made a serious attempt to ensure that consultations were inter-disciplinary in character because it believes that that is one of the essential characteristics of the way in which Christians should reflect on social and ethical issues. One of the main reasons for issuing invitations on this occasion however was that those invited had worked with Ronald Preston at one time or another during his distinguished career. The result was a consultation and a list of contributors to this volume which left a good deal to be desired in terms of inter-disciplinary balance but a group of Ronald Preston's friends and collaborators who, almost by virtue of that fact, shared his concerns if not always his opinions and were well equipped by their learning and experience to contribute to the debate.

At the consultation itself each of the papers, circulated and read beforehand, was introduced briefly by its author and then discussed. It has since been revised for publication. There was one exception. M.M. Thomas, the Indian theologian, a friend and colleague of Professor Preston's from early days together in the Student Christian Movement and, later, in the affairs of the World Council of Churches, wrote a paper but was unable to come to the consultation or subsequently revise his paper in the light of the comments made. Distance defeated us. Since his paper added an important dimension to the discussion, a shorter version of it has been included as an Appendix to this book. The publication in 1980 of the Brandt Report *North-South: A Programme for Survival* reinforces its relevance.

In preparing this publication the editor has had to bear in mind that the reader could hardly be expected to read Ronald Preston's book, *Religion and the Persistence of Capitalism* in order to make sense of this one. In Chapter 2 therefore the argument of that book is restated insofar as it is germane to the arguments of this one, but the proportions of it are different and at certain points it is taken further in response to what others have since written and said. In particular, when discussing a way forward for our Western type of political democracy, it takes up the themes of justice (and equality), participation and sustainability, brought to our attention by the Church and Society studies of the World Council of Churches.

It may be useful to indicate briefly the contents of the other six chapters which follow Ronald Preston's.

Duncan Forrester is concerned with the distinctive contribution of the theologian to discussions of this kind — how he addresses himself to social and political issues. He finds the present performance of British social theology unimpressive and suspects that the inter-disciplinary approach going back to J.H. Oldham may leave the theologian doing little more than organising discussion between experts whose opinions he may think of more highly than he ought to think. Wary of applying Biblical and Christian insights too directly, Forrester examines the concept of 'middle axioms', informed by the faith and by the facts and attempting to establish an agreed middle ground between very general insights and principles, and specific programmes for action. Acknowledging the fruitfulness of this approach, Forrester suspects that it is too ready to underestimate the extent to which the experts' accounts of their own disciplines are influenced by the social context out of which they come and to assume the given, *a priori* nature of Christian faith. He wants to see this kind of Christian contribution complemented by the insights which can only arise out of Christian action where, by attempting to be faithful to the Gospel, we discover what the Gospel is. The vices of the social scientists who cannot see things straight because of their particular involvements thus become the virtues of the Christian activists, given the right commitments; though presumably if their committed action is to be at all reflective they must soon be involved in intellectual disciplines similar to those which make use of middle axioms, relating existing theological insights to contemporary details.

Gerard Hughes, in a tightly argued paper, takes up the familiar complaint about the way in which capitalism fosters, not to say relies upon competition, acquisitiveness and self-interest. It is antipathetic to the Christian ideal of human perfection. This raises questions about the relationship between capitalism and egoism on the one hand (are they inseparable?) and between egoism and Christianity on the other. Hughes deals mainly with the latter, maintaining an important distinction between the motivation and the justification which egoism offers for what we ought to do. Does it for example appeal to or ignore and even undermine our altruistic inclinations; and if it is not to be dismissed as a non-moral view or as mere expediency, can egoism ever supply in Christian eyes an adequate basis for morality? He concludes that egoism and Christianity are not incompatible in any crude or obvious sense, and that Christianity need not therefore be opposed to capitalism on those grounds, rather on the grounds that it tends, if it does, inexorably to create situations of injustice.

Edwin Barker underlines the importance for democracy of an emphasis on obligations as well as rights, and a sense of personal responsibility among its members for everybody's welfare expressed mainly through participation but also, where individuals and groups have considerable power, by restraint. Writing more informally than others, and from a local vantage point as secretary of a diocesan council for social responsibility, he discusses some of the difficulties that hinder responsible participation in such areas as local government, the social services, education and industry, and the problems created by size, departmentalisation, professionalism, rising unemployment and the powerlessness which many experience in our society. Barker also reviews a number of suggestions for maximising opportunities for the exercise of personal responsibility. These include devolution of powers from central to local government and from statutory to voluntary bodies, co-ownership, and the fostering of more appreciative attitudes to 'work' which is not productive in the most obvious sense. Examples of what has been achieved on the international scene through voluntary and personal service give him hope for the future.

Paul Abrecht brings to the discussion the wider perspectives of ecumenical debate and the World Council of Churches MIT (Massachusetts Institute of Technology) Conference on "Faith, Science and the Future" with which he has been so closely involved. He examines the concept of 'sustainability' and offers a mainly negative critique, shared by insiders as well as outsiders, of Western-style capitalist economies. He articulates the fear that they are 'unsustainable' as a matter of fact because, for example, non-renewable resources will run out so that economic growth cannot be sustained (a fear discussed by Ronald Preston who has more confidence that new technological breakthroughs will solve this range of problems). But the main criticism is that capitalist economies cannot be sustained on moral grounds. It is increasingly difficult to argue in their favour when they are tied to a technological revolution which is too risky and beyond social control, and to an affluent life-style which is maintained only at the expense of the less developed parts of the world. The dream of securing human happiness by economic growth and the achievements of science and technology is fading, and at present there is no compelling vision to take its place. The search for a society which is 'sustainable' as well as 'just' and 'participatory' is equally a priority for socialist countries which shared the earlier optimism about what science and technology could achieve; and for Third World countries which, although they may suspect they are now to be denied what others already enjoy, are nevertheless part of an international system which makes them increasingly dependent on Western technology.

Kenneth Medhurst, a political scientist, analyses the present but turns towards the future as well. He recognises that our democratic institutions are under strain caused above all by our economic problems, and that some of the trends which these problems have provoked, such as attempts to plan the economy, improve industrial relations, and regulate wages by bringing government into the bargaining process, have not made for greater equality. Where rising expectations are disappointed as they must be, there is frustration; and where traditional restraints, mutual trust and shared moral understandings are eroded, potentially destructive forces are at work. What alternative options are open to us? Medhurst reviews three: reducing the role of the state; the command economy; and the incorporation of major interest groups into a decision making process presided over by the state. He then commits himself to a fourth: the fraternal society, in the hope that the comparatively neglected notion of 'fraternity' can ease the tension between the more familiar ideals of 'liberty' and 'equality'. He concludes by indicating some practical policy implications such as a diffusion of decision making responsibilities which balances centralised government agencies with de-centralised ones; industrial democracy as a prelude to greater productivity and the redistribution of wealth; and equal educational opportunities which may at last erode the deeply entrenched class structure of our society accompanied as it is by unequal access to society's material and cultural rewards.

John Atherton regards the persistence of poverty and inequality as a challenge to social democracy and the Christian churches alike, since both say they want a more just society but apparently form an unholy alliance which condones and even contrives to maintain the status quo. He examines the nature of poverty as, for example, relative deprivation, and its extent in Britain which is surprising. When it comes to seeking explanations, the culprits range from a rigid class system, through public attitudes to the poor, to their lack of economic and political power as compared to their civil and political rights. For Atherton the way forward involves a vision inspired by moral imperatives and tested by the criteria of justice, participation and sustainability. It must be matched by a programme which effectively achieves the priorities which the vision requires. He favours a command economy carefully understood, a strong interventionist state, a radical extension of participation and power sharing, and an advance beyond conditional welfare for the few to the collective provision of basic human needs. If the Church is to contribute to all this it must advance its own social thinking by re-examining amongst other things its philanthropic response to the poor which may uphold rather than reform a defective social order, and at least in the case of the Church of England, it must put an end to its identification with middle class individualism.

Agreement and Disagreement

Too much should not be claimed for the coherence of a volume of essays. The writers of these belong together in the social democratic tradition. They believe the economic activity of the market place should be controlled for social purposes by democratic political institutions. They are not in entire agreement over whether capitalism has a future or whether there is much to be gained from continued economic growth.

At least five of the essays however are agreed (and there is no reason to suppose that the others disagree) that our Western societies ought not to continue as they are. They are already changing, not always for the better, and they need to change a good deal more. Justice, equality, sustainability and participation (for all the difficulty of introducing it into areas where it has scarcely existed before) emerge as shared ideals.

Added to this is a large measure of agreement as to where the battle should be joined, interestingly so in the attention given for example to a more equal social provision for human needs, to be enjoyed by everybody as of right. The most striking divergence of opinion is over the command economy which for Preston and Medhurst solves few problems but which Atherton thinks worthy of a more sympathetic hearing. His approach is more ruthless than that of the rest.

There is of course another area of common ground and it was mentioned at the outset. All the contributions to this volume wish to bring the insights of the Christian tradition to bear responsibly on the crucial issues of our life together, learning from everyone else whilst making their own contribution, and respecting what both faith and careful empirical analysis requires of them. This shared endeavour is exciting as faith comes alive in the modern world. It is also perilous since the Christian is no more guaranteed against error than anyone else and unsound judgments in these matters can cost lives and a great deal of human happiness. Given our imperfections and limitations there is bound to be disagreement about what policies should now be pursued but failure to agree is less worrying than failure to tackle pertinent isues and raise the right questions. This we hope we have done.

2
Capitalism, Democracy and Christianity

Ronald H. Preston

Capitalism has spread over the world and is associated with different political systems, but in its origin and innovative forms it has been associated with the growth of our Western type of political democracy. A question mark is put against the future of both as we near the end of this century. It is therefore natural to link a discussion of the two together. But what of the third term in the title? Christianity has lived under many different economic and social systems in the past, and does to-day; nevertheless it also has been associated with capitalism and democracy,[1] because it was out of the only civilisation which has been deeply influenced by Christianity, that of Western Europe and its offshoots, that both of them have arisen. Christianity has had a deeply formulative role in our culture, and still has a considerable one. The number of Christians is significant, and churches are substantial institutions. References to it crop up in surprising places. For instance, as this chapter is being written in the summer of 1980 the Conservative Centre for Policy Studies has just issued a pamphlet by Nigel Lawson, MP, *The New Conservatives,* in which he says "if Socialism is the creed of the perfectibility of man, Conservatism is the creed of original sin and the politics of imperfection". (We shall have reason later to query this notion). There are therefore good historical and contemporary reasons for treating capitalism, democracy and Christianity together.

Part of a concern for a sound Christian social witness, shared by all the contributors to this book, is for a proper appropriation of distinctively Christian insights, but in doing that an equal concern arises, that of relating these to other views of man and society which command the allegiance of men and women to-day. Part of a Christian understanding of life is that God does not put us in the social order primarily as Christians, but as human beings. The Christendom situation in which there was a broadly unitary view of life, and that a Christian one, was but a temporary episode in one civilisation in human history, and only then covered a part of the globe (though a dynamic part). Remnants of it survive, but more of the outward appearance than the inward reality. Attempts to re-create an equivalent situation in Moslem countries, notably Iran, attract attention at the moment, but their long-term prospects are poor. For the most part, and certainly in the old Christendom countries, we live in a plural society. Christians are inextricably involved in the bundle of humanity with those of other faiths and none, and their understanding of God must lead them to believe that God wills the well-being of humanity as such, and not only of Christians, and it must lead them to seek some common basis and commitments which will further that well-being. They will want to find allies among adherents of other faiths and of various types of humanist outlook (not excluding types of Marxism), by seeking for a level where their convictions overlap with some of the convictions of adherents of these other faiths and ideologies.

This book has a Western background. The group behind it are almost all citizens of the United Kingdom and, though they want to look at issues in the broadest perspective, it would be folly to suppose that they can divest themselves of their political, social and cultural background and become universal men. That is why the contributions of M.M. Thomas and Paul Abrecht are particularly valuable. Nevertheless attention is focused on the problems of capitalism and democracy in the contemporary British context. As time has gone on the interlocking of the two has become closer. One of the conclusions of this book is that the attempt to isolate the institutions of capitalism as an economic system is doomed to failure, and that the economic issues which present themselves today require political as much as, if not more than, economic decisions, if only because of the outlook and situation of the electorates which Western governments have to accommodate.

Capitalism itself, however, is more than a technical system of markets and the like for managing the economy; it has carried with it an over-all ideology which brought a crusading zeal in its earlier and classical days against what it regarded as effete privilege and sloth. It has never been without exponents of a similar zeal in these later days against efforts to use the state to manage the economy, especially in a socialist direction; indeed there has lately been an increase in such attacks. As soon, however, as we are dealing with an ideology it is necessary to appraise it in the light of other ideologies or 'faiths'; I use both terms in the sense of overall interpretations of life. Those Christians who have been critical of capitalism have fastened on the possessive individualism it stood for as a false view of life. It was from a discussion of the Christian critiques of capitalism that the discussions on the future of social democracy embodied in this book began.

Some Related Issues

The title of my F.D. Maurice Lectures of 1977, "Religion and the Persistence of Capitalism", refers to a continuing Christian critique of capitalism whose progress can be marked by two previous books. The first is R.H. Tawney's *Religion and the Rise of Capitalism* of 1925, which has become a classic of British twentieth century historical writing, and has been reprinted many times and translated into many languages. The second is V.A. Demant's *Religion and the Decline of Capitalism,* published in 1951. It seemed to me, after another quarter of a century of unprecedented economic growth in the Western world, that the decline of capitalism had been prematurely heralded in 1951, and that it was time to look at the matter again. Hence the title of the Maurice Lectures. Two things were involved. The continuing Christian critique of capitalism; and an empirical analysis of the current state of affairs. The two are, of course, connected but they are not the same thing. The first involves a more theoretical critique of attitudes, presumptions and pre-suppositions; the second a more empirical analysis of 'what is going on'. Many Christian critiques of capitalism have run the two together, and assumed that because it should be theologically condemned it must be breaking down, and have seized uncritically on any handy theory which purports to show that it is breaking down. Connections are not so simple. It is a hazardous matter to understand one's own times, more difficult than an historical study such as Tawney's, since it involves the study of a whole culture and society in which everything relates together. It is only possible by drawing on much corporate private discussion, in addition to as many published studies of the contemporary world as one person can master amid many other pre-occupations. As far as the two sides of the task are concerned it would be possible, for example, to conclude on the one hand that capitalism is flourishing, and on the other to approve or condemn it; or that it is weakening, and either needs supporting or hastening to its end. And various intermediate positions are conceivable.

In brief my conclusion was to agree with the Christian critique that its overall philosophy should be condemned, but also that some of its key institutions are of permanent usefulness to any economy. As to its current state of health, my conclusion was that it is changing its nature in some important respects in advanced industrial societies, so that we are faced with a continuum of positions between what is often called a social market economy and a democratic socialist one, rather than with clear cut alternatives. For the problems raised by advanced industrial economies are complex and occasioned by their relative success. This analysis is fortified by a comparison with what is theoretically opposite to a capitalist economy, a centralised command economy of a socialist type, which shews that very similar problems are raised, and that it is no better at solving most of them.

In an important sense the Christian critique of capitalism has now become part of the wider ecumenical discussion, through the World Council of Churches, of the Just, Participatory and Sustainable Society. This is referred to in the Maurice Lectures, but since they were given the important world conference sponsored by the World Council of Churches (WCC) on "Faith, Science and the Future" was held at Massachusetts Institute of Technology in July 1979.[2] Paul Abrecht was more responsible for it than any other single person, and this adds to the significance of his chapter in this book. The global context of these issues brings home the necessity of facing up to the responsibilities of the relatively affluent world (to which we belong) for the two thirds of the world which is not affluent, when pre-occupation with the inflationary and unemployment problems of our advanced industrial society can lead us to forget them. The contribution of M.M. Thomas reinforces this. Even so, since selectivity is essential, the main focus of this book remains, as already indicated, that of the West. The WCC discussion has taken up further issues, which began by raising the problem of the relation of human beings to the rest of nature, and has spread out to a consideration of the whole ideology of modern science, and its embodiment in structures of technological power, chiefly military power, which are in danger of getting out of our control. The theological and philosophical issues of the relation of man to nature are hardly touched on here;[3] but Abrecht, in the course of his chapter, raises the issue of science as power, though it is not the focus of the discussion in this book.

It should also be noted that since the persistence of capitalism began to be queried in the light of the Christian religion, the persistence of religion itself (including the Christian religion) has come to be queried by some sociologists of religion. I refer to the debate on secularisation, its origin, nature, theological status and likely outcome. That, again, is something which cannot be covered in this book.[4] Suffice it to say that in my view the theory that there is an overall process at work in human history leading via industrialisation and urbanisation to a form of secularisation which means the withering away of any or all religions has not been demonstrated, nor do I think it is demonstrable. One of the themes of the Maurice Lectures is that all these over-all theories of society are unfounded, and implicit in them is the conviction that it is extremely unlikely that such overall theories of society can be established. Sociologists are less confident these days of the possibility of doing so than were the founding fathers of sociology in the nineteenth century. To say this, of course, at once puts a question mark against a central claim of Marxism, by far the most influential of such alleged scientific theories. I do not think there are any grounds for supposing that either capitalist economies or their polar opposite command economies are inevitably collapsing through their inherent contradictions, nor that human history in general is necessarily moving forward on some indefinitely forecastable path, nor that religion in particular as part of human life is on the way out. However these are issues related to the theme of this book which need to be noted but cannot be pursued in the present context. Everything cannot be dealt with at once. So I turn to a re-statement of the argument to which the rest of the chapters of this book are a response.

Christian Criticisms of Capitalism

The capitalist economy is often referred to as a market economy because the device of the free market is at the heart of it. Any society has to solve a basic economic problem, how to allocate resources which are relatively scarce compared with the many possible uses of them. Which goods and services are to be produced? How to match the demand for them with the supply of them? How to distribute the rewards of producing them? How to allocate resources between present and future consumption, that is to say between current and capital goods?

To an economist the real cost of something is the alternatives which have been foregone among all the things that might have been chosen instead of what was in fact chosen. The only purely *economic* value is efficiency in the use of resources, that is to say not using more scarce resources than are necessary. This is a value other things being equal, and it is perfectly possible that society may decide that other values are to a greater or lesser extent more important to it than economic efficiency. For instance the pursuit of it regardless of all else might well lead to inhumanity in the treatment of certain individuals and groups. It is, however, wise for society to be aware of the economic cost of what it is doing, and to know what aims are economically compatible and what incompatible with one another. For instance a lot of people at the present moment want full employment, a stable price level and free collective bargaining when the three are incompatible.

The device of the free market as the lynch pin of capitalism was to create a system, set in a basic framework of law and order, where these basic economic decisions were made automatically by the play of the market. Independent producers reacted to the making of profits and losses in the market as a result of decisions made by myriads of consumers deciding for themselves how to spend their money. Central authority had little to do with it, apart from providing the framework of law and order. Of course things were never as simple as that. Some collective needs, like defence, cannot be provided in this way; and it was soon discovered that protection against cholera could not be, and that a considerable public health system was needed. Also in practice working people banded themselves together in trade unions to protect themselves against the icy indifference of the market to basic human needs, especially as the economy developed in a roughly ten year cycle of boom and slump, against which otherwise they had no protection. Also, on the management and ownership side, there were constant attempts to protect particular firms and industries against changing economic demands, by tariffs and quotas, or to keep out competitors by cartels, oligopolies and monopolies. And overall there were the great inequalities of income, magnified by the even greater inequalities of wealth brought about by inheritance possibilities, that distorted the market by allowing the wealthy to attract resources to luxury articles whilst the poor had not enough money to bid for necessities. All this is familiar, but it is necessary to rehearse it once again in order to understand the first Christian criticisms of it, and because it is still the language of free enterprise talk to-day. In Max Weber's term it is an 'ideal type', that is to say it is a social institution considered in the light of its distinguishing characteristic in a 'pure' form, even though the form is never in practice expressed in that pure way. The ideological justification of the free market is generally thought to go back to Adam Smith, who was well aware of its possible defects, but thought that it was the least bad way of running an economic system. Moreover he held that an 'invisible hand' ensures that if everyone pursues his own self-interest the result will be what the common good requires. After the middle of the nineteenth century a further and more brutal argument was brought in to justify the free market, a kind of social Darwinism which held that it was by this device that 'nature' eliminated the economically unfit.

The first Christian arguments against all this, under the influence of F.D. Maurice, were to say that the assertion that these economic laws, setting everyone in competition with everyone else, are a divine institution, is a lie; so is the idea that an invisible hand brings general good our of individual self-seeking. It was further thought that the making of profits as the criterion for production is immoral; in the phrase commonly used, production should be for use and not for profit. Allied with this was fundamental criticism of the appeal to self-interest as the main motive in life; rather service to one's neighbour should be the motive. These points have been repeated again and again by Christian socialist groups, and are still made to-day. This is not the occasion to discuss them fully, or others to be made shortly, since this chapter can be no more than a general survey of issues. Suffice it to say that they do not face up to the fundamental economic problems of any society in the allocation of resources, nor do they make clear what is unChristian in competition as such, provided it is set in a basically just social framework. There is also a distinction to be made between profit as a directive which decides to what ends scarce resources are to be devoted, and profit as an incentive or motivator. However even the latter need not be *private* profit; it could, to take one example, be part of a co-operative enterprise; but even if it is appropriated privately there seems nothing unChristian in making a surplus, or profit, out of one's activities, whether they be in the form of wages, dividends, royalties, patents, or preaching fees! Moreover the talk of service as a motive seems to pre-suppose that society could be run as if all were active Christians, because it seems to suppose that an appeal to self-interest is unChristian. This brings us to the points discussed very fully in the chapter by Gerard Hughes. There has been a long discussion in the course of Christian history on the place of self-interest in the Christian life, especially how to interpret Jesus' summary of the Jewish Torah in the form of the second of the two great commandments, "You shall love your neighbour as yourself". It is well known that the great moralist Bishop Butler in the eighteenth century held that if a person truly acted from "cool self-interest" he would arrive at the same line of conduct as if he had acted according to what benevolence required.[5] Hughes does not go quite so far. He holds that there is little to choose between what an altruistic motivation and an egoistic one would lead to; but he holds that there is *some* difference when one considers a theory of social justice based on needs. He concludes that one can rehabilitate egoism, and capitalism with it, quite a long way, but not far enough.

In fact the situation is worse than that because capitalism, as usually presented, appeals to a crude form of egoism in the form of a competitive individualism which ignores the social matrix of human life, as will be mentioned shortly. Meanwhile it should be noted that the gross inequalities of wealth and income to which it gives rise, and which have proved very hard to modify, undermine the pure theory of the market. The story of the last hundred years has been one of modifying the distribution of net income to produce the institution of the Welfare State. This has still some way to go; it is largely a re-distribution of income within the working class, whilst the relative income positions of the lower paid worker has hardly changed at all. Wealth has proved even more intractable. All we have done since the end of the Second World War is to re-distribute the wealth of the top 1% among the top 5%. Fuller details and references to all this are given in the Maurice Lectures, and in John Atherton's essay in this volume; indeed there are many sources available. Inequalities of wealth and income mean inequalities of power and consideration. There is no divine hand bringing the common good out of competitive individualism. In so far as the socialist case is concerned with a more egalitarian society its case against capitalism as we have known it so far, stands, even if the other criticisms I have mentioned are much too simple. Moreover we are now the first generation to be confronted by a global frame of reference. References to a 'village world' and 'space ship earth' have become commonplace; they have their limitations, but they also make a fundamental point. Consideration of human welfare and social justice cannot stop at national frontiers. Christians cannot believe that it is God's will that the 'two thirds world' should live in abject poverty whilst the 'one third world' lives in relative abundance. What is the responsibility of the relatively rich and how should they discharge it? The rich are usually not quick to pursue justice for the poor unless the poor are in a position to put pressure on them. One of the worries to-day is that the poor countries are lacking in economic and political weapons. This is the issue to which M.M. Thomas' chapter is addressed.

I have mentioned so far the rather simplistic traditional Christian criticisms of capitalism. A much more serious one is that it is cutting off the moral bough it is sitting on. This is a major point made by Demant. He pointed out that the competitive individualism of the free market ideologies pre-supposed centuries of Christian teaching on the organic relation of persons in society; what it assumed as 'natural', in the sense of happening automatically and not requiring human ordering, was in fact a complex net of non-contractual moral, legal and religious bonds. It did nothing to foster these, and in fact actively undermined them. It has been parasitic on moral resources which it weakens. Edwin Barker's chapter pre-supposes, if what he wants is to be achieved, a generally accepted view of the nature of society and a common acceptance of the basis of social cohesion within which conflicts of interest can be expressed and dealt with. He points out that a sophisticated industrial society is increasingly vulnerable to groups who are tempted to use their power without prudence and proportion, be they doctors or lorry drivers. This increasing moral weakness is being realised by nonChristian writers. Fred Hirsch, in a book to be mentioned shortly, finds three sources of moral renewal in society: traditional social ties, religious teaching and a sense of civic duty. The first is growingly eroded by the speed of social change and increased nobility; the second he hardly thinks worth discussing; that leaves only the third, and a frail hope it is. Again Bryan Wilson in discussing religion and secularisation raises the question, Where is there a source of disinterested goodwill that society needs? In a book of 1966, while not a believer himself, he thought that religious sects could be such a source, but ten years later he was even more convinced that all forms of religion are on the way out in urbanised, industrialised societies and, since he does not like what he sees in these societies, he is pessimistic about them because of their lack of moral resources.[6]

There is, then, a serious case against capitalism at this point, advanced by both Christians and non-Christians. As already mentioned, some Christians who have been convinced of the moral wrongness of capitalism, usually on the more *simpliste* grounds, have gone on to assume that it is collapsing out of its inherent weaknesses, not to say contradictions. Of course they cannot reach this conclusion on purely Biblical or doctrinal grounds. They have to come to some conclusion about 'what is going on'. There is no escape from some estimate of the evidence; and thus from drawing upon contemporary experience, including the evidence of experts. There are inevitable hazards in this. Evidence is often confusing and hard to interpret. Experts differ, and sometimes they speak beyond their expertise. Then there are cranks around, and it is not always clear who is a crank and who is an expert. Christians who are sure of the wrongness of capitalism are so sure that it must break down that they are apt to ignore these difficulties and take over uncritically some theory that purports to show it is breaking down. But its demise is permaturely announced. The mills of God do grind, but they often grind slowly. It took four hundred years before the overthrow of the Roman Empire heralded in Chapter 17 of the Apocalypse in the New Testament came to pass, and then it was accomplished by those who partly wanted to share its benefits.

In the depth of the depression, after the Wall Street crash, many Christians took over a monetary theory worked out by an engineer, Major Douglas, to explain the paradox of "poverty amidst plenty", as the phrase went. It was a theory that could be refuted by any first year student of economics, and is now quite dead.[7] But by far the most influential theory of the inevitable breakdown of capitalism is the Marxist theory. On this there is an immense literature, the upshot of which is to shew that whilst there is a good deal of value in the various elements in the Marxist theory (and it was even more valuable in the last century because it was drawing attention to factors at that time almost entirely ignored), it fails to prove its main case. Nevertheless outrage at the injustices produced by the bucanneering capitalism of Latin America has led the liberation theologians there to take over the Marxist analysis of what is going on quite uncritically. Perhaps it is the moral indignation paradoxically built into Marxist 'science' which leads them to do this. In brief they say that Biblical faith gives them the motivation to commit themselves to the cause of the poor, but they need a 'science' to tell them the context of to-day in order to put the commitment into practice. That 'science' cannot come from the Bible, it must come from a contemporary source. The 'science' is Marxism. Its claim to be a 'science', in the sense of a basis for prediction and therefore for action, is accepted almost without discussion. It apparently seems self-evident.[8]

Christians in the affluent West have shewn a tendency to take over two other and very different theories of the breakdown of their present economic system, both of which made an impact in 1972 and subsequently. One was the first report of the Club of Rome (a private body) *The Limits to Growth.*[9] It worked with a series of factors, population size, food production, industrial production, the amount of pollution and the rate of use of non-renewable resources, and purported to shew that, assuming these grew over the years steadily at the same annual rate as they had been growing when the study was made, society would reach an impasse within a hundred years. It has been the subject of detailed discussion, and has had an immense influence over readers of the 'quality' newspapers. It also has had a big impact on the Church and Society studies of the World Council of Churches. Subsequent reports from the Club of Rome have considerably modified the picture, but it was the first one that made the stir. Its mistake was to overlook the fact that technological innovation also proceeds at the same rate, and that while there must of course be limits to the resources of our world, since it is finite, we have a very imperfect idea of what those limits are.[10] In the same year, the journal, *The Ecologist,* published in the January issue "A Blueprint for Survival".[11] It was concerned with the danger to human life through the fouling of earth, air and water beyond their natural sources of self-cleansing and recovery, and the dislocation of the ecosystem through the repacious exploitation of nature by human beings. The ecologists issued an important warning. We did behave brashly in the years of expansion following the Second World War. Our monitoring devices did not keep pace with our technological developments. Once this became clear, however, it is not in principle difficult to correct, nor particularly expensive in economic resources. This is not to say that the dangers will be coped with, since it requires both national will and international co-operation to do so, but in principle there is no reason why they should not be, and some progress has been made in doing so. Examples are the effect of the Clean Air Act of 1951 in this country, and plans for cleaning up the Mediterranean. There is also among many ecologists a conservative picture, which needs challenging, of the balance of nature as more or less unchanging and threatening disaster if altered in any major way. In any event neither the Club of Rome nor the ecologists have shewn that the present economic systems of the world are necessarily collapsing or likely to collapse.[12]

There is, however, one recent example of an analysis of modern capitalism which does reveal a contradiction, though it is too recent for Christians as yet to have seized upon it. I refer to Fred Hirsch's *The Social*

Limits to Growth,[13] and I quote what I said of it in the Maurice Lectures:

> He points out that the paradox of the relative affluence that we have achieved is that it is unsatisfying when widely spread, once the basic necessities of food, clothing and shelter are secured. Perhaps we might go further and add to them our modern entertainment devices like television, or labour-saving devices like washing machines. Beyond these, and it is not certain what percentage of the economic productivity of the economy this amounts to, there arise what he calls "positional goods" which are either absolutely scarce or socially scarce. He refers, for instance, to the enjoyment of scenery, the pleasure of suburban living, and access to leadership positions. In these "positional goods" the problem arises that, to use his favourite phrase, "if everyone stands on tiptoe no one sees better". The positional good depends on relative scarcity; the more people possess it, the greater the amount of time needed to amass enough to possess it and then to consume it. Also this increase on the one hand leads to less sociability between people and, on the other, acts as a stimulus to wage inflation. To see economic advance, or rather social economic advance, as individual advance writ large is to set up expectations that can never be fulfilled. Adam Smith's invisible hand only worked in the earlier stages of capitalism.[14]

Hirsch has made a powerful case not so much for the social limits to growth as to the social limits to private consumption. He does not shew that the free market capitalist system is breaking down, but that it is operating with increasing friction, and the suggestion is that we would move it more away from the emphasis on private accumulation and consumption. To put it bluntly, the policy advocated by Mrs. Thatcher's administration in 1980 is the precise opposite of the way we should go.

The upshot of the argument so far is that there are criticisms to be made of the moral blindness of capitalism, of the gross inequalities of wealth and power it perpetuates, and of the social frictions which increasing affluence are intensifying. Nevertheless there is no reason to suppose it is inherently breaking down. It has in fact made it possible to transform the conditions of life for one third of the world's population, even though many injustices remain. Properly handled it could continue to produce economic growth which would provide the basis for removing crippling poverty from most of the rest of the world within a generation. But will it? If it is not breaking down is there an alternative analysis of what is happening to it? and how far does its ideal opposite, the command economy, succeed any better in solving basic economic problems?

Capitalism: Surviving but Changing

An alternative analysis of what is happening to advanced industrial societies must depend on judgements made by any one who offers it which are based on personal experience, reading and reflection, and even more on co-operative group work which draws on a wide variety of relevant experience and reflection. It has no privileged status and has to be critically appraised as to its plausibility, as does the Marxist or any other analysis. It is inherently vulnerable because of the sheer difficulty of understanding the complexities of one's own time. With these provisos I re-state the thesis of the Maurice Lectures. In the three to four years that have elapsed since they were first written the immediate diagnosis looks less favourable, in that the economic down-turn is more severe than it appeared then that it would be. But the diagnosis was not meant to be a short term one, and in the longer run — for example up to the year 2000 — it still seems that the over-all trend in the wealthy countries will be economic growth, perhaps averaging over the whole period about 3% per annum. So the question still remains, What will the wealthy do with their wealth in terms of their own societies, and in terms of their responsibilities to the 'two-thirds world' of newly developing or less developed countries (NDC's and LDC's)? LDC's contain 61% of the world's population, and there are more in absolute poverty in them now than there were in 1970.

Capitalism is surviving, but changing its nature. There is a growth in ownership by institutions, and the divorce between ownership and management and control has become wider. More information about firms is having to be given to trade unions, and in some form or other the development of worker participation in policy making will grow; in this the West Germans led the way after the last war under the name of *mitbestimmung*. Technological advance continues, for example in microprocessing and in recombinant DNA procedures; and training for tomorrow's jobs is a matter of urgency. So is advance in energy technology, for the Organisation for Economic Co-operation and Development (OECD) world should aim to reduce its dependence on oil from one third of its energy consumption to at most one quarter.

Something of a stalemate has been reached in industrial relations. What is often referred to as the excessive power of trade unions really means that they have achieved parallel power to management, and industry can no longer be run with little reference to them, even in an economic recession when jobs are at stake. Workers can stop management taking certain positive actions but cannot compel it to keep the works running, whilst management can stop workers realising benefits of money wage increases by passing them on in higher prices, but it cannot enforce an increased output from the same machinery and plant. Neither side can impose its will on the other. A new stage of industrial relations has been reached requiring more participation and more consensus, and thus involving more time and effort than before. Without reasonable procedures and agreements, and without a spirit of prudence and proportion, it could easily lead to mutual destruction; with them there is the prospect of a much healthier and humane society than industrialism has so far produced. There is no inevitability either way. The same situation exists in the professions, indeed even more so, for the professions have built themselves into a position where those in work are in an almost impregnable position. This whole picture is very far from the notion of the free market of the classical capitalist economy. Even multi-national companies, whose social accountability remains a big problem, are having to be concerned with more than profits and growth, and to be much more conscious of their public responsibilities.

All this does not mean, however, that the new social capitalistic system is unworkable. Take Japan for example. Its economic growth since 1948 has been remarkable. It has a higher taxation rate than any other 'free market' industrial country,[15] an élitist civil service which exercises a good deal of bureaucratic power over business and industry, together with good social services, and only 1% of robberies committed in the USA. This is not to suggest that it is an earthly paradise, far from it, but it does suggest the danger of simple generalisation. What the present British administration abhors as inimical to enterprise and growth exists in Japan without the alleged deleterious effects.

Capitalism is changing in that a stalemate in industry is being paralleled by a state of schizophrenia in the electorate. As taxpayers, the electorate responds to calls to cut taxes and rates; at least the more affluent part of the electorate does. The affluent worker with high weekly wages is shewing the same signs of grumbling about the weight of taxation as has so long characterised the middle classes. Yet the electorate as consumer values the social benefits provided by taxation, notably the Health Service. This is much abused because its very success has made expectations of it unrealistic, but it has transformed the medical situation of the bulk of the electorate compared to what existed before. There is also schizophrenia in the trade union movement as a whole between concern for the low paid workers by some and insistence on the maintenance of differentials by others. Further, the protection of jobs, many of them obsolescent, is at war with the desire for the greater benefits that a more dynamic and innovative economy would bring.

These ambiguities make the demands on governments very difficult. Even if we assume that they are pursuing sensible and far-sighted policies, a big assumption, there is no guarantee that the electorate will give them sufficient backing to carry them out. There are signs that electorates are becoming more fickle, and reacting against whatever administration has been in power. Politicians have largely themselves to blame for this, for they rarely spell out underlying economic factors which constrain actions; they are prone to pander to the desire of all of us both to have our economic cake and eat it. But however blame is apportioned for the difficulties, it remains the case that we do not suffer from governments with too much power, but with too little. The obvious example is that of achieving an incomes policy and, together with it, a re-alignment of established differentials. There are so many inevitable institutional rigidities in the modern industrial state, necessary because people will not be pushed around in the way that was possible in the past, that some form of prices and incomes policy is essential. (The idea that monetary policies can solve them belongs to the myth of pure laissez-faire, as does the trade union riposte of free collective bargaining.) The difficulty of bringing about such a policy is evident, but it will have to be attempted, even though anything arrived at will be pretty rough and ready, and subject to continual argument and re-negotiation. We shall have to work towards some participatory forum where such policies can be argued out. Differentials may largely have to be left to be dealt with by the tax system.

If we look briefly at how far industrialised socialist economies raise the same problems as the capitalist ones, and how far their command economies (the opposite 'ideal type' to the market economies), are successful in solving them, the resemblances become quite striking, both in the nature of the problem and the difficulties of finding a solution to them. Of course it is not easy to be clear about what is happening in all of them, particularly China; whilst some things are clear, others are problematical. One thing which is clear is that the phenomenal economic progress made by the USSR since 1917, when it was very backward, is not due to the merits of socialist economic analysis, but to the political power of the state, which enabled it to enforce a rate of forced saving on the Russian public for decades, which no government subject to dismissal by an electorate at the polls could have got away with; voters would not have put up with such a prolonged scarcity of consumption goods. For the rest, the development of computer techniques makes the centralised planning of a command economy much easier in precision and scope, but the management of innovation no easier. An established bureaucratic vested interest in the *status quo* develops which is hard to shift; it resists any reforms which would weaken its power. Economic dissent is easily labelled political deviationism, with all the unpleasant consequences that brings. In 1961 the Programme of the Russian Communist Party was suggesting that by the 1980s full communism would have arrived. Not only is it as far away as ever, it is a vanishing mirage. In Yugoslavia, where a significantly decentralised management system has been in operation, vested interests in established jobs has developed, whilst the Party wants industry to succeed but is wary of rival centres of power if it does. Indeed there are differences of interest between worker and management, and between the worker as producer and the worker as consumer which are endemic in society so long as the basic economic problem of the allocation of scarce resources with alternative uses remains, and there is no sign that the command economies are more successful in solving it than are the market ones. Even in controlling inflation, where the political authoritariansim of the command economies was for a long time more successful than the market economies, the rise in prices produced by the action of OPEC (Organisation of Petroleum Exporting Countries) has been too much for controls, and in East European countries the inflation rate varied between 11% and 19% in the year 1978-9.[16] In China a period of fossilisation followed after the 1949 communist take-over until 1966, followed by the ten years of anarchism of the cultural revolution, and since 1976 a period of what might be called radical moderation. There appears now to be the growth of greater inequality of incomes, more bonus schemes, more attempts to meet consumer demands, more urban unemployment (especially among school leavers) and more urban crime. There is also a campaign against large families, with the slogan "one is best, two is most"; and with the third child economic sanctions begin to operate. Poland has had major outbreaks of worker and consumer resistance to the policies of its communist government, in 1956, 1970 and 1976 and in the summer of 1980 there were 120 strikes in a month, of just the kind to which market economies are prone, but add to those a demand for more independent trade unions.[17] On the whole, however, advanced command economies do much better at equalising wealth, and are in a better position to deal with Hirsch's problem of the social limits to growth. For the rest they seem to face much the same problems as advanced market economies, with the additional disadvantage of a dangerous concentration of political and economic power in the same hands, the abuse of which it is very difficult to check. John Atherton's chapter favours a command economy to tackle the urgent problems of relative deprivation in our society, but does not shew how it would work.

Christian socialists in Britain tend to favour a five-fold programme, each element of which has some merits, but also difficulties which they do not shew much sign of facing.[18] **i** Equality of opportunity. This by itself would lead to a meritocracy, which would be a most unpleasant society. What needs spelling out is what society will do with those of average talent or less; those who have hitherto earned their living in unskilled physical or mental dead-end jobs which are now disappearing. They are at least 'half our future'. **ii** Workers' ownership. Ownership by workers is not by itself a solution of the conflicts of interest in society, as has been shewn ever since the failure of the Producers' Co-operatives set up by F.D. Maurice and the Christian Socialists in 1848-54. By itself it is an expression of a vested interest which has to be counterbalanced by a wider communal one. **iii** The community control of wealth; what this means has of course to be spelled out; but it has to deal with the dangerous centralisation of political and economic power, already mentioned. **iv** A planned socialist economy; the same point applies; in addition there is the question already discussed as to how it proposes to solve the basic economics of the allocation of resources. There seems no reason in principle why many of the devices of the market system in a suitable framework and no longer idolised, should not be adopted. **v** Full participation in decision making. This is akin to the demand of the World Council of Churches for a Just, Participatory and Sustainable Society, though a great deal of work needs to be done on the structures of participation. It is entirely right that those whose interests are affected by decisions should participate in making them, but in an advanced industrial society a great deal of it cannot be done by direct participation. Society cannot be run like a Greek city state. The right forms of indirect participation have to be found. Problems that need solving include access to relevant information, taking decisions in time and with a longer view than immediate concerns require, relating to other interests in the forum of public discussion, and allowing the management sufficient authority to operate effectively.

Meanwhile there has been a recrudescence of a conservative philosophy of both an individualist kind (which used to be called liberal) and an organic one. Some of it is rather a lightweight stress on private property, the right of inheritance and individual freedom. But there is a more solid conservative view which regards society as a deep and turbulent river flowing through time in a way which is very little understood, so that the task of politicians is merely to keep things afloat, a view associated in the recent past with Walter Oakeshott;[19] or which stressed, with K.R. Popper, the sheer difficulty of predicting the future, and therefore the necessary limitations on the power of the state.[20] This is fair enough as a warning to over-exuberant planners and technocrats, but it is quite unsatisfactory as a general position. Governments cannot avoid all kinds of major 'interferences' with the economy, whatever they may say, nor are electorates willing to accept that they live in the best of available worlds, and that no organised efforts at targets and policies to improve it are possible. State intervention is inevitable; the need is to improve its quality.

The two most influential exponents of the new conservatism are Milton Friedman and F.A. von Hayek. The former is an advocate of the old liberalism, qualified by a negative income tax which would guarantee an unconditional but very basic income to all, in order to cope with the unfortunate as well as the feckless. For the rest we are back with the claim that competitive markets transform the self-interested actions of individuals into social benefits, and that policy making is too difficult for policy makers, it had better be left to the free market. Put choice back into the pockets of the people! Sewers, schools, houses, roads, town planning, libraries, fire and ambulance services, hospitals and so on. Only law and order and defence would be exempt.[21] Hayek is less of a libertarian. His celebrated book of a generation ago, *The Road to Serfdom,*[22] was a warning that centralised planning would lead to political totalitarianism, but now he is more alarmed that democracy has become an unprincipled auction by rival parties to satisfy organised groups whose demands are mutually incompatible and insatiable. He has published a trilogy, *Law, Legislation and Liberty,* of which the third volume appeared in 1979, after the Maurice Lectures, which referred to the first two.[23] He is conservative in stressing the hidden wisdom in existing institutions, their traditions and rules. However he allows there must be innovation, though it had better be cautious. Indeed he criticses conservatives for being too fearful of change, too deferential to established authorities, and too nationalistic. But he will not allow the free market system to develop in a social market or social democratic, let alone a democratic socialist, direction. He wants a free market, which he thinks of as a fundamentally human invention as significant as language or laws. It is not merely that it distributes known resources among known wants (a computer could now be envisaged as doing that, as we have seen), but it is a great innovating technique for promoting new possibilities. To Hayek rewards are a mixture of effort, ability and luck, and nothing worthwhile can be done about the distribution of them. He thinks that the pursuit of social justice is a mirage; but in my view it in no way follows from a role for a free market that a greater re-distribution of wealth is not desirable, nor that much collectivisation cannot be justified. To quote from the Maurice Lectures:

> He is not willing to trust the citizen as a voter in the way in which he is as a consumer, because the issues of political decision are dangerously remote from the voter, whereas his economic decisions in the market are immediately present to him, and because each of us is irremediably ignorant of many facts on which the attainment of our ends depends. Indeed he stresses the unforseen consequences of decisions, and our proneness to assume knowledge we do not possess.[24]

Once more we have to say that it is one thing to draw attention to difficulties in social market techniques and policies, as against an easy utopianism, but quite another to give up the problem with political naivete! No government could adopt such a policy. It cannot avoid much more deliberate management of the economy. Nor would electorates allow it. No one but a tiny group of intellectuals would put themselves at the mercy of an impersonal mechanism, operating almost in a social vacuum, in matters vitally affecting their lives and interests. Interests will insist on organising and representing their views. There must be a public forum where these are contested, and governments must create structures for this, whilst accepting final responsibility for policies of 'interference'. If it is not made an idol, the market and its allied institutions can be a useful mechanism within this overall aim.

We conclude that the new right offers not new wisdom but old shibboleths. Bearing in mind the warning already made about the necessarily provisional character of any suggestions, what way forward can be suggested for the market economies in coping with problems, so many of which are so similar in advanced industrial societies, whether they are market or command economies?

A Just, Participatory and Sustainable Society

The pursuit of social justice has a long history as part of the classical as well as of the Judaeo-Christian tradition.[25] Very broadly speaking there are three general models of distributive justice; legal right, which corresponds to a more hierarchical society, merit, which corresponds to a more libertarian and individualist one, and need, which corresponds to a more collaborative one. It is unlikely that society will function without elements of all three models. The question seems to be, What is the mix to be, and which wants fostering? In my judgement it is the element of needs which should be fostered, for the simple reason that we are much more conscious of our rights and our merits than we are of common needs; and as far as these last go the resemblances between human beings are much more significant than their differences. This is neatly expressed in the social formula of the Marxist utopia, "From each according to his ability, to each according to his need". So the problem here is to move in a more equalitarian direction. This is not the place to consider in detail devices to bring this about. They include a combined progressive and negative income tax, combined with a capital transfer tax, levied on the beneficiaries.

A modest annual wealth tax is also a possibility; a heavy one has serious economic disadvantages, since it can lead to a spending spree or to emigration. Another possibility is an expenditure tax to catch the playboy. Death duties work very slowly and tend to catch only the innocent or the unlucky, who have not found a way of forestalling them. Maybe a short, sharp capital levy is better. Labour governments have made little or no progress in this matter. One reason is that there is a lack of enthusiasm for equalitarian measures in the country and in the Labour movement itself, where much of the resistance comes from the skilled blue collar and the white collar unions. Political parties in order to get elected, are driven to appeal to the centre, and since a significant move towards greater equality could not be achieved solely by re-distributing from the rich, much of it would be at the expense of the centre. It is significant that one third of the trade union members must have voted Tory at the election of 1979.

Equalitarian policies are ambiguous because the concept is an elusive one and cannot be pursued without regard to other concepts such as right and merit. But in my view we need more equality, and it requires a strong political educational push to make it electorally possible. It needs to be pursued not only in the realm of taxes and subsidies but in conditions of work, where on every count blue collar are disadvantaged as compared with white collar workers. It is the best way of modifying the problem of positional goods raised by Hirsch.[26]

Sustainability is a requirement which has only recently come to the fore owing to the scare raised by the ecological and limits to growth arguments about the dangers of the exhaustion of non-renewable natural resources, of disturbing the balance of nature, and of polluting beyond nature's powers of self-cleansing. It also arises in the shape of the need to foster basic moral and civic virtues, without which society can hardly hold together, except by sheer force, and that has its limits in an advanced industrial society. I say no more about this last point, which has already been discussed, but something needs to be said about the other problems of sustainability.

The first thing is to get the sums right. Even with sophisticated techniques of forecasting, the hazards of extrapolating ahead, even fifteen years, are great. The further beyond that, the greater the hazards. One major reason is that extrapolation is an inherently conservative activity, since it can only proceed on the basis of present trends, whilst we are continually surprised by unexpected technological innovations, unexpected not least by the pure scientists out of whose previous work the technological innovation has come. This is a human limitation which we cannot surmount, though we can foster a mental flexibility to cope with it. However we can at least try to make our extrapolations from the present as accurate as possible. There has been a tendency to make exaggerated claims, or always to take the most pessimistic of the possible forecasts. Christians are often prone to this; perhaps they have an inarticulate thought that only dramatic headlines will galvanise their constituency into action, since most people prefer not to have their accepted ways upset by disturbing thoughts. The notable conference of the World Council of Churches in the USA in 1979 was not free from this. The chapter in this book by Paul Abrecht is particularly fruitful in this connection. He draws attention to the fears now being expressed by dissenters from within the affluent world, including the scientific world which had added force to them; fears of the costs and risks of technology; alarm at the extent to which it is tied to the military establishments, and that it and the scientific and technology personnel have gone beyond social control; and in economic terms that the rich countries have become accustomed to standards of affluence and welfare which are impossible for the whole world, and impossible for the rich countries to sustain without robbing the poor countries of resources for their future development. None of these fears is groundless. They amount to saying that with increased power to human beings goes increased risks if they misuse it. It is an old point in a new context: not everything that can be done should be done. Limits must be thought out and respected.

The issues of science and faith are not the focus of this book, but economic and political issues are. It is quite true that at this moment the world cannot afford another USA, which with 6% of the world's population uses up over 40% of its resources. What has yet to be shewn is that the 'two-thirds world' will not get on better with *disciplined* growth by the advanced societies than by other means. For apart from the political difficulty of persuading electorates in wealthy countries, in so far as they are parliamentary democracies, to stop economic growth, or actually to reduce their standards of living, it is not clear that by doing so it would actually benefit the rest. The problem seems, rather, to get them to adopt the right economic policies and not live selfishly in a wealthy ghetto. A vision is required to move them, as well as reasoned arguments. Surely the vision of the abolition of primary poverty, which modern productivity is now shewing to be over the horizon, should be something to move us. Furthermore doing something about the scandals of relative poverty and deprivation on our own doorstep is likely to make us more, rather than less, alert to the larger vision.[27]

This involves taking some responsibility for the future and not merely thinking of the present generation. When all the reservations about forecasting are borne in mind, we are capable of thinking at any rate as far ahead as our grandchildren as we get to grips with present problems in the immediate context of the next ten or fifteen years. It also involves an attitude to risk taking, epitomised by questions of the development of nuclear energy. Should commercial fast breeder reactors be built and should research into nuclear fusion be pursued? There are also questions of genetical engineering, following upon the cracking of the genetic code by Crick and Watson. One can do no more than mention these issues, involved as they are in the question of sustainability.[28]

Participation raises its own crop of questions; of conflicts of interest within an overall consensus; of structures of participation at different levels, direct and representational. Through most of history most people have been pushed around all their lives by small élites. We are only at the beginning of working out structures of participation. The underlying concept of man expressed in political democracy is only very slowly beginning to be thought about in terms of the world of daily work where a significant part of a person's life is spent. There are the problems of accountability, and of the control of technocratic élites presiding over rapid technological innovation, of multinational enterprises, and of central government control as against local channels of participation. With regard to the less developed countries there is the question of the obstacles to distributive justice within them because of local élites, and whether it is possible for the affluent to use any pressure to undermine them without provoking a reaction on the grounds of paternalism.[29] Furthermore there is the growing problem in wealthy societies of those who are in effect being elided out of participation in the full sense as citizens by having no work to do, and that in societies who have propagated a work ethic, and are all too ready to be more pre-occupied with what they call scroungers than with tax dodgers. It seems as if we need to develop new social values which cease to make such a sharp division between work and leisure, and to provide a social wage without direct reference to either. But more than that is required. There is a vital difference between chosen leisure and enforced leisure because society has apparently no need or place for those concerned. With the disappearance of unskilled jobs, the manufacturing base will be covered by a much smaller labour force, and we shall move more and more into a service society. Almost all the unskilled have personal and human qualities which can be called upon. Those who have not are indeed among society's casualties and must be treated gently and humanely. There is an almost unlimited scope for personal service (take mental hospitals as one example), but it needs to be paid for as a proper job, not regarded as a voluntary filler-in of time when one is on unemployment pay. There is plenty of scope for voluntary service in leisure time on top of a paid job, but it is no substitute for one. It is paid service which is needed, and it is communal not private consumption which is chiefly involved. We are back again at Hirsch's point on the social limits to private consumption. Obviously waste must be avoided, and there is every ground for seeing that taxes and rates are not spent wastefully but, apart from this, zeal for cutting both in favour of private consumption is the precise opposite of the way we should go.

To sustain the economic basis for this, society needs to be efficient and adaptive, and it is not easy to combine this with participation. This is partly due to the fact that usually in our society change bears unduly harshly on particular individuals and groups. How real is the fear of this is evident in the professional world where, with all its buttressed security, a *frisson* sweeps through it at even the slightest hint of a possible redundancy, something that most wage earners live with all the time. It requires a far-seeing electorate to see the needs for efficiency and adaptability, and it will only be possible in so far as society systematically eases the adjustments that particular citizens have to make. Participation therefore opens up a very large number of problems which will test political, economic, social and industrial maturity to the full.

The Bible and the Modern World

The last question to be faced in this chapter is what is distinctively Christian in all this? Earlier we mentioned that this is not necessarily the crucial question for Christian social ethics, since the Christian is not primarily concerned to advocate in this field something that no one else can share. Nevertheless it is an important question, and the non-Christian may well want to know what the connection is between the Christian faith and these reflections on capitalism, democracy, and Christianity.

What is the Christian gospel? In essence it arises from the ministry and message of Jesus. He saw himself as proclaiming in word and deed the Kingdom of God, that is to say the way God rules the world. It is a paradoxical way of graciousness and hope for all, and a challenge to reverse the usual standards of human reckoning and rule. God himself rules by service and suffering. The ethic of the Kingdom is non-reciprocal; it does not depend upon doing good to those who do good to you, but continues to do good even if it gets no return (though of course it longs for one). Ruling in the Kingdom means being a servant of all and not lording it over one's subjects. The parables are designed to bring out in varied ways the paradoxical nature of the Kingdom of God. Jesus' hearers are called to trust in God's Kingdom, in his way of ruling the world, and to have no other security. He gathered a nucleus round him of citizens of the Kingdom, and they formed in turn the nucleus of the Church, which is the agent of the Kingdom, subject to it, but part of the Gospel. The Kingdom was good news to all society's rejects, whom Jesus actively sought out. His horizon was foreshortened, in that he probably thought there was little time left for life on this earth, and there is no ongoing picture of society in his ministry, nor any teaching of the relation of the Church (which soon burst the bounds of Israel) as the agent of the Kingdom of God to the kingdoms of this world in which it is placed. However, the Church had to face these problems from its earliest days, as we can see from the various epistles of St. Paul and later New Testament books like Acts and Revelation. The problems discussed in them — questions of marriage and the family, and attitudes to the state and to daily work — are very illuminating, but they are church centred and only marginally related to on-going civic society, which was not the focus of attention. Moreover for the most part the thought was conditioned by the foreshortening of time and the expectation of the imminent end of the world. It cannot be transferred neatly to our own day. The only substantial New Testament writing which has abandoned this foreshortening is St. John's Gospel, and it concentrates on the heart of Jesus' significance and the heart of his ethic, and does not go at all into detailed application.[30]

It is impossible, therefore, to move directly from the Bible to the modern world. Criteria have to be derived from it, which are then brought to bear on that world, after it has been empirically investigated, as has already been mentioned.

What are the chief criteria? In brief I suggest the following as examples. **i** Concern for the poor, in the sense not only of the materially poor but all society's rejects. It is an awkward question for theologians and the Church to face as to how far they have in fact stood for them. The liberation theologians say pointedly that without this prior commitment one cannot begin to think authentic theology. **ii** Concern for community, and the diminution of social and cultural barriers, so that people will be at home with one another; the slogan of the French Revolution, 'liberty, equality and fraternity', has much to be said for it in this connection, and it is fraternity to which least attention has been paid, as Kenneth Medhurst's chapter points out. **iii** Concern for abuses of power, but not hostility to power as such, because more power in the hands of men does not diminish the power of God; it seems that God is self-effacing and wants men to be creative in the world and with respect to nature and, in this sense, to 'come of age'.[31] **iv** Awareness of the power of sin, and therefore alertness to the perennial conflicts of interest that arise between people and groups whose love of neighbours as themselves is only crudely developed. The cross of Christ is at the centre of the Christian Gospel (or good news); another paradox. **v** A reserve about human policies and causes, because the Kingdom of God is always seeking a political and social expression in terms of right dealing or justice between man and man, but is so far reaching that it is never exhausted in any political or social set-up but transcends it, and points towards reform and further expression. This reserve is *not* because of a social pessimism, quite the contrary. The Christian does not believe that God has set limits to what men may achieve in society if they are faithful, but equally he is aware of the extent to which they can fall if they are not faithful. Nazi Germany is a vivid instance of this in this century. Moreover, gains achieved by one generation are not automatically sustained by the next, they require a fresh commitment. However the Christian realises that the possibilities of love increase the more love is explored, so that they are not exhaustible in this life. The Kingdom of God finally transcends time and space; and it is in this perspective that worship arises.

It should be noted that there is a two-sided doctrine of man in these insights; his greatness under God and his sin and folly. This latter is often expressed in the confusing term 'Original Sin'. To return to Nigel Lawson, whom I mentioned at the beginning, he makes a common conservative claim that socialists believe in the perfectibility of man whilst conservatives are the realists who allow for original sin. It is true that many socialists have been and are utopian about man, and they would do better to pay attention to both parts of the Christian understanding of him instead of only one. They should certainly not let conservatives appropriate original sin, for one of its obvious implications is that no one is good enough to exercise power over another unchecked, and that means that hierarchies, of which conservatives are fond, must come under continued scrutiny.[32]

There is no way to move from these criteria direct to the modern world. The Christian cannot produce his own solution to political and social problems directly from them. The Church cannot say the last word, only a penultimate one.[33] It can also ask searching questions, perhaps even one more than anyone else is asking. It likes to think of itself as the conscience of society, but it needs first to be careful that it is sufficiently critical of itself; and in a plural society it needs to be alert to the consciences of others. For the rest, it should join in corporate investigation into what is going on, and *if* reasonable agreement is obtained it can arrive at a middle position between the basic gospel criteria and detailed policies. Usually, though not always, detailed policies involve so many uncertainties of fact and interpretation, that it is not likely that there will be general agreement about them, even among those who agree about the end to be sought. Christians may very well agree about the end, but it does not follow that detailed policies designed to achieve it can be 'officially' adopted as 'Christian'. But it is possible that at the middle level there will be reasonable agreement among those who have seriously investigated the question. The agreement will include an analysis and evaluation of social facts, and trends and possibilities, and a recommendation as to the general direction to be aimed at. Individual Christians as citizens, and in certain cases churches as institutions have to go further into detailed implications, as the World Council of Churches has done with its Programme to Combat Racism.

This middle level is sometimes referred to by the confusing term 'middle axiom'. I myself use it for want of a better. Duncan Forrester in his chapter discusses middle axioms critically without necessarily wanting to veto them altogether. Rather he wants to hold them together with the opposite procedure, which is to act faithfully first, in order to know what the Gospel is. This, however, does not solve all the problems. The liberation theologians, who are foremost in stressing the need for prior faithful commitment (to the poor), are the ones who stress that while motive comes from the Bible, study of one's own times is necessary in order to implement the commitment. We are back once again at the problems of empirical investigation, and the obstacles to arriving at agreed detailed policies as distinct from the possibility of an agreed middle ground.

I think Forrester is right in saying that Christian social theology can start with a negative judgment of features of the *status quo* in the light of our criteria. But it ought not to stop there, and if we wish to move from a negative general condemnation to a more positive contribution we must strive to arrive at a reasonably agreed middle ground, not expecting complete agreement but sufficient to be weighty; it will indicate facts and trends in the question under discussion and suggest the tendencies to be encouraged, but without getting as far as detailed policies.[34] I do not think there is an escape from this middle axiom position inaugurated by J.H. Oldham. Inter-disciplinary as it is, it had nothing to do with the attitudes of linguistic philosophy, as Forrester suggests; nor does it necessarily pre-suppose a static understanding of faith; and it is less likely to result in merely echoing the current values of the intelligentsia, by reason of the co-operative process by which it proceeds, than is the attempt to move directly from the Bible to some detailed conclusion about the modern world, which is notoriously open to that very defect, just because of its unreflective nature.

Summary and Postscript

To put the theme of this chapter in a nutshell much of the peculiarly Christian critique of capitalism has failed, though the falseness of its ideology — which is a basic point — has been exposed. Nevertheless it has useful devices which need to be appropriated by any advanced industrial society. Capitalism is not breaking down from inherent contradictions but is changing its nature: and command economies are facing very similar problems; they, too, are running into difficulties but not collapsing. The possibilities of friction in advanced industrial societies so that they become unworkable are great; but so are the opportunities. Many changes are needed if we are to work towards a just, participatory and sustainable society, not least in an equalitarian direction, which is the strong point of the socialist case. In this sense social democracy needs to move in the direction of a democratic socialism freed from an utopian ideology. This will require political skill, moral purpose, and the sustaining powers of a terrestrial aim and (a Christian would add) a transcendent hope. The abolition on a global basis of primary poverty should be the immediate terrestrial aim. The Christian should expect to play his part in these tasks in a plural society and a plural world, sustained by a faith and hope which may well commend itself to others.

To this summary a postscript is perhaps necessary. Marxist mythology holds that all this is impossible because holders of economic power will not give it up; only revolutionary and probably forceful change can establish a society on a new basis, that of the command economy. The trouble is that such an economy brings us back to much the same problems. Also an advanced industrial society does not lend itself to revolutionary change. Better, therefore, to work hard to move our institutions along the lines I have indicated. The Marxist thesis about power has not been proved or disproved as far as an advanced industrial economy is concerned. So far in this country supporters of the *status quo* have realised in time when it was necessary to give way. They need to continue to do so. But a bewildered and uneasy electorate needs a great deal of political and economic education, and much more vision, if it is to have the stability and stamina both to insist that changes be made and also to realise the nature and limits of these changes. Reforms achieved reveal new problems. There is no end to the quest for social and economic justice.

Notes

1. One of the best short discussions of this relation is still that of Niebuhr, Reinhold, *The Children of Light and the Children of Darkness,* London, Nisbet, 1945. The Foreword contains the much quoted sentence "Man's capacity for justice makes democracy possible; but man's inclination to injustice makes democracy necessary".

2. The sources for the MIT Conference are chiefly Abrecht, P., (ed.), *Faith, Science and the Future,* Preparatory Reading for the Conference, Geneva, World Council of Churches, 1978; Shinn, R., (ed.), *Faith and Science in an Unjust World,* Vol. 1, Plenary Presentations at the Conference, and Abrecht, P., (ed.), Vol. 2, Reports and Recommendations, both Geneva, World Council of Churches, 1980. They contain an unique range of material both in global reference and issues covered.

3. On man and nature the best general discussion is probably Passmore, J.A., *Man's Responsibility for Nature,* London, Duckworth, 1972; the best Christian one is Montefiore, H., (ed.), *Man and Nature,* London, Collins, 1975. A lively debate goes on in both 'secular' and Christian circles, with a range of positions taken in each.

4. A lively debate also rages on the issue of secularisation and religion, and all recent books on the sociology of religion deal with it. It was focussed in its earlier stages by Wilson, B., *Religion and Secular Society,* London, Watts, 1966, and Martin, D., *The Religious and the Secular,* London, Routledge and Kegan Paul, 1969.

5. See his sermons, a convenient edition of which, together with a critical introduction, is Roberts, T.A., *Butler's Fifteen Sermons,* London, SPCK, 1970.

6. The first Wilson book is cited in note 4 above; the second is *Contemporary Tansformations of Religion,* London, Oxford University Press, 1976.

7. The Canadian province of Manitoba had a Social Credit government for years, but Federal institutions prevented it doing damage.

8. A good deal of Latin American liberation theology is now available in English. The best single volume is one of the first to be translated, Gutierrez, G., *A Theology of Liberation,* London, SCM Press, 1973. He is a Roman Catholic; on the Protestant side a good representative is Bonino, J.M. *Revolutionary Theology Comes of Age,* London, SPCK, 1975. (In USA the title is *Doing Theology in a Revolutionary Situation,* Philadelphia, Fortress Press, 1975). Bonino is now one of the five Presidents of the World Council of Churches.

9. New York, New American Library, 1972.

10. A good critique of the issues raised by the Club of Rome comes from the Sussex University Science Policy Research Unit: Freeman, C. and Jahoda, M., (eds.), *World Futures: the Great Debate,* London, Martin Robertson, 1978.

11. Reprinted as a Penguin Book (London) with a new edition in 1977.

12. Another good survey of current social and economic issues in a global context is Ward, B., (Lady Jackson), *Progress for a Small Planet,* London, Penguin Books, 1979.

13. London, Routledge and Kegan Paul, 1977.

14. *Religion and the Persistence of Capitalism,* London, SCM Press, 1979, p.34.

15. In mid-1979 the top rate of Income Tax was USA 50%, West Germany 56%, France and the UK 60%, and Japan 85%.

16. In the Maurice Lectures I conceded greater power to control inflation to the command economics than has since proved to be the case; this is partly because the East European COMECON countries can get no more than 65% of their energy requirements from their own resources (a proportion which is falling), and so cannot isolate themselves from OPEC price rises.

17. At stake in Poland is a problem endemic to economic life, how to manage change? Command economies are run by a bureaucratic system which is designed for routine administration. Change is always a threat to existing authorities in any sphere (the Church included); in the command economies there are no alternative sources of power, such as independent trade unions, to facilitate the process. These economies face the same economic restraints as the market ones but are ill equipped to meet them. If pay rises of, for example, 20% are granted without more goods being available it merely fuels inflation. Strict price controls are a possible policy, but if the goods most people want are priced too low the result is queues, black markets, and bribery. If the prices are then raised abruptly even the combined political and economic power of the state cannot prevent trouble, as in Poland.

18. They are not alone in this. Many of the socialist critics of the Labour Government of 1974-79 are in the same boat. For example, as this chapter is written there has appeared a critique by Coates, D., *Labour in Power: a Study of the Labour Government 1974-9,* London, Longmans, 1980, which includes much acute analysis. But when it comes to the socialist alternative his very brief treatment amounts to saying that the entire working class will run their own industries and communities on democratic lines "consciously and articulately deciding for themselves the priorities of social production and welfare". This sidesteps all the basic economic, industrial and political problems. It is no nearer to them than the Beatitudes of the Sermon on the Mount; all the detailed work has to be done.

19. See Oakeshott, W., *Rationalism in Politics,* London, Methuen, 1962.

20. See Popper, K.R., *The Open Society and its Enemies,* London, Routledge and Kegan Paul, 1945, and *The Poverty of Historicism,* London, Routledge and Kegan Paul, 1957.

21. See Friedman, M., *Capitalism and Freedom,* Chicago, University of Chicago Press, 1962.

22. London, Routledge, 1944.

23. The three volumes are *Rules and Orders,* London, Routledge and Kegan Paul, 1973, *The Mirage of Social Justice,* London, Routledge and Kegan Paul, 1976, and *The Political Order of a Free People,* London, Routledge and Kegan Paul, 1979.

24. Preston, op.cit., p.27.

25. A good treatment is Miller, D., *Social Justice,* London, Oxford University Press, 1976, especially Part 1.

26. The profoundest 'prophet' of equality is still R.H. Tawney whose classic book with that title was first published in 1931; the fourth revised edition appeared in 1964, London, Allen and Unwin. The details are, of course, out of date.

27. The Willy Brandt Independent Commission on International Development Issues, *North-South: a Programme for Survival,* London, Pan Books, 1980 re-states forcefully what has been known for some time; the problem is to get the wealthy nations to take it seriously.

28. These issues are all dealt with in the literature of the MIT Conference of 1979 (see note 2 above). See also Gribbin, J., *Future Worlds,* London, Abacus, 1980, largely based on the University of Sussex Unit (see note 10).

29. An encouraging example of the weak beginning to exert an influence in the third world comes from the Indian state of Karnataka. Usually in an Indian state powerful landed castes enjoy most of the political spoils; the poor have habitually followed them, and the leaders of their own castes have often been bribed by them. In Karnataka the Congress Party has been driven, in order to get power (i.e., out of self-interest), to break the dominance of the landed castes by an alliance of poor peasants, artisans and untouchables. The untouchables have been persuaded, by putting them into important ministries, to work with their enemies, the poor castes. In two years they began to form their own interest groups and produce their own representatives. (This information comes from *The Economist,* March 29th, 1980, which remarks that public pressure is forcing pragmatic politicians to become liberals.)

30. See especially the 'Farewell Discourses' of John 14-17; and 1 John 4.

31. The phrase, which has been much discussed, is associated with Bonhoeffer, D., *Letters and Papers from Prison,* enlarged edition, London, SCM Press, 1971, p.326f.

32. Cf. Reinhold Niebuhr's saying about political democracy (see note 1).

33. Dietrich Bonhoeffer makes a great deal of the difference between the ultimate and the penultimate in his *Ethics,* London, SCM Press, 1955.

34. There is no conveniently available treatment of middle axioms; I can do no more than refer to my article on them, "Middle Axioms in Christian Social Ethics", in *Crucible* (the Journal of the Church of England Board for Social Responsibility), January, 1971, reprinted in *Explorations in Theology 9,* London, SCM Press, 1981.

3

What is Distinctive in Social Theology?

Duncan B. Forrester

What is the distinctive contribution of the theologian to the discussion of questions of public policy? What is the theological *proprium* which at one and the same time encourages the theologian to claim to be heard, and gives his input into the discussion its peculiar shape?

In church circles in Britain the answer to these questions is commonly assumed to be obvious: of course Christianity is relevant to life, indubitably it has a distinctive and invaluable contribution to make in politics and economics. But when a reason is asked for this confidence, when the enquirer asks *how* Christianity bears upon the issues of the day, *in what way* it becomes relevant, again and again no answer is forthcoming, save a mass of pious and banal verbiage. In public life, on the other hand, the very term 'theology' is bandied about as an epithet for irrelevant, unrealistic and self-indulgent theorizing; and it is taken for granted that theology proper has no contribution to make except, perhaps, in the area of personal ethics. No one expects the theologian to say a relevant word. The nice story that F.D. Roosevelt used to phone Reinhold Niebuhr each morning during the war on a 'hot line' to Union Theological Seminary, New York, to ask, "What's the Word of God for today, Reinie?" is worlds away from our present situation in Britain.

For many people in Britain today the Christian contribution is typified by either the vapid pietism of the 'Archbishops' Call to the Nation' in October 1975, or the unstructured mass of information and pinkish opinion which resulted from the 'Britain Today and Tomorrow' project of the British Council of Churches.[1] It is not altogether surprising that E.R. Norman won such widespread approbation for his thesis that the theologians' *proprium* is to devote themselves to the "ethereal qualities of immortality", and whenever they stray beyond that they are to be found as mouthpieces of the *zeitgeist* and nothing more.[2] As we observe the explosion of ecumenical social thinking around the world, and compare it with the sparsity of creative Christian social thought in contemporary Britain, we should be rather ashamed of ourselves, and ask some hard questions about why so much of the British tradition of social theology appears to have run into the sand, and why we have such difficulty either in emulating or applying to our context the lively thought on social and economic matters emanating from other parts of the world.[3] We do indeed need to apply ourselves with renewed seriousness to the question of how the theologian addresses himself to social and political issues, and the distinctive contribution he has it in his power to make.

A Distinctive Way of Doing Social Theology?

Under the influence very largely of that remarkable ecumenical statesman, J.H. Oldham, there has been dominant in ecumenical circles, particularly perhaps in the Anglo-Saxon world, the idea that the best way of 'doing social theology', of developing a Christian approach to social issues, is to gather together groups of people with varied and relevant skills and experience to discuss the matter in hand and make recommendations. Such groups always include 'experts', indeed sometimes they are composed exclusively of experts, primarily social scientists and those with experience in industry, administration, and so forth. They are expected to establish the facts of the situation and understand how these facts are analysed and understood in the secular world, prior to attempting a Christian judgement upon them. The groups are multi-disciplinary, and often include non-Christians who are willing to offer sympathetic expertise.

This method of working has produced really significant results; it underlies, according to Ronald Preston, nearly all substantial work done by the churches in social ethics.[4] And there is a solid theological rationale for the method. Interdisciplinarity, which is integral to the approach, is still far from common either in academic or in public life. It is far commoner for the various disciplines, specialities and professions to delimit their areas of competence and expend extraordinary amounts of energy on boundary maintenance and disposing of trespassers. The resultant fragmentation, competitiveness and misunderstanding results in whole ranges of important questions which lie in a kind of no-man's-land between specialities being unattended to, and other issues rarely being illuminated by the co-operative application of a number of different approaches and skills. Interdisciplinarity involves tearing down barriers of suspicion and competition as a way to a fuller encounter with truth; and, as such, it reflects (even if not under explicitly Christian auspices) something of the destruction of the dividing wall of hostility of which we read in the second chapter of the letter to the Ephesians, together with a care for the wholeness of truth, for the recovery of an unfragmented vision.

There is a similar significance in the fact that this way of doing social theology is almost invariably ecumenical. The older efforts to develop confessional systems of social ethics — a Calvinist, Lutheran, or Anglican ethics, for example — have been superseded, and virtually all the denominations are now committed to working in the field of social theology in a thoroughly ecumenical fashion. This gives a very much broader base for the endeavours, both theologically and geographically. It also creates tensions, as the comparatively narrow gauge consensus among Europeans and North Americans from which most earlier ecumenical work in social ethics sprang is replaced with the vastly more variegated ecumenical scene of today. Yet tensions may be healthy, the growing pains of a social theology growing out of Eurocentrism towards a greater universality and a wider scope and relevance.

And the group approach reminds us that theology is a participative affair. Theology, and *a fortiori* social theology, is too important a matter to be left to the theologians.[5] Policies, suggestions, and programmes of social action are not the product of the theologian isolated in his study, or of ecclesiastical potentates acting without consultation. At least, the experts must have their say; at most, there may be really wide discussion and a serious effort to listen to the poor and needy, to see the issue through their eyes, from the bottom of the heap, as it were.

At this point a problem arises. The whole approach from Oldham to recent times has an inbuilt elitist tendency: it is the *experts,* the articulate and skilled ones with relevant experience, who are to be brought together and allowed to share in shaping social theology. This may be far preferable to leaving the issues exclusively in the hands of ecclesiastics or theologians, but it, like all elitism, has its dangers, particularly in its failure to take with adequate seriousness the fact that experts too have their interests, which often give a skew to their views. They are not, as intellectuals, the eagle-eyed, dispassionate, objective and altruistic Guardians dreamed up by Plato in the *Republic,* but men and women, with skills and insights, but also occupying a social position which can limit their insight and empathy or even distort their values. Broadening the base for ecumenical ethical discussions has already brought right into the ethical workshop a whole range of tensions and conflicts of which in the quite recent past many people were quite unaware — and that before real participation, particularly of the poor, has even started.

The commitment to participation which Oldham inaugurated and which has begun to snowball in recent days reminds us that theology is a function of the Church and, in this case most explicitly, part of the Church's disturbing service to the society in which it is set. We are having in this generation to look again at the nature of the Church's involvement in society, and its role in social conflicts. The earlier ecumenical ethics may have had more than a trace of ecclesiastical triumphalism as well as intellectualism. Today the Church, particularly perhaps in a country such as Britain, has to establish its right to be heard, and this cannot be done by speaking alone. The being and activity of the Church shape and confirm or refute its social and political statements; they must flow out of action if they are to be capable of instigating action and carrying conviction.

The Theologian in Search of a Role

Oldham inaugurated a way of doing theology which has developed so far and proved in many ways so successful that it has become necessary to enquire what role there is for the theologian within it. The traditional authoritative position of the theologian as representing the Queen of the Sciences, or the *magisterium* of the Church, has to be set aside at the very beginning. His initial function is to bring people together; he is more of an impressario than an actor: he gets the right people on stage at the right time, while he himself stays in the wings. Bringing people together is indeed a Christian thing to do, especially when it involves removing misunderstandings and opening up possibilities of communication. There is something genuinely attractive and Christian in the idea of the theologian as having a servant-role: the modest and self-effacing theologian, more given to listening than to talking, sees himself as a catalyst and an enabler.

One can see why this image of the theologian as initiator, catalyst, and finally mouthpiece of a consensus has proved attractive. It is a useful corrective to the not infrequent arrogance and triumphalism of the past. It has produced impressive results — of that there is no doubt. But is it enough to suggest that the distinctive contribution of theology is a way of organising discussion? Does the theologian not require a role larger than that of initiating and servicing discussion? Can social theology be entirely consensual and not at all prescriptive? Is there, perhaps, a relation between the prevalence in the Anglo-Saxon world of linguistic philosophy and the fashionableness of this understanding of the theologians' task? There do, on the face of it, seem to be some interesting parallels between this way of doing theology and the linguistic philsophers' rather self-conscious modesty about their role. Eschewing the system-building, the grandoise schematizations and the bald imperatives of the past, the linguistic philosopher presents himself as a kind of technician of language and of argument. I once heard the inaugural lecture of an eminent professor of moral philosophy. He depicted his task, and that of his discipline, as helping people to think more clearly, argue more cogently, and use language more precisely in moral discourse. This, he argued with grace and fluency, has nothing whatever to do with making people good, or helping them to act in a better way. Such matters were entirely beyond the sphere of his proper professional interest. Socrates' question, "Can goodness be taught?" he left to the moralizers; it was no concern of the moral philosopher. His modesty involved writing off a great part of the traditional content of the subject he professed, a narrowing which depended on a new and total split between teaching people to think straight and teaching, or helping, people to be good. It is obvious how deeply the content and presentation of much contemporary British theology has been shaped by the encounter with linguistic philosophy; my contention is that this encounter has also influenced the way many theologians see their role. Like the philosophers, the theologians see themselves as the enablers of discussion; people who are good at gathering others together, experts at guiding debate. But often enough they, or other participants in the exercise, seem doubtful what their *proprium,* their own distinctive contribution, may be to the discussion. In the past Anglo-Saxon theologians were often *too* sure; now the pendulum has swung to the other extreme. And is not the new modesty, even uncertainty, on the part of the theologian a major source of the tendency which Preston discerns for theologians to swing from refusing to recognise the proper autonomy of secular disciplines to an uncritical and adulatory reliance on them?[6] A dialogue on such a basis is no more productive than a situation where the theologian pontificates in splendid isolation, disregarding entirely the contribution of others. It can easily lead to the theologian becoming nothing more than the initial enabler and final mouthpiece of the group, reflecting more or less accurately their opinions, attitudes and prejudices. If this is theology at all, which is extremely doubtful, it is based not upon tradition or on Scripture, but on the informed opinions of intelligent people of good will. It is therefore peculiarly open to the charge, preferred so repeatedly and acidly by E.R. Norman, of simply reflecting the conventional values of the intelligentsia, decked out rather unconvincingly as Christian ethics.

Fortunately there are those who, while rejecting the idea of the theologian as a solo performer, and affirming the value of wide ecumenical and interdisciplinary consultation in the framing of Christian opinion on social issues, have had a special concern for the theological *proprium,* the distinctive contribution of the theologian to the discussion. The late Ian Ramsey, for instance, was himself deeply involved in a series of groups which produced notable statements. "I cannot exaggerate," he said, "the necessity for trans-disciplinary groups, nor their significance, nor their theological and ethical value, any more than their novelty and difficulty . . . Such groups will recognise the need for a classical theology which gives us the necessary professional background, and also for what has been called a 'contextual' theology where believers develop the facility for latching onto the multiple discussion of a problem. Such a discussion not only aims at a creative decision; in reaching such a decision it discovers also new possibilities of theological articulation. It is in this contextual theology that there will be found the growing points of our faith and the intimations of a new culture, a culture Christian, scientific, technological and humane."[7] This call for a dual theological input, 'classical' and 'contextual', needs to be carefully heeded; it suggests that the theological *proprium* is dangerously distorted if either component is omitted, or if the balance between them is wrong. Ronald Preston has also, of course, been involved creatively in a great deal of this kind of group wrestling with intractible ethical problems, taking as an operational principle that "moral theologians do not lay down a law from above, they try to clarify issues from within, in association with those of relevent experience of them, whether experts or lay folk."[8]

The 'Oldham method' certainly provided a role for the 'contextual theologian'; what was increasingly in doubt was how 'classical theology' fitted in, and whether the contextual method without a strong classical input counted as theology at all. The theologian operating in accordance with the 'Oldham method', however highly (and rightly) he rates it as a way of doing social theology, must have a special care for his own *proprium,* the distinctive contribution that he may make *qua* theologian both to the clarification and to the resolution of issues.

In a recent article M.M. Thomas attributes to "the Anglo-Saxon theological ethicists like Ronald Preston" the raising for him of the question of distinctiveness, of the theological *proprium:* "the question whether there could not be ideologies and patterns of politics which were more or less informed by Christian insights about man as created, fallen and redeemed, and open constantly to the judgement and renewal of the Gospel of Christ. While power politics was a realm in which accumulated sin and necessity played a large part, was it not possible to make the ethic of power politics less tragic and violent by its transformation by the ethic of forgiveness and grace? Could not collective politics itself receive grace for its renewal".[9] "The Christian faith," as Preston himself puts it in his recent book, "is the source both of spiritual strength and of critical insights which can be brought alongside the expertise and insights of others in the search for a just and sustainable society." He calls for a renewed grasp of the insights of faith and for detailed attention to the complicated matters of their interaction with other disciplines and their application as policy.[10] Ramsey, Thomas and Preston are clearly and emphatically affirming that it is not enough for the theologian to bring people together, to be an enabler and a catalyst; he must also have a care for his own proper and distinctive contribution to the discussion, lest the result be well-informed and genial, but hardly an expression of the Christian Gospel.

Direct Social Theology

There are Christian thinkers who affirm the possibility of a more or less direct passage from fundamental Christian insights to political and social applications. Karl Barth, for instance, boldly sought to apply with remarkable directness doctrinal insights to political and social problems. Believing in "the analogical but extremely concrete relationship between the Christian Gospel and certain political decisions and modes of behaviour",[11] Barth longed for a Christian social and political teaching which "takes its bearings from the Christian centre". The Church, he argues, must "stand for social justice in the political sphere" because the Son of Man came to seek and save the lost; it must affirm the equality of citizens because it is "the fellowship of those who live in one faith under one Lord on the basis of a Baptism in one Spirit"; because of the diversity of the gifts of the Spirit the Church will support the separation of judiciary, legislature and executive; because Jesus Christ is the light of the world, "the Church is the sworn enemy of all secret policies and secret diplomacy;" and so on.[12]

Others, too, espousing a strong doctrine of the authority of Scripture, argue that social and political imperatives may be taken directly from the Bible and it should be allowed to shape the social and political orders.[13] But one does not need to be from the fundamentalist wing to believe that insights from the Bible or the Christian tradition are of *immediate* relevance to the present situation. The Christendom Group, an Anglo-Catholic body influential in England from the 1930s to the 1950s, believed (as did many Roman Catholic thinkers of roughly the same period) that their rather idealised picture of the Middle Ages as a time when society more or less faithfully reflected and expressed Christian belief provided relevant guidance for today.[14]

All those who support a 'direct' social theology share many things in common. They are much concerned for the distinctiveness of Christian social thinking, which they hope to preserve by ensuring that it is rooted in, and shaped by, Christian sources rather than the contemporary environment. Theology is usually understood as something given, as revealed truths which do not change. Social and moral theology therefore becomes *applied* theology, the application of Christian principles, dogmas or the Bible to the resolution of social problems and the shaping of society. Christian truth is something given, and it is infinitely more important for the social theologian to understand this 'given' than it is that he should have a sensitive appreciation of the society in which he operates or the complexities of the problems. Theological truths are unchanging and perennially relevant. This highly prescriptive kind of theology could well claim to be classical theology, although it is doubtful if this is what Ian Ramsey meant by the 'classical theology' he believed to be the necessary complement to 'contextual theology.'

The objections to direct social theology are manifold, and cumulatively they form a telling indictment. Space forbids to follow through these criticisms in any detail here but, put very briefly, they suggest that direct social theology operates with untenable and rigid notions of the nature of theological truth or biblical authority. On the other hand, there is a dangerous reluctance to come to terms with the complexities of social and political issues, and an unwillingness to acknowledge the damage that absolutist solutions frequently involve. For all its naivity and dangers, direct social theology has two clear strengths: it takes seriously the desirability for Christian social thinking to be distinctively *Christian,* and it can promote a truly Christian intransigence in saying quite simply that Nazism, or apartheid, or racism is incompatible with the Gospel of Jesus Christ. This suggests that direct social theology may have a special capacity to sustain a necessary Christian 'No' in circumstances which call for this. It is better at following an ethical *via negativa* than at producing blueprints of the good society. As Bonhoeffer put it: "The Church cannot indeed proclaim a concrete earthly order which follows as a necessary consequence from faith in Jesus Christ, but she can and must oppose every concrete order which constitutes an offence to faith in Jesus Christ, and in doing this she defines, at least negatively, the limits of an order within which faith in Jesus Christ and obedience are possible."[15]

Indirect Social Theology

Those who find direct social theology dangerous and believe that the Bible, doctrine and the Christian tradition do not give immediately applicable answers to today's problems, are not less committed in seeking a social theology which is distinctively Christian. Thinkers like Ronald Preston, J.H. Oldham, William Temple, George Bell, John Baillie, J.C. Bennett and many others have serious reservations about the boldness with which dogma, the Bible and theological insights are applied to political problems by theologians such as Barth. Mediation, they teach is necessary; basic Christian principles must be filtered through 'middle axioms' or the like before they can be put to work by the political decision-makers.

Middle axiom thinking on social ethics involves four stages or levels. The first is the basis for the whole operation. It is the Christian faith, understood variously as a system of doctrine, or the teaching of the Bible, or the Gospel. We should not expect this foundation to be spelled out with too great precision, for what is involved is something like 'the essence of Christianity': what all Christians have in common, the deposit of faith, rather than any denominational or confessional, and therefore divisive, development or interpretation of the faith. This, then, is a foundation on which all — or most — Christians may agree, and on which they may base co-operation across sectarian and theological differences. From this is derived the next stage: fundamental ethical principles which are authentically Christian, even if they may also be shared by many non-Christians, because they are implied by the formulations of stage one. These are principles of great generality and affirm such things as the dignity of man and social structures such as the family and the nation within which man is enabled to achieve his destiny in fellowship. As William Temple put it: "Freedom, Fellowship, Service — these are the three principles of Christian social order, derived from the still more fundamental Christian postulates that Man is a child of God and is destined for a life of eternal fellowship with Him."[16]

Between general statements of principle derived from the Gospel, and concrete decisions come the 'middle axioms'. "It is these," writes J.H. Oldham, "that give relevance and point to the Christian ethic. They are an attempt to define the directions in which, in a particular state of society Christian faith must express itself. They are not binding for all time, but are provisional definitions of the type of behaviour required of Christians at a given period in given circumstances."[17] Ten years later J.C. Bennett described middle axioms as "those goals for society which are more specific than universal Christian principles and less specific than concrete institutions or programmes for action."[18] Examples of middle axioms cited by Bennett were opposition to racism and the need for an international organisation to bring order to international relations. Temple devotes the sixth chapter of *Christianity and Social Order* entitled "The Task Before us" to the elaboration of a series of what are in effect 'middle axioms' concerning family life, the sanctity of the individual, education, fellowship, and the economic system.

Temple relegates to an appendix his "Suggested Programme". He does this because he sees the derivation of policies and practices from middle axioms as the most contentious stage of the process and believes that this last stage is to be undertaken by individual Christians rather than the Church, in the light of the best expertise available. Inevitably there will be disagreements among Christians about the application of Christian principles; but disagreements at this level he sees as in no way impugning the validity of the principles which have been percolated through middle axioms.

This scheme presents a clear and in many ways very attractive statement of the theological *proprium* in ethics and its limits. The theologian's distinctive contribution is to bring his developed understanding of doctrine and of Scripture, together with the fundamental general ethical principles he has distilled from the Gospel, to meet and interact with the expertise of the social scientists. This interaction takes place to some extent in the formulation of middle axioms, but more radically in the development and implementation of policies and programmes. Charles Elliott has criticized Temple (and by implication other middle axiom theorists) for presupposing a value-free social science which may safely be entrusted with the modest role of implementing middle axioms.[19] While there is something to be said for this argument, and it may well be a just criticism of some social ethicists, it neglects Temple's affirmation that there will usually be several competing solutions to any given social problem, each backed by the opinions of experts, and each claiming to be derived from middle axioms. Temple is concerned that guidance should be given to Christians involved in decision making, but well aware of the dangers of labelling one school of economics or sociology or one political philosophy as 'Christian' in an unqualified way. The theologian should beware of pushing his authority too far, of becoming imperialistic and denying a proper autonomy to other disciplines.

For myself, I am more concerned at the ivory-tower misunderstanding of the nature of theology which may be engendered or encouraged by the middle axiom approach. It sometimes suggests that the theologian is rather like Moses coming down from the mountain and veiling his face with middle axioms because the glory of his countenance is too great for the people to behold! It is as if theology were done in olympian detachment and without dynamic interaction with praxis. The resultant pure truths are then transformed into ethics and finally applied, with necessary modifications, in practice and policy. This would involve far too clear a distinction between doctrine and ethics: while doctrine may provide the principles for Christian behaviour no possibility is allowed for praxis to be regarded as a criterion of Christian truth. Is it any longer tenable to think in static terms of an unchanging deposit of faith which may be investigated and expounded as a 'pure science' without reference to its context, and then applied, put to work as it were, by a kind of theological technology? Is not the relation between doctrine, ethics and action far more dynamic and dialectical than the middle axiom model would suggest? In terms of the quotation from Ian Ramsey cited earlier, what we need is a careful spelling out of the relation between 'classical' and 'contextual' theology.

The proponents of the middle axiom model in the '40s and '50s seemed to operate with a rather static notion of a deposit of Christian truth which is of timeless validity and relevance. They discern correctly, and significantly, that the Gospel does not provide us with a blue-print of the Christian society, or a text-book on how to build the Kingdom. But they seem still to assume that Christianity provides us with a world view, a more or less coherent map of reality on which marching instructions for political and social behaviour may ultimately be based.

The presuppositions concerning the Church involved in middle axiom thinking deserve further exploration. There is no doubt that the Church is taken with deep seriousness, but a sharp distinction is made between the proper role of the Church as custodian and proclaimer of the Gospel, and its improper but frequently asserted claims to be itself an agency of social and political action. Temple is particularly emphatic that the Church must not commit itself to particular policies. The making of actual political decisions and the implementation of policies must, he claims, be left to the experts and to the individual Christian acting without specific ecclesiastical endorsement of his actions but with general encouragement to involve himself *qua* Christian in politics. Temple seems to believe that dogma and general principles unite, while policies and praxis divide; and in such a world the unity of the Body must be maintained above all political conflicts. Different, even contradictory, conclusions may be derived from shared Christian principles; theology provides no resource for resolving these conflicts; therefore the Church can and must allow its members great diversity in their practical commitments. "It is of crucial importance," he writes, "that the Church acting corporately should not commit itself to any particular policy."[20] The task of the Church, and therefore the theological *proprium,* is "to inculcate Christian principles and the power of the Christian spirit."[21] Implementation is then passed on to the individual Christian citizen.

As a rule for normal circumstances this sharp distinction between the Church and the individual Christian may very well stand; but there are surely situations in which the Church, as Church, must get involved politically, and where detachment for the sake of preserving the life and unity of the Church can amount to disobedience, situations where costly institutional identification with the lot of the poor and the oppressed is the only Christian way for the Church. Both Barth's emphatic espousal of political preaching,[22] and the activities of the World Council of Churches' Programme to Combat Racism would seem to be excluded by Temple's argument. The Church by its nature and according to its mandate is neither absolutely above nor totally immersed in the political fray. Furthermore, the Church is itself a political entity whose existence is, in Barth's words, "of ultimate and supremely political significance."[23] This means, among other things, that the Church itself, no less than society, is *semper reformanda,* subject to judgement and renewal in the light of the Gospel. Serious social ethics has no place for churchly triumphalism, nor can it accept as a matter of principle that the Church may never speak on matters of policy, or take sides in politics.

Conclusion

Middle axiom thinking developed through 'Oldham groups' has had a long period of dominance in social theology, and has produced significant fruits. But the elitism of the Oldham approach has begun to attract criticism: there is a new suspicion of 'experts' in the air, and no longer is the objectivity and disinterestedness of their judgements taken for granted. Rather, it is assumed that where you stand affects what you see, and efforts are being made to see how theology can be done 'from below', that is, in solidarity with the poor and oppressed, seeing things through their eyes and closely related to action on their behalf. Simultaneously there has been a swing back to the direct derivation from Scripture or doctrine of practical imperatives, sometimes involving a refusal to recognise that the problem to which middle axioms were a solution exists at all. There is an endeavour to stand the middle axiom progression from theology to action on its head: in the attempt to live and act faithfully, in Christian praxis that is, one comes to know what the Gospel is — or, in the words of John's Gospel, "He who does what is true comes to the light" (John 3.21). It is not, therefore, simply a matter of deriving prescriptions for political and social action from independently established Christian truth, or of applying a theory to society. Rather, there must be a dialectic between theory and practice such that, in Moltmann's words, "the new criterion of theology and of faith is to be found in praxis."[24]

In words strangely reminiscent of Marx's insistence in the *Theses on Feuerbach* that the task of philosophy was not to interpret the world but to change it, for only then does it become intelligible, William Temple, despairing of his earlier idealistic attempts to make Christian sense of the world, wrote in 1939: "The world of today is one of which no Christian map can be made . . . Our task with this world is not to explain it but to convert it."[25] The real distinctiveness of Christian social theology lies not only in a direct or indirect derivation from Christian roots of its principles of social action, or even in a proper relation between a 'classical' and a 'contextual' theology. It must be rooted in the dialectic between faithful Christian practical engagement with the great issues of our time, and the Christian tradition in all its complexity.

Notes

1. Edited and commented on in Beeson, T., *Britain Today and Tomorrow,* London, Collins, 1978.

2. Norman, E. R., *Christianity and the World Order,* London, Oxford University Press, 1979.

3. An excellent discussion of the present state of ecumenical social thinking is Abrecht, P., "Ecumenical Co-operation for Social Responsibility", *Crucible,* July-Sept., 1979, pp. 105-112.

4. Preston, R.H., "Anglican and Ecumenical Styles in Social Ethics", *Crucible,* July-Sept., 1978, pp. 117-126.

5. As John Drury reminded us in his *Angels and Dirt,* London, Darton Longman and Todd, 1972, p.17.

6. Preston R.H., *Religion and the Persistence of Capitalism,* London, SCM Press, 1979, p.24.

7. Cited in Edwards, D.L., *The British Churches Turn to the Future,* London, SCM Press, 1973, p.38.

8. Preston, op.cit., p.23.

9. M.M. Thomas, "European Theology in the Experience of an Indian Layman and Ecumenist", *Religion and Society* (Bangalore), XXV: 4, p.84.

10. Preston, op.cit., p.62.

11. Barth, K., *Against the Stream,* London, SCM Press, 1954, p.42.

12. Ibid., pp.36-40.

13. Good examples are Sir Frederick Catherwood's books, *A Beter Way: The Case for a Christian Social Order,* London, Inter-Varsity Press, 1975, and *The Christian in Industrial Society,* London, Tyndale Press, 1964.

14. A recent example of a similar endeavour, but from the orthodox tradition, is Geervarghese Mar Osthanthios, *Theology of a Classless Society,* London, Lutterworth, 1979. Here it is argued in singularly naive fashion that the classless society, more or less as understood by Marx, is a direct demand and implication of the doctrine of the Trinity.

15. Bonhoeffer, D., *Ethics,* London, SCM Press, 1955, p.324.

16. Temple, W., *Christianity and Social Order,* London, Penguin Books, 1942, p.54.

17. Visser't Hooft, W.A. & Oldham, J.H., *The Church and Its Function in Society,* London, George Allen and Unwin, 1937, p.210.

18. *The Church and the Disorder of Society,* The Amsterdam Assembly Series, III, London, SCM Press, 1948, p.158n.

19. Elliott, C., "Vision and Utopia", *Theology,* May 1978, pp. 712-9. See also the correspondence with Ronald Preston resulting from this article in the Nov. 1978 and Jan. 1979 issues of *Theology.*

20. Temple, op.cit., p.18.

21. Ibid., p.23.

22. "It is a bad sign when Christians are frightened by 'political' sermons — as if Christian preaching could be anything but political. And if it were not political, how would it show that it is the salt and the light of the world? The Christian Church that is aware of its political responsibility will demand political preaching; and it will interpret it politically even if it contains no direct reference to politics." Barth, K., op.cit., p.47.

23. Ibid., p. 19.

24. Cited from *Religion, Revolution and the Future,* in Kee, A., (ed.), *A Reader in Political Theology,* London, SCM Press, 1974, p.54.

25. Cited in Ramsey, A.M., *From Gore to Temple,* London, Longmans, 1960, p.160.

4

Christianity and Self-Interest

Gerard J. Hughes S.J.

An outline sketch of one Christian response to the contemporary social order might take the following shape. Our Western societies are ultimately based on capitalism. As an economic system, capitalism places great stress on the profit motive, with the consequence that a society based on capitalism comes to stress the importance of enlightened self-interest, and is led to develop a picture of human beings which is fundamentally egoistic in character. The practice of capitalism encourages the development of just those traits of self-reliance, competitiveness and acquisitiveness which are typical of an egoist morality. In contrast, Christianity upholds an ideal of human perfection which is radically at odds with this egoistic picture of man. A Christian social order should be founded on altruism, on a loving concern for the weak, the poor and powerless. Only such an altruism can foster the social structures which will enable us to avoid the injustices which, as experience surely teaches us, are the consequence of capitalism. In the last analysis, Christianity must reject capitalism as contrary to the Gospel.

It is the purpose of this paper to assess at least some of the complex hidden strands in this argument. The argument contains two major assertions: the first is that Christianity is incompatible with an egoist view of morality; and the second is that capitalism necessarily presupposes such a view of morality either in theory or, at least, in practice. The truth of the second of these assertions is a question which must in the end be established within the disciplines of economics and political sociology. All that as a philosopher I can hope to do is to throw light on the matter by presenting the issues to which these disciplines must address themselves in as clear and provocative a manner as I can. In the second part of this paper I shall try to formulate some such questions. The major part of this paper, however, will be concerned with the relationship between Christianity and egoism as a moral theory, and only indirectly with the relationship between egoism and capitalism. I shall argue that egoism is a much more subtle moral theory than is often supposed, and that if egoism is in the end incompatible with Christianity it is at any rate not crudely and obviously so. It will follow that, even if capitalism is fundamentally egoist in its presuppositions about human nature, it will still not be a simple matter to show that capitalism is incompatible with Christianity.

My strategy will be to show, first of all, that egoism as a moral theory is not *obviously* repugnant to our ordinary moral sensibilities nor, indeed, to our Christian moral perceptions. (I have already tried to discuss elsewhere[1] the thorny question of whether there is anything distinctive in a Christian view of morality, and I shall not raise the issue again here. I intend my remarks in this paper to be neutral with respect to that set of problems.) This conclusion should not surprise us. Egoism as a moral theory has a long and not totally undistinguished history and is still actively discussed by moral philosophers. No theory which is obviously and crudely wrong would have survived so long, for it is a characteristic of all reasonably successful moral theories, as it is a characteristic of successful scientific theories, that *in general* they reach reasonable conclusions. If a moral theory is unsatisfactory it will either be because it is a very partial account and fails by being incomplete; or else that in some few — possibly extreme — situations it leads to conclusions which are nevertheless seen as clearly false. I shall argue that this is the case with egoism. If it is false, it will be because of the conclusions to which it leads in certain extreme cases, not because it is manifestly mistaken right across the board. And if egoism is to suffer in comparison with a Christian morality, it will in all probability not be because Christian ethics is right and egoism wrong on most questions, but because Christian ethics can more safely be pushed in extreme cases than egoism can. Having tried to show that there is nothing to choose between the two theories in 'ordinary' situations, I shall therefore go on to see whether there are grounds for differentiating between them in their handling of extreme cases, cases which are nevertheless of considerable social and political importance.

A convenient point of departure is to be found in Ronald Preston's recent *Religion and the Persistence of Capitalism* in the course of his debates with Tawney on the one hand and Rawls on the other. In the third of his Maurice Lectures, Preston writes,

> Still less can capitalism be said to be the economic expression of Christianity; only the belief in the 'divine hand' ever gave that view plausibility. Capitalism relies far too exclusively on self-interest, ignoring the necessity of other motives on which (as we have seen) it must implicitly rely in practice but does nothing to cultivate, and indeed actually undermines. On the other hand, socialist theories, whether Christian or secular, have tended to work with an over-optimistic view of man which assumes that it is only because of capitalism that self-interest is so powerful; change to socialist structures and it will disappear, together with the conflicts of interest which go with it.[2]

Rather than this, Preston argues that we must adopt a more nuanced view,

> Society needs to be organised so that the equivalent of the 'unseen hand' makes self-interest and the common good coincide, in order to prevent altruism from being put under a greater strain than it can bear.[3]

In passages such as these, we can see clearly enough that Preston is willing to give some, but far from total, support to the kind of outline argument that I sketched at the beginning of this paper. The critique of capitalism from a

Christian point of view is related to the disputes about the place of self-interest in morality. It is especially noteworthy that the notion of motivation is introduced into the debate, a point which Preston emphasises in his criticism of Rawls:

> Motivation is obviously important as far as it goes. For instance Christians, in common with other men, must have a concern for justice, and it is quite possible that Christians can give a much firmer motivation to the search for justice than can be given on a purely secular basis. Efforts to establish a rational basis for the pursuit of justice, such as John Rawls' notable study, *A Theory of Justice,* are extremely important, but it is hard to believe that they provide a sufficient motivation without some greater dynamic than can come from the kind of rational contractual political analysis which Rawls attempts.[4]

Again,

> To my mind [Christians] may well think that Rawls is too individualistic. People are persons in relations, they are social beings. Why should not their altruism, their *agape* if you like, be called upon as well as their rationality and their self-interest? After all, *agape,* as Christians understand it, may well be deepened by Christ, but it draws out from man what is already there. And while we have seen that it is naive to expect society to run on *agape* alone, it is impoverishing to man not to call on it at all.[5]

These passages from contemporary debate are in interesting ways parallel to the dispute between Butler and Hobbes. Butler perhaps invokes the 'divine hand' to ensure that self-love and benevolence will not ultimately conflict, but his general concern is to show that even without the divine hand they do not conflict in the way commonly supposed. Butler, too, seeks to achieve this result by arguing that Hobbes has simply ignored the altruistic inclinations that we have. Butler might well have shared the common view that Hobbes' picture of man was sub-Christian in this respect; but he is nevertheless at pains to make sure that the altruistic motivation upon which he insists is not put under too great a strain. Significantly, too, Butler bases his case against Hobbes on a particular view of motivation. We may surmise that he would agree with Preston about the inadequacy of a morality based merely on rational justification in the manner of Rawls' theory of justice.

The Christian critique of capitalism so far sketched out derives from two quite different objections to the moral egoism on which it is taken to depend. One objection concerns the adequacy of an egoist account of moral motivation; the other, not carefully enough distinguished from the first, turns on the adequacy of egoist accounts of self-interest as a justification for what ought to be done. The first part of this paper will examine these two questions in turn; and the results of this inquiry will then enable us to formulate some precise questions about the nature of capitalism which the Christian critic might like to put to economists and social psychologists.

Self-Interest and Motivation

a Egoism and 'Altruistic' Motives

It used to be the received opinion in moral theory that whereas egoism could easily provide motivation for being moral (and, indeed, this was one of the main advantages of egoist theories), other views of morality would have great difficulty in doing so. Other moral views could indeed answer the question 'Why be moral?' by giving reasons, even good or decisive reasons; but in the last analysis they have to concede that, if this question represents a request to be shown a motive for acting as one ought, no such motives can be given to cover all cases. I think that there are good grounds for challenging both limbs of this traditional view.[6]

That egoism can give a motivational answer to the question 'Why be moral?' would seem almost to be a tautology. For is not egoism the view that each person ought to act in his own interests? And surely one always has a motive for acting in one's interests — indeed, what better motive could there possibly be? But the matter is not so simple.

It is certainly true that the classical egoist positions have laid great stress on the importance of motivation in ethics. As part of his general programme to integrate ethics with human biology and psychology, Hobbes took it to be essential to provide a motivation for every action that a person ought to perform. A person is obliged to do only those actions which he is able to do, and he is able to act only if his action springs from those drives which are connected with pleasure and pain. It is therefore particularly noteworthy that Hobbes is so careful to provide artificial motivation for man's moral behaviour in the state by ensuring that the ruler has at his disposal a series of deterrent punishments, and, presumably, an efficient system for detecting transgressions of the social contract. The implications of this for Hobbes' view of motivation are important.[7]

On Hobbes' account, 'motivation' is a causal notion, and is connected with emotions such as fear, aversion, love, envy and pity as well as with other desires which we would not normally class as emotions. To experience an emotion or a desire is, other things being equal, to be moved to act, and this is to have a motive for acting. Dispositional statements, such as that a person is envious or lustful or desirous of his own well-being are statements about the motives a man has only because they are linked with the truth of causal statements about occurrences of such emotions on particular occasions. To be able to act on a particular occasion, a person must at that time experience a desire. It will not suffice that he is in dispositional terms favourably disposed to act in such and such a way. The truth that a man is in general inclined to act in his own interests does not of itself entail that at some particular time he will actually experience any inclination to perform an action which his own interests require him to perform. Hobbes' remark that Good and Evil are the names we give to our appetites and aversions is not to be taken as a claim that at any given moment a man experiences an appetite to do what is in his long-term interests or has an aversion to acting in a way prejudicial to those interests. Hobbes is well aware that not all agents are so clear-headed about their interests, or so free from the temptation to pursue the immediately attractive. It is for this reason that he is careful to provide a system of sanctions for law-breaking which, he hopes, will induce fear on each occasion (or, perhaps more reasonably, on sufficient occasions to prevent such widespread lawlessness as would lead to the breakdown of stable government).

It is quite clear from this that Hobbes must have distinguished sharply between a process of reasoning which would justify the conclusion that it is not in a man's best interests to break the law, on the one hand, and, on the other, the occurrent desires which are needed to enable him to act on each particular occasion as his long-term interests require. Reasons for keeping the laws of the state are always available, but Hobbes saw clearly enough that his theory of motivation required much more than this. It is not obvious that all the criticisms directed against Hobbes have been so clear about the precise point that they wished to establish against him. Butler and Hume seem to have accepted Hobbes' general position that a man had to have an occurrent motive if he was to be able to act, and to have concentrated on showing that Hobbes had given an inadequate account of the motives that men have. Thus Butler sought to undermine Hobbes' egoist account of motives. Once we clearly distinguish between the object of a desire and the pleasure that comes from having a desire satisfied, we can see that the objects of our desires are not solely concerned with our own interests. And of course it is true that to desire the happiness of John and Mary is not the same as to desire the pleasure of seeing them happy; the two desires have different objects, and the first could be satisfied in circumstances in which the second would not be. But it seems to me that this point is not perhaps crucial to anything which Hobbes need have been concerned to defend. He needed to defend two distinct theses: **i** that on every occasion a man requires to feel inclined to do what he ought to do if he is to be able to do it; and **ii** that there is an egoist justification available for every true claim about what a person ought to do. The first thesis is not threatened at all by Butler's contention that some of the inclinations in question are inclinations of benevolence. Indeed, I should have thought that a Hobbesian would wish to argue that, since the stability of society is so important to each of its members, they will wish to have a programme of moral education which will result in people feeling *inclined* to the law-abiding behaviour which will preserve that stability. Hobbes, just as much as Butler, will favour individuals developing inclinations to act in ways which the agent himself might well describe in 'altruistic' terms; allowing, and, for that matter, helping others to pursue their goals is part of the price each egoist has to pay for the social stability which is in his own best interests. If there is a difference between Butler and Hobbes, it seems to me that Butler is claiming that such inclinations are innate, whereas for Hobbes, I think, they would have to be the result of a moral education.

But what of the second thesis? Do not Butler's criticisms undermine at least this part of Hobbes' view — and it is the most central part? Perhaps they do — though if they do it is not, I think, that Butler has automatically established this by establishing his point about motivation (assuming he has established even that much). It is important to note that the second thesis is one about the kind of justification that can be given for saying that a person ought to act in such and such a way; it is not a thesis about the motives he has. I shall deal with the question of justification in connection with egoism in the next section. For the moment, the point I wish to make is simply that Butler at least directly threatens not Hobbes' view of the necessity of motivation for moral behaviour, nor even the range of motives that Hobbes could allow himself, but, so far as I can see, only the comparatively peripheral point about whether such altruistic motives are part of man's natural constitution.

More radical critics, such as Kant, might wish to claim that motivation in the sense of inclination is not part of morality at all, and is not even a necessary condition for moral action. Bernard Williams, with his customary neatness, makes this point, and calls attention to an important ambiguity in the term 'motive' in the following passage:

> Kantians make the distinction between motivations which are emotional, grounded in desire, and particular, as against motivations which are universal, rational, and of principle. The step to morality involves a discontinuous step to the latter. For Hume, there are desires of different degrees of generality, involving objects with different degrees of remoteness and independence from the subject: the slide towards morality is a slide along these continua. Connected with this is the point from which we started, that for Kant impersonal and intrapersonal altruism is grounded in the structure of practical reason; for Hume it is grounded in a special sort of desire or sentiment.[8]

Williams concludes his article by suggesting that "it is not the Kantian leap from the particular and the affective to the rational and universal that makes all the difference; it is rather the Humean step — that is to say, the first Humean step — from the self to someone else."[9]

Whatever be the truth about Williams' conclusion here, it is important to notice the two senses of 'motive' to which he calls attention. In the first sense, in which 'motive' means 'inclination', Hobbes certainly did not believe that men naturally had altruistic inclinations; but then, neither did he believe that they always had inclinations to act in their own best interests. I surmise that he would have happily accepted that men could and should be educated in such a way that some of their inclinations could be described as altruistic; after all, Hobbes was all in favour of the Christian virtues. But he was realist enough to consider that no amount of Christian education would suffice to motivate the moral life without the additional help of publicly enforced sanctions. In the second, Kantian, sense 'motive' is used in the sense of 'justification'. Hobbes clearly saw the difference between the two — witness his claim that he alone, with his egoist theory of justification, succeeded in really explaining why it is that the Christian virtues *are* virtues.[10] Here Hobbes seems to me to see more clearly than Butler, and no less clearly than Kant, that one *needs* a rational justification for such claims.

b Two Alleged Criticisms of an Egoist Account of Motivation

In the light of this, we may return to the criticism that capitalist theories, because they will rely on self-interest, cannot provide adequate motivation for the practice of morality, and especially of Christian morality. We can distinguish two quite separate points that might be intended, corresponding to the two senses of 'motivation'.

A The criticism of capitalism is based on a view of the place of inclinations in morality. In particular: **i** Capitalism ignores certain altruistic inclinations that man innately has, or fails to inculcate such inclinations where they are not innate. **ii** In so doing, capitalism is forced to appeal to inclinations which are too weak to lead men to act in the way required by Christian morality — especially perhaps, the Christian stress on equality, and the concern with those in the greatest need. **iii** In the longer term, capitalism in practice tends to undermine, and even to eradicate, the altruistic inclinations which men naturally have.

B The criticism of capitalism turns on the kinds of action which can be justified within a capitalist framework. In particular: **i** Capitalism, since it justifies actions solely in terms of self-interest, simply cannot of its very nature provide a setting in which *moral* issues as such will even arise. **ii** There are certain moral values, or moral obligations, which are important, and central to Christianity, which no theory couched solely in terms of self-interest can account for.

The issues raised by B will be considered in the next section. For the moment I wish to concentrate on A. I think that the passages from Preston which I quoted in the introduction to this paper read most naturally as expressions of A-type criticisms. The fear that altruism might be put under a greater strain than it can bear sounds like a remark about the strength and weakness of men's inclinations, rather than about the cogency of various arguments which might be invoked in favour of the common good. The criticism of Rawls, that he appeals too narrowly to rational considerations, and places no reliance on the *agape* that is already in man, sounds like a plea in favour of a quite un-Kantian approach to motivation in ethics, combined with a claim that altruistic inclinations are innate. And the whole of the first passage, which speaks of the powerfulness of self-interest, and the cultivation of more altruistic motives, seems to me to have in mind inclinations rather than justifications. There are strong reasons, then, for supposing that we are dealing with the criticisms I have listed under A. How far can this version of the case against capitalism be made out?

Two recent articles by Andrew Oldenquist and Laurence Thomas offer arguments which have a bearing on the set of criticisms listed under A.[11] Their focus is upon egoism, not upon capitalism directly. But if it be granted (in this and the next section I shall assume it is granted) that capitalism is based on self-interest and thus is related to egoism, the criticisms advanced in these articles against egoism in ethics will apply also to capitalism as a basis and framework for human living. And I shall assume, further, that if capitalism fails as a basis for moral living it must also fail when judged by Christian standards.

Oldenquist's main contentions may be summarised conveniently in terms of two pairs of assertions:

a In order to function as an egoist, an entity requires a concept of the self as unique; that is to say, it must be able to distinguish between itself and any other entity, even one that is only numerically distinct from it.

a[1] Any entity lacking this concept of a self could at most act in such a way as to discriminate between *kinds* of entity.

b One can define a notion of 'group egoism', in which every individual member of a group acts in such a way as to favour the interests only of members of that group, but without distinguishing between itself and other members of the group.

b[1] Certain kinds of human behaviour could be described as group-egoist from one point of view, even when they can be described as altruistic from another.

I shall not give the arguments which Oldenquist offers in support of these four assertions, largely because I agree with them and because they do not in themselves affect the points I wish to make. Entities of the kind mentioned in a[1] are described by Oldenquist as 'perfect Kantians', and he underlines the apparently paradoxical consequence of a[1], that (contrary to what one might imagine from reading Kant) 'lower' beings such as robots, or, possibly, ants, must necessarily act in conformity with the highest Kantian principles; whereas for human beings to act in such a way will require of them that they suspend their notion of themselves as somehow unique selves.

In connection with the second pair of assertions, Oldenquist draws upon recent researches in sociobiology in support of the view that certain entities, for example individual genes, seem to operate as perfect Kantians in the way described. They are apparently programmed to function in a way that maximises the chances of future replication of that particular gene-type, but the programme makes no distinctions between individuals of that type. Moreover, this behaviour of gene-types can influence the behaviour of the organisms whose genes they are. Oldenquist points out that if one looks at the behaviour of an individual gene, or an individual ant, then, as individuals, they appear to be perfectly altruistic. But if one looks at them in either case as individuals of a type, and concentrates upon the type, this impression of altruism disappears. The gene-type, or the ant colony, regarded as a super-individual, is thoroughly egoistic in its behaviour; in this sense we can speak of 'group-egoism'. Oldenquist suggests that such human behaviour as group-loyalty, or certain kinds of patriotism, or family loyalties, can be looked at from two points of view. From the point of view which focusses on individual members of the group, such behaviour might be considered to be altruistic; but from the group-egoist point of view, in which the individual above all is aware of the group as *his,* or a parent conscious of the children as *his* or *hers,* and hence is interested above all in distinguishing between the members of that group and those of other groups, patriotism or family loyalties can be considered egoistic in character.

Sociobiologists might argue that a person is inclined to act in his own interests because he is genetically programmed to feel so inclined; and they might further argue that the inclination to sacrifice oneself for one's children or close relatives has the same genetic basis. The individual will, on occasion, feel torn between his own personal interests and those of his children, for example. And, in the case of self-sacrifice for the sake of one's country, or one's gang, or whatever, there will characteristically be difficulty in describing the behaviour either as simply altruistic or as egoistic. It depends on whether one focusses on the individual or the super-individual.

The most immediately relevant part of this argument for our present purposes is the suggestion, if the sociobiologists are right, that each of us has innate dispositions favouring a Kantian altruism in respect of our blood relatives. If this is so, it might be thought that an egoist morality would have to ignore such tendencies, and this might provide some evidence in favour of Butler and against Hobbes. On the other hand, is Oldenquist not also right in his contention that, from one point of view, there is an egoist flavour about certain instances of self-sacrifice which might otherwise have been taken almost as paradigm cases of altruism? For the most perfect altruism not merely does not distinguish between the self and other similar individuals for the purposes of moral discrimination; neither does it single out for preferential treatment any group just on the grounds that that group is *my* group. (Incidentally, this argument seems to me to raise important questions about the possibility, and perhaps even the obligatoriness, of altruism in respect to animals; but for our present discussion, I shall restrict my comments to altruism in respect of human beings.)

In short, there is perhaps some evidence to show that egoism (and capitalism in so far as it is egoist) would require us to ignore certain instinctive inclinations which are in one way altruistic in character. But these inclinations cover only a rather limited range of human behaviour; and even that behaviour is not wholly without its egoist side to it. On the other hand, altruism would have us ignore ourselves as unique individuals; and if there are instincts which urge us to the preservation and well-being of the self, and not merely of our selves as individuals of a certain genetic kind, then altruism will require us to ignore such inclinations too. All in all, if the criticism is that capitalism ignores some of our inclinations, because of its egoist basis, it is also true that altruism will have us ignore others, some of which are linked to behaviour we might consider morally admirable.

Rather a different line of argument against egoism is advanced in the second article, by Laurence Thomas. His conclusions may or may not provide any support to a thesis about the relationship between egoism and innate dispositions, but it purports to show that at least a certain set of acquired dispositions of an altruistic nature are required by us as human beings. The steps in his argument may be briefly put as follows:

a It is in each person's interests that he have a healthy personality.

b A healthy personality includes those dispositions essential to friendship, and, in particular, includes the ability to enter into relationships involving trust.

c Relationships involving trust are incompatible with the disposition to use another person whenever it is in one's interests to do so.

d Hence, the disposition required of an egoist is incompatible with a healthy personality.

This amounts to an argument that egoism, in practice, will prove to be incoherent, and incoherent in a particular way because of the altruistic dispositions which all human persons require to have in their own interests. It is not part of Thomas' claim that any of these dispositions are innate; but, whether they are innate or acquired, they are essential to our healthy development as functioning human beings. Since, on any reasonable view of morality (and all the more so if morality is spelt out in terms analogous to the Christian ideal of love) psychological health is a legitimate moral goal, Thomas' paper can be seen as an argument for the view that egoism would inevitably run counter to what a true Christian morality would require.

The argument is extremely interesting and original. But it fails, I think, and does so for a reason that Thomas considers as a possible objection, but, in my view, fails to deal with. Rightly, Thomas sees that an egoist would try to meet this argument by asking why the egoist could not simply agree that to develop a capacity for friendship was in his interests. If this were agreed, d in the above argument simply would not be true. The egoist could back up his rejoinder by saying that it is no part of his view that he should not have, or should not need, friends. Thomas certainly has not shown that a healthy personality needs to have *everyone* as a friend. He has shown that we need, all of us, to cultivate the dispositions necessary for friendship, but that is a long way from showing that such dispositions are incompatible with being prepared to use or exploit people other than one's friends. It is surely implausible to maintain, as Thomas would have to, that to be the kind of person capable of having friends is incompatible with ever exploiting anyone.

Thomas' line of reply to this objection is to say that we do not, in friendship, consider the interests of others *in order to* be psychologically healthy (as an egoist would be driven to maintain); rather, it is *because we* are psychologically healthy that we consider the interests of our friends even, at times, at the expense of our own. And, of course, in this Thomas is surely correct. To be favourably disposed towards one's friends only because they serve one's own interests is, as the medieval theologians following Aristotle would have put it, no more than *amor concupiscentiae;* and that, if it can be called friendship at all, it is friendship of a very low grade. But I do not think that this suffices to defend Thomas against the objection. It is one thing to ask what the disposition of friendship consists in — it consists in the willingness to trust and act unselfishly in the interests of one's friends because they are one's friends. But it is quite another thing to ask on what grounds one might consider such a disposition worth having.

Thomas, so far from ruling out an egoist answer to *this* question, seems to give one himself in step a. The point is one very close to the theological debate in the middle ages about whether it was possible to have a perfectly unselfish love of God. The difficulty of answering this question was exacerbated by the fact that it was commonly accepted doctrine that all men, by a necessity of nature, had a love for that being who alone could satisfy all their desires. Despite the differences in their terminology, and the occasional confusions to which this led, their answer appears to have been to distinguish between the object of an inclination, and the reason that could be given for saying that an inclination was a valuable one to have. Thus, the object of perfect love (perfectly altruistic *agape*) was the goodness of God in and for itself; but such love is a supreme value for us because to have it satisfies man's deepest needs. In essence, the point is the one already made above in connection with Butler and Hobbes. An egoist can, and may well find good reasons for saying that he should, develop dispositions of an altruistic nature.

In short, and to sum up the arguments of this section as a whole, I see little reason to suppose that an egoist is less well placed than an altruist to integrate his moral theory with any plausible view either of man's innate inclinations or of those dispositions of an altruistic kind which a human being should, desirably, set himself to acquire. The application of these conclusions to the critique of capitalism with which we began I shall leave to the final section of this paper.

Egoism and the Justification of a Christian Morality

I shall now turn my attention to thesis B (see above p.53). Perhaps the criticisms to be made of capitalism and its reliance on self-interest should be interpreted in terms not of motivation, but of the kinds of reasons which would be required to justify a Christian view of our moral and social obligations.

Two attempts to show that any such egoistic justification of social morality is out of the question can still of occasion be heard, but can, I think, be fairly summarily dismissed. These correspond more or less to Bi above. The radical rejection of egoism as a contender in the justification stakes is based either on the claim that egoism cannot count as a morality at all; or else, it is based on the closely related claim that egoism could account at most for such notions as expediency or prudence; and these notions are either non-moral notions, or else comprise much less than morality does.

Two of the best and most recent discussions of the more general charge that egoism simply does not count as a morality at all (for example, because it is not, as morality by definition is, other-regarding) come to conclusions which are in one salient respect remarkably similar.[12] James R. Flynn lists up to twelve possible elements which various people might wish to include by definition in their concept of the moral as distinct from the non-moral. He points out that, as a matter of history as well as of logical possibility, different people may want to adopt wider or narrower definitions by including a smaller or larger number of these elements. The value of the list is that it enables any given dispute to be readily identified; it enables the disputants to agree on their terminology, and to argue the precise pro's and con's of including any given element, since there is a definite price to be paid at each stage. It is then possible to have a substantive discussion about what might otherwise turn out to be no more than a confused argument about differing terminologies. Dorothy Emmet's recent book has as one of its main conclusions that morality is an essentially contestable concept; that in fact it involves several elements, and that the mature moral conscience is one which is adept at knowing which one to highlight in which kinds of circumstances. Common to Emmet and Flynn is their agreement that nothing substantive can be settled by definitional *fiat;* and that one would have to see in practice what a particular view of the scope of the moral amounted to before one can with any clarity see the advantages and disadvantages of adopting that view.

It therefore seems to be quite fruitless to suggest that egoism should be excluded by definition as a non-moral view. If there is any substantive dispute between egoist and other conceptions of morality, this is best brought out in other ways, and in particular by considering just what an egoist would and would not have to rule out as nonsensical questions in the realm of social morality.

The same point in general terms has to be made about the way in which phrases like 'reasons of expediency' or 'purely prudential considerations' are contrasted with 'properly moral considerations'. If this is simply a matter of defining prudence and expediency as non-moral by *fiat,* it will fail for the reasons given. Moreover, it is not at all clear that any such definition ought to commend itself to us on wider grounds. I here refer to an article by W.D. Falk[13] which, despite the fact that it first appeared as long ago as 1963, still seems to me to be the best available treatment of these two terms, if not of the term 'moral' on which his views are much more open to criticism.

We may take prudence first. Prudence, says Falk, is by no means to be identified with self-interest. It is a much narrower notion, at least in its modern, if not in its medieval, usage. (In its medieval usage, prudence is, of course, one of the four cardinal *moral* virtues.) Prudential considerations have to do with the avoidance of risks, and the advisability of a safety-first policy in life. It will clearly be the case that to be prudent in this sense will often be what one's self-interest requires. Equally clearly, one might well ask whether self-interest *always* requires one to be prudent in this sense: is a certain amount of risk-taking not perhaps essential — say, in falling in love, or in creative activity, or in crucial choices in one's career? Unless one defines prudence as just the right amount of playing safe, it seems obvious that it will at times be in one's interests not to be prudent. If prudence is used, then, in the somewhat pejorative sense in which someone can be criticised for being too prudent, then there are no grounds for supposing that considerations of self-interest and prudential considerations coincide. We will sometimes be led in our own interests not to be prudent. Moreover, there are some 'oughts' of self-interest which are more stringent than merely prudential 'oughts': those, namely, which enjoin on us the avoidance of *certain* harm, and not just the risk of harm. On the other hand, if prudence is identified with self-interest by definition, then no *independent* argument can be mounted against the morality of self-interest in terms of prudence.

Similar considerations apply to expediency. In one common use, to act merely out of *expediency* is contrasted with acting out of *principle.* The expedient is the convenient; and what is convenient is such a variable factor that it is not susceptible of being encapsulated in principles. But in this sense, there is nothing morally disreputable in taking into consideration reasons of expediency, nor is there any reason to suppose that considerations of self-interest will be limited to such considerations. Again, 'expediency' is at times used to mean short term interests in contrast with long term interests. But here again, there is every reason for not identifying expediency in this sense with self-interest as an egoist would understand it. Falk points out that Hobbes' 'men never act except with a view to some good for themselves' is by no means equivalent to 'they never act except with a view to what is expedient'.

Falk's final point is to notice that there are many cases in which it would be quite out of place to say 'He acted in such and such a way, but only out of prudence (or, only out of expediency)'; for there are occasions on which reasons of prudence or expediency are just the ones which ought to have influenced us.

No sharp contrast can be drawn, therefore, between prudence or expediency and moral considerations; and there is no reason in any case to suppose that an egoist would ever think it his duty to consider only reasons of prudence or expediency. What is perhaps true is that we commonly regard moral considerations as being at least in part over-riding and important precisely because the whole of society has a stake in them. The peculiar 'force' of moral utterances has indeed a great deal to do with the fact that one of their commonest functions is to urge us to consider other people and not just ourselves. Perhaps it is this feature, more than any other, which might give the impression that egoism could in principle never give a complete account of morality.

Yet the egoist can accept and account for a great deal of this. After all, Hobbes himself would not speak of morality or moral obligation except in the context of an organised society; yet his account of the justification of that society is an egoist one. The general point is that on any reasonable version of egoism it will be true that the egoist will require a stable social structure (in his own interests he will require this) in which people are brought up to respect the institutions of society and their obligations within society. They must be brought up in such a way as not to act in a manner which would contribute to the breakdown of society. A Hobbesian society will therefore have to inculcate these feelings of respect; and it would be neither surprising nor inconsistent with egoism if people came to perceive their obligations as constraints upon themselves for social reasons, and hence to associate the term 'moral' with just such constraints. Just as Hobbes' account of the origins of society is a mythical story for the sake of dramatising a philosophical analysis, so too we might say that the resulting picture of a society each of whose members is a clear-sighted long-term egoist with an accurate understanding of the egoist justification for every detail of the social contract is equally mythical in character. That the ultimate justification for every obligation, virtue, and social pressure is an egoist one need not in the slightest prevent the ordinary man in the street thinking in altruistic — even *agapeistic,* one might add — terms about what he ought to do, or from having an emotional commitment to acting in such a way. In such a society, most of the features of our use of the term 'moral' would also be found, and there is no reason, therefore, to suppose that thesis Bi is true in any degree.[14]

The crucial point, then, turns out to be that mentioned in Bii; are there any obligations which morality, or Christian morality, would consider essential and which could not be accounted for on egoist assumptions? The answer to this question, as might have appeared from what has already been said, is neither simple nor clear.

An egoist need not base his view of his true interests on his desires; it is logically open to him to adopt any other theory of value he wishes, for egoism as such is a theory of obligation, not a theory of value at all. Still, the classical theory of egoism did, as a matter of fact, adopt a desire-based theory of value, and it seems to me that such a view is probably the most defensible. I shall therefore continue to discuss egoism in those terms, while making the general cautionary remark that objections to egoism should not be made to hinge on any particular theory of value an egoist might have adopted.

I have already argued that an egoist will not base his view of ethics on just any desire he happens to have, but, at most, on desires generally as offering the best evidence of where his long-term interests lie. I have suggested that such desires could consistently include the desire for friendship, and desires to sacrifice himself for his family and for his friends. Moreover, an egoist born into any given society will learn to some extent to identify his own interests with those of the group — whether tribe, or class, or nation — and will be able in principle to give an egoist justification for such loyalties. His morality will not, typically, be felt on a day-to-day level as selfish or narrowly self-seeking. And, as Hobbes makes clear, it will include at least *some* theory of social justice. The crucial question, then, is whether an egoist theory of social justice could possibly be an adequate one.

What would an egoist theory of social justice be like? David Millar[15] helpfully gives a threefold classification of theories of social justice: there are theories based on established rights (exemplified by Hume); theories based on deserts (exemplified by Spencer); and theories based on needs (exemplified by Kropotkin). In Millar's own view, I think, any theory based on rights must in the end be reducible to one of the other two. This is a view which an egoist would be expected to share. The egoist would have neither motive nor reason for recognising the existence of any rights as ultimate; rights must depend on the interests of individuals. It is perhaps more difficult to see whether an egoist is committed to one of the other two types of theory. Hobbes, I think, opted for a theory based on needs, but does egoism of its very nature require such a view of justice?

One might perhaps argue that an egoist could well adopt a theory based on deserts, since it could not be in his interest not to get what he deserves. However, there are difficulties in this view. If one allows that it is possible to deserve things which are not in one's interest (punishment, for example), there will be no way in which an egoist would consider allowing as primitive such a notion of desert. Moreover, there are many things which are in a person's true interests but which he could not in any sense be said to deserve. It seems to me more natural that the egoist would consider the notion of 'interest' — to which his commitment is basic — as the only fundamental one; and the notion of interests is more closely linked to that of needs than to that of deserts. Of course, an egoist could accommodate a theory of justice which included reference to deserts, as he could one which included reference to rights, provided that both were derived and not primitive notions within the theory.

I surmise, then, that the truth of the matter will not be too badly distorted if we rephrase the question 'Which obligations could an egoist theory of justice not account for?' to read, 'Which obligations could not be accounted for by a theory of justice as needs which an egoist would accept?' The qualification 'which an egoist would accept' is an essential one, clearly, for there might be a theory of justice based on needs which would be acceptable to a Rawlsian, or to a utilitarian, but which would not be acceptable to an egoist. We can therefore get closer to an answer to our question by seeing how various theories of justice based on needs would differ.

A Hobbesian egoist will recognise that no society will be viable unless it can offer something to each contracting member which makes it worth that individual's while to contract in rather than take his chance in the jungle of the state of nature. It must be rational for each person, in his own interests, to subscribe to the contract. Rawls' model of justice recognises this; and so does the utilitarian principle that each is to count for one, and nobody for more than one. The egoist would differ from Rawls, however, in that the egoist could justify helping the least advantaged only in those circumstances — say a mounting and potentially violent discontent on the part of the least advantaged — where not to help them would imperil the stability of society as a whole. And *that* situation would arise, on the egoist model, only when the least advantaged members of the society gained no more from membership than they could hope for in the perpetual war of the state of nature. But in a situation in which the least advantaged were better off than that, the egoist would have no reason to submit to Rawls' maximin principle whereby all surplus resources were to be given out in such a way that any differentials had to be shown to be to the advantage of the worse off. One might put the point from another angle: the egoist might feel that to submit to a Rawlsian maximin requirement, even granted Rawls' stipulations about the veil of ignorance, would be to display a quite excessive degree of prudence. It would be to over-insure against the discontent of the masses, and it would also (at least in the case where the disadvantaged were a comparatively small proportion of society) be a failure to see that the risk of finding oneself among the disadvantaged, when places in a Rawlsian society were randomly determined, was a very small risk indeed compared with the potential benefits of being among the better off. Even less would an egoist be disposed to accept a still more restrictive (from his point of view) theory of justice such as a utilitarian might propose.

There are thus at least three areas in which an egoist theory of justice based on needs might seem to be inadequate.

First it will refuse to prescribe any way of distributing surplus resources. Second 'surplus' will be defined in terms of a minimum level of well-being only marginally better than the state of nature. This might be thought to be too low to be an adequate theory of human rights. Thirdly in a situation of such scarcity that even minimum standards cannot be secured for all, the egoist theory would have nothing to say about justice at all.

I shall consider these difficulties in reverse order.

Situations of Extreme Scarcity

Such situations are taken to be ones in which it is impossible to provide for everyone even that minimum level of human well-being which would be an improvement on the terrors of a Hobbesian jungle. I think it is true to say that in such a case a Hobbesian egoist would have no theory of justice to offer. If the material basis to make the social contract workable simply is not present, then there is no rational alternative to trying to promote one's own interests by whatever means come to hand. On the other hand, is it so clear that any theory of justice has a clear solution to offer in such cases? Suppose, for instance, that a situation were to arise in which it became impossible for us to produce the level of energy, or food, to sustain the population of the world. What would be the just way to distribute those resources which were available?

One might canvass the merits of a strictly egalitarian solution, in which resources were equally distributed; or, as a slight variant, where resources were so distributed that everyone declined at a roughly comparable rate, and died, other things being equal, at more or less the same time. I see little reason to suppose that this solution is the most just, or that it is the one which Christian morality would enjoin. On what grounds is it preferable, for example, to a solution in which, on the basis of some principle of selection, resources were distributed in such a way as to ensure the continued survival of a fraction of the population, perhaps at a level which would, foreseeably, be sustainable indefinitely? Of course, the difficulty with this alternative is to discover a just principle of selection to use. Is there reason to hope that one could be found, and, even if it were found, could it be enforced? It is surely hardly surprising that we are not able to handle such cases; apocalyptic situations of this kind are quite beyond the reach of our ordinary moral principles, and we should not expect to find them clear-cut. Still, it is perhaps hardly fair to criticise an egoist for not offering a solution (or, in effect, being resigned to seeing the problem sort itself out in terms of practical thuggery and the survival of the fittest) if no other theory can in fact do much better.

Of course, a Christian looking at our present state, in which we have begun to understand that even such an apocalyptic situation may not be totally remote, will at once wish to urge, in the cause of responsible stewardship, that we bend every effort to husbanding existing resources and discovering new ones in order to ensure that such choices never have to be made. But neither need a Hobbesian have any thirst for the eschaton in this gruesome sense. It is in no man's interests to bring about a situation in which we would inevitably regress to a state of nature. On this point, egoist and Christian would entirely agree. Overall, then, it is not clear that at this level egoist theories of justice would be any more defective than their competitors.

The Account of the Minimum Level

I have already suggested that there is a certain admixture of egalitarianism even in an egoist theory, in so far as an egoist will recognise that, since he has to live with his fellow egoists, an arrangement will have to be reached in which each person has a stake. In theory, the minimum level required for this to be true is whatever level can be seen as marginally preferable to taking one's chance in the state of nature. What might such a level be in practice, and how would it square with a Christian view of basic human rights?

I suspect that there is something of a divergence between the implications of Hobbesian theory here, and what a Hobbesian egoist might have thought would actually happen.

The main characteristic of a Hobbesian state of nature is radical insecurity with respect to all one's goals, even the preservation of one's life. Of course, the rationalism of the egoist at this point allows for a certain room for manoeuvre. If I happen to be very strong, or very intelligent, or very good at exploiting others or persuading them to gang up with me, then there is a somewhat greater chance of me doing well even in the jungle; yet, on the other hand, the more successful I am, the more I will threaten the interests of others, and arouse their fear and their envy. There will, then, be some point at which, if I am modest in my ambitions and fairly well endowed by nature, there will be a comparatively small risk in doing comparatively well. It is Hobbes' view that the state will always, and must always, be in a position to make me a better offer than this. The minimum that a state must offer, then, to be attractive will vary somewhat according to the talents and risk-taking temperament of individual egoists. If it is to appeal to most people, the level of benefit must be preferable to the risks of the alternative, and this might suggest that the level cannot be *too* low. Yet the horrors of the state of nature are painted in such dark colours by Hobbes, that he almost seems to suggest that *any* level of security would be worth having.

In practice, Hobbes seems to envisage people contracting away very many of their powers, and receiving in turn a very high level of benefits. He envisages a state in which one's obligations coincide with the virtues of Christianity, and with the life of society more or less as he knew it. There is plainly in his mind a considerable difference between the minimum level to make any social contract worth while and the maximum level at which it will still be worth while to give away one's rights in exchange for social benefits. For Hobbes, the justification in both cases is precisely the same. At any point, whether in the state of nature, or at a minimum level of social living, the individual will have reasons for increasing the scope of any contract he enters into just if so doing will maximise the benefits he may hope to receive.

It is understandable that Hobbes should have considered that the society justified in the pages of his writings should have coincided to a considerable extent with the society he knew. In practice, however, I suspect that things may not always work out so neatly. Suppose a situation in which the majority of members of a society found it to be in their interest to keep a minority in a state very close to the minimum point at which the least advantaged were only just better off than in a state of nature. On egoist grounds, they would agree to do just that, and the minority would also agree to it. Though the majority would perhaps be stoking the fires of a future revolution, the underprivileged would also have to reflect that in a state of war they would be yet worse off, and there would perhaps be little guarantee that the result of a revolution would not be some new exploitation. Of course, the majority might have to invest more and more of their resources in an efficient police force, to remind the others of how much they have to lose by revolution; and there would come a cut-off point where the risk of a successful revolution would be so great that the majority would have to make concessions in their own interests. If contemporary South Africa can fairly be taken as an illustration of this mechanism at work, it appears that the minimum level in practice is somewhat above what pure Hobbesian theory might suggest, but a long way below what Hobbes presumed an enlightened egoist would wish to see. The degree of exploitation required to engender the popular revulsion which would force additional concessions out of the exploiters would seem to be quite unacceptably high from any reasonable Christian standpoint. Of course, with his maximal account in mind, Hobbes might well argue that the whites in South Africa have not been particularly enlightened egoists, and that, had they been, much more would have been conceded much sooner. But I think it is important to recall that at least one way of judging a moral theory is by looking at the kind of results it would produce in practice, and not just in theoretically ideal situations. Egoism in practice, like any theory, will have to allow 'for the normal degree of ignorance, shortsightedness and sheer backsliding to be found among men.

I conclude, then, that in practice the level of minimum subsistence likely to arise in a society governed by self-interest is lower than that which considerations of self-interest could ideally justify, and is in fact unacceptably low. While it is true that there is no generally accepted theory of justice which gives a clear and satisfactory account of what such a minimum level of human rights should be, and, *a fortiori,* no Christian theory of this kind, it seems quite unthinkable that any Christian moralist could accept egoism at this point. Some theories can be known to be false, even if we are not yet in a position to outline one which is true.

Distribution of Surplus Benefits

For the sake of argument, we may waive the above difficulties against egoism, when considered from a Christian point of view. To make this supposition more realistic, we might consider a situation in which, with the rapid increase of access to information and education, oppressed peoples would become discontented with their lot much earlier and much more effectively. In these circumstances, the amount of exploitation which could be enforced by a group of practising egoists would be much lower than it is even at present (and it has clearly been falling somewhat in recent years). Granted, this example cannot be considered *very* realistic. As perhaps the present state of human rights in the Soviet Union suggests, provided that the general level of security and living conditions is reasonably high, and the state is very powerful, the minimum level, even if only for a small minority, might well be very much lower. Still, suppose that we grant to the egoist that the arguments so far adduced fail to be conclusive. It can still be said that egoism will be unsatisfactory on other, independent, grounds.

These are that egoism fails as a theory of justice because it provides no guidance whatever about how surplus benefits over and above the minimum level are to be distributed. And the same point might be made about even the much higher level envisaged as normal by Hobbes; there might still arguably be much too much room for injustice in the way in which egoists are allowed to operate within the framework of the social contract. If Christianity has strong views about distributive justice even at this level, then it will find egoism unacceptable here too.

I have already suggested that an egoist would have no good grounds for accepting a Rawlsian maximin principle, or even for allowing that the social contract be negotiated beneath a Rawlsian 'veil of ignorance', designed precisely not to allow talents of particular kinds to count in the delineation of justice. No egoist who considers himself well endowed with intelligence, drive, initiative and persuasiveness will be willing to put himself under moral restrictions of a kind designed to put him on a more equal footing with his less fortunate competitors. He is much more likely to wish to propagate a moral theory in which it is accepted that, if people like himself succeed, they well deserve their success because they have made the most of their talents, have worked hard, and so forth. He will try to convince others that a more restrictive view of social justice will destroy the spirit of free enterprise, encourage scroungers, or undermine the essential human quality of self-reliance. Note, he will not promote a theory of justice in terms of deserts in this way as though deserts were the ultimate justification; for the egoist, the ultimate justification will still be his own interests and needs. But it will suit the egoist's book admirably to promote a moral outlook which does allow for deserts in a comparatively unquestioning manner, and which does not question the social justice of a system in which the talented or powerful can rise to positions of great affluence.

Still less would an egoist be willing to accept a more utilitarian concept of social justice — say, one which combined a theory of maximising benefits with a view about diminishing marginal utility. Thus, should a utilitarian argue that surplus resources should not be up for open competition, but should be given mostly to those lower down the scale, on the grounds that £10.00 to each of ten poor people has a greater utility than an extra £100.00 to a millionaire, the egoist with some hopes of making his own fortune will take that as a reason for rejecting the whole utilitarian way of looking at the matter.[16]

Supposing a satisfactory minimum level (such as might be enshrined in an account of basic human rights, for instance) what would the Christian moralist say about the distribution of surplus benefits? He might consider an appeal to his generally altruistic assumptions. However, a purely formal altruism will not help him here. A purely formal altruism might indeed urge him to consider all cases alike, and that he should not make any allowance for the fact that certain interests are *his* interests rather than someone else's. But a purely formal altruism will not of itself tell him which *kinds* of interests to take into account. To answer this, the Christian might try to develop additional criteria for discrimination — for example, that his first concern should be for the worst off, or for those who try hardest, or for those who are morally most admirable. But each of these criteria looks somewhat shaky. The Gospel concern for the poor and the downtrodden is clear enough; but it might well be argued that it is a concern for those who are oppressed; and in the situation we are considering, in which there is a satisfactory minimum level for everyone and it is only surplus benefits which remain to be distributed, there are no 'oppressed' in the Gospel sense. Again, if by 'those who try hardest' is meant those who make most efforts to better themselves, the Christian will find himself on very uncertain ground. As I have suggested, this is a view to which an egoist himself might well subscribe; and, further, it makes the dubious assumption that everyone is capable of trying hard. On one interpretation, this assumption will turn out to be a tautology, and hence will not serve as a criterion for differential treatment; and on any non-tautologous interpretation, it is not apparent that there is anything particularly deserving in a person who has this ability. Nor does the view that benefits ought to be distributed to favour the morally admirable fare much better, despite the fact that it might appear an excellent way of fostering sound morality. Plainly it would be highly invidious in practice and would leave the way wide open to Victorian mistakes about the 'undeserving poor' or the modern equivalent of those mistakes which would regard unemployment as evidence of moral weakness, or to some other similar error which our contemporary culture blinded us to. Moreover, such a proposal is also theoretically objectionable; if moral worth is a matter of the kind of effort that is made rather than of the actual performance, then this proposal amounts to no more than the preceding one about 'trying hard'; and if moral worth is measured in terms of actual performance, it seems to involve an un-Christian lack of compassionate understanding towards those handicapped in this respect by upbringing or the misfortunes of a niggardly nature.

Impatient with all this quibbling, the Christian might be tempted to say that there is a radical egalitarianism in Christianity which requires that all surplus benefits be distributed equally. This, perhaps, is ultimately what is meant by the command to love others as one loves oneself. Here, however, the Christian is likely to meet all the objections from the egoist that such a policy will have the effect of undermining self-reliance and creativity and industriousness; and Christians themselves have argued against certain versions of the welfare state on just these grounds. Moreover, it might be argued that such egalitarianism is simply psychologically beyond our reach, since it requires us to ignore too many motives of an individualist and group kind. Finally, it may be that the very notion of 'equal distribution of benefits' cannot be given any determinate sense, and that Rawls manages to gloss over this only by the artificial device of considering only financial rewards.

With some hesitation, I conclude that on this point there is no way in which Christian morality can provide a view which is both clear and clearly better than anything an egoist could also provide. The most that can be said — though I think it is a significant point, is that although this question and the preceding one about minimum levels can be kept logically separate as I have done, they are not in practice causally independent of one another. It could well be maintained that the kind of laissez-faire individualism which an egoist would recommend will, in the longer term, tend to produce a situation in which the minimum level itself is more and more threatened. Power would become concentrated to such an extent that the most talented, or lucky, could become progressively more able to lower the level at which the least advantaged could safely be kept. This, of course, has the effect of reducing this point to no more than a special case of the preceding one, in practice if not in theory. So I suggest that it is the problem of minimum levels alone which is of decisive importance in asking whether a Christian would inevitably find a morality based on self-interest inadequate.

Capitalism and Christianity

I shall briefly conclude by applying the results of the discussion to capitalism. Which features of capitalism are essential to it, and which are no more than the contingent results of the historical circumstances in which capitalism is to be found are questions which are beyond my competence. I shall not, therefore, be in a position to make my conclusions immediately practical or suitably general. At most, I hope to pose questions which economists and sociologists might find interesting.

I shall not even question, nor shall I support, the assumption underlying this entire discussion, that capitalism can fairly be said to be based on self-interest, though David Millar has an interesting chapter in which such a connection is shown to be less inevitable than might at first sight appear. He suggests that capitalism has become less egoistic in character as it has been transplanted from a society which viewed social structures in the light of a model of market transactions to a society in which society was seen more organisationally. Hand in hand with this transition, he suggests, has gone a tendency to view justice less in terms of deserts than in terms of needs; and this has had a notable effect on the ideology of capitalist enterprises themselves. I am in no position to evaluate these contentions: I mention them because, if they are true, they would tend to undermine a basic premise in Tawney's critique of capitalist morality.

At any rate, Preston seems to be quite correct in criticising Tawney, if Tawney's view is interpreted as a thesis about the motivation to which capitalists can appeal. Preston's criticism is that motives of self-interest are also important. As we have seen, there is perhaps a certain amount of evidence to show *why* this might be true; and if this evidence is accepted, there seems to me to be no reason to accuse Tawney of over-*optimism*. It is no reflection on human nature if part of that nature involves motives of self-interest, or group egoism. Tawney's fault is a failure in realism, failing to see that self-interest has a good side, and that such motives are valuable, not somehow disreputable. Human nature is not *worse* than Tawney hoped: it is just different.

On the other hand, it seems to me that Preston and Tawney underestimate the extent to which egoists (and not merely egoists, let it be said; the same point can be made about Preston's criticism of Rawls) can appeal to motives which are 'altruistic'. Once the distinction between motives and justifications is made clear, and once it is admitted that motives can be learnt as well as innate, it seems to me that there is little to choose between Christian and egoist motivation. I therefore see no reason why capitalists cannot, and many reasons why they should, seek to encourage feelings of genuine concern for others. We have already seen, in our own day, companies arguing that they wish to have a concern for their workers, for the interests of the countries and communities in which they work, for the environment, and so on; and to the extent that they believe such policies to be in their interests, it is also in their interests to encourage among their employees a genuine emotional commitment to these goals. The point is no different from companies wishing their employees to feel uncomfortable at the very prospect of cheating their customers, because it is in the interests of the company to deal honestly. Evidently, egoists, and capitalists insofar as they are egoists, cannot appeal to anything other then self-interest in justifying their policies, or in justifying their view of the motives they wish their employees to have. But that is quite a different assertion from saying that those motives themselves have to be motives of self-interest. If Millar is right, we are already seeing a development in precisely this direction; and that is just what Hobbes himself would have expected to happen.

I have also suggested that if the criticism made of capitalism is that it will justify its actions on grounds merely of expediency or prudence, this charge is either simply question-begging, or false, or else dissolves into a quite different charge about the kinds of behaviour which capitalism could justify. It is here, if anywhere, that the criticisms of capitalism should be mainly directed.

One problem which I have identified is the problem of extreme scarcity. I have argued that neither egoists, nor, I suspect, Christians have any clear moral view about what should be done in such a situation; but both Christian and egoist have strong views about the necessity of trying to ensure that such situations do not arise. Egoist and Christian can make common cause, then, and (in rather different tones of voice) ask the capitalist whether he is aware of his own long-term interests in this respect. Moreover, and this is a question that I cannot answer, they might inquire whether capitalist systems, as they operate in practice, are driven by their own economic logic into producing such a situation willy-nilly, as it were. For example, would the introduction of a radical energy programme be incompatible with the operation of capitalism, whether as we know it, or in any form whatever? This I take to be a socio-economic, not a moral question, and I must leave it to others to discuss.

The second problem I have tried to raise is this. There seems to be a good deal of evidence to show that capitalism, as it has actually operated, has been responsible for a great deal of exploitation, as a result of which many millions of people have been forced to live at a minimum level which is quite unacceptable. I have suggested that there is nothing in egoism which logically entails that this should be so; but that the practical effects of a society living by egoist principles might be that it will be so. Recently it has, as I mentioned, become fashionable for capitalists to renounce such behaviour. Can we say that the faults of capitalism are behind us, and were no more than the consequences of the historical situation in which capitalism arose, and of the inexperience and ignorance of the capitalists of the past? Is it the case that capitalism can renounce all exploitationist policies — say towards the fourth world — and still survive intact? Or is it rather the case that to transfer enormous resources to the fourth world would inevitably mean the demise of any capitalist system? Or do we simply not know, one way or the other? I suggest that the final assessment of capitalism from the Christian point of view must in the end turn on this consideration.

Finally, I wish to enquire whether, even were it possible to solve the problems mentioned in the previous paragraph, and secure an acceptable minimum level for even the least advantaged, would capitalism even then tend inexorably to re-create just the situation of injustice from which it had escaped? If so, it would be a system to which a Christian could subscribe only with the most severe reservations, and only under stringent restrictions.

Notes

1. Hughes, G.J. *Authority in Morals*, London, Heythrop Monographs, 1978, ch.1.

2. Preston, R.H., *Religion and the Persistence of Capitalism*, London, SCM Press, 1979, p.47.

3. Ibid., p.105.

4. Ibid., p.49.

5. Ibid., p.129.

6. Perhaps the most convenient collection of recent work on the subject is Gauthier, D.P., (ed.), *Morality and Rational Self Interest*, Englewood Cliffs, Prentice Hall, 1970.

7. See the most illuminating paper on Hobbes by K.R. Minogue, "Hobbes and the Just Man", in Cranston, M. and Peters, R.S., (ed.), *Hobbes and Rousseau*, London, Papermac., 1973.

8. Williams, B., "Egoism and Altruism", in his *Problems of the Self*, Cambridge, Cambridge University Press, 1973, p.260.

9. Ibid, p.265. Another essay in this same collection, "Morality and the Emotions", also contains material relevant to my discussion here.

10. Hobbes, T., *Leviathan*, I. 15.

11. Both appear in *American Philsophical Quarterly*, 17, (1980): Oldenquist, A., "The Possibility of Selfishness", pp.25-34; Thomas, L., "Ethical Egoism and Psychological Dispositions", pp.73-78.

12. Flynn, J.R., "The Realm of the Moral", *American Philosophical Quarterly* 13, 1976, pp.273-86; Emmet, D., *The Moral Prism*, London, Macmillan, 1979. Dorothy Emmet's discussion is by no means limited to asking whether egoism is a morality; but she raises this question among others in attempting to say what the term 'morality' might be held to include.

13. Falk, W.D., "Morality, Self, and Others", originally in Castaneda, H-N, and Nakhnikian, G., (ed.), *Morality and the Language of Conduct*, Detroit, Wayne State University Press, 1963; also in Pahel, K. and Schiller, M., *Readings in Contemporary Ethical Theory*, Englewood Cliffs, Prentice Hall, 1970, pp.360-90; see, too, the useful reply by Frankena, W.K., "The Concept of Morality", Ibid., pp.391-401.

14. See Minogue's paper for a version of this view, (reference in note 7 above).

15. Millar, D., *Social Justice*, Oxford, Clarendon Press, 1976.

16. For various helpful comments on Rawls, see Daniels, N., (ed.), *Reading Rawls*, Oxford, Blackwell, especially in this connection the papers by R.M. Hare and A.K. Sen.

5

Personal Responsibility for Social Welfare[1]

Edwin Barker

In his search for the origins of *homo sapiens,* the archaeologist, Richard Leakey, distinguishes man from his probable *hominid* predecessors by his capacity to recognise that altruism and self-interest were complementary qualities — two sides of the same coin. The recognition of this personal responsibility for social welfare, including, of course, the person's own welfare, led to the first affluent society centuries ago.[2]

The second Commandment, "Thou shalt love thy neighbour as thyself", is consequently not an exhortation but a simple statement, based upon experience, of what distinguishes *homo sapiens* and of what is, in man's social attitudes, essential for his well-being. As the late Bishop of Leicester (R.R. Williams) pointed out "..... we should have, and could have, no picture of God's character, as contrasted with his 'eternal power and divinity', except through those who have seen the social demands on God's people as expressions of the voice and mind of God."[3]

This relationship between egoism and altruism is a requirement of true human society and is embodied in the second Commandment as an expression "of the voice and mind of God."

The theme of this essay is, therefore, not new. It is descriptive of the nature of man in society, of what is distinctive about human society and of the essential criteria of social welfare. But the context changes and we are required to embody these longstanding insights in the contemporary scene and to indicate the consequent social policies and programmes in our own times.

There is a reciprocal relationship between our expectations of what society will provide and do to maintain our life and dignity and what, as a necessary condition for such provisions, society requires of us. Pre-conditions of entry into the Promised Land, flowing with milk and honey, are the worship of Him who promised and the acceptance of the consequent social disciplines and personal obligations. This remains true. The context is now different but commandments to be obeyed retain their essential function as a vital part of the social equation. Social welfare requires the acceptance of personal responsibility within the providing society. There are no inalienable rights, no human rights without their accompanying personal responsibilities and duties.

Insistence on rights and responsibilities demands of necessity, the formation of 'interest groups' for without such groups there are no means to discern and insist upon them. It is, therefore, evident that our concern is with politics and, at this moment in history, with social democracy. Attempts to embody social welfare in our society in recent years, have, however, produced their crop of problems related to personal responsibility, which, unless we solve, could threaten the continuance of what they set out to achieve. Self-interest without altruism destroys the possibility of satisfying self-interest.

All these issues concerning the future of social democracy arise in the context of specific social concerns on which church bodies are invited by politically executive authorities to comment. This is clearly the experience of the Bishop of Coventry's Council for Social Responsibility, a consultative group which seeks to respond to such invitations, and the argument of this essay rests on this local experience.

Local Government — a case in point

Our nineteenth century form of 'local' government, designed to bring the individual closer to the social decision making process, and thus responsible within and for it, is a case in point. Historically local government is a response to size. Within a small community it is possible for all its members to share in making and enforcing the rules necessary to combine liberty and ordered development. When the size is that of a nation, a city, or a county, this is no longer possible and representatives are elected to make rules for all of us. Those given this power are a majority of those elected. We, therefore, get a double dose of majority rule. Our representatives are those preferred by a majority of us and the decisions are made by a majority of them. There is a third element of majority rule, within the political parties. Consequently, within a very short time after this form of local government was devised, complaints arose about the apathy of the electorate. The whole system of representation, whilst maintained as a hopeful basis for responsible citizenship, was at the same time implicitly challenged by the low attendance in the polling booths. Representation does not ensure direct democracy and consultation.

In the mid nineteenth century Local Authorities were required by central government to undertake specific tasks, for example to cope with the typhoid epidemic. The Medical Officer of Health, in this case, had to report plans for this purpose to both the Local Authority and the Minister. Their execution required the permission of the Minister. Even at this stage it appears that Local Authorities were given responsibilities without powers and the Medical Officer of Health had a measure of independence from local control. Similar independence was maintained for Chief Constables. Other Local Authority officers never were, and still are not, independent. Their duty is to the employing Council provided, of course, that the Council's decisions are lawful and practicable. In the case of the Treasurer of Bognor Regis, for example, he could not claim to represent the rate-payers as over against the Council. In another instance, however, the City Engineer could affirm the physical impossibility of building a bridge at a point determined by the Council because of the unsuitability of the physical site. These general ties, therefore, hide the subtle interplay between elected councillors and their officers in the decision making process. In discharging their responsibilities to their employers they are required to maintain their own professional standards and these must be accepted by the elected body. Whilst in the case of engineers this presents no problems, the same does not always obtain, for example with social workers, as we shall see later.

The whole structure of local government, when viewed in the light of expectations and of its admirable intentions, has creaked from the start and some recent changes have further revealed its continuing weaknesses. The enlargement of the areas covered in recent years has removed councillors even further from their constituencies and electors. The growth of the political party system has polarised issues and has enhanced emphasis on a united front irrespective of whether it services social need. Management techniques have been introduced and the Town Clerk has become the Chief Executive, thus further blurring the line between policy and administration. Along with these developments power is continually being taken away from Local Authorities and transferred to central government or to appointed bodies. Obvious examples are the National Health Service, and the Regional Water Authorities. The consequence is that local public interest and participation wanes still further.

The services to be rendered here also become more technical as is evidenced by the transition from the old Poor Law to Social Services Departments. This has both reduced the scope for councillors' decision making and has tended to undermine the status of voluntary agencies. Compensation for some of these challenges to personal and local responsibility is being sought through a growing mechanism of consultation. This is notable in planning and is extended by the issue of Green Papers and consultative documents. Whilst by these means a measure of acceptance necessary for government may be achieved, the traditional view of social democracy, in which elected people are expected to govern, is being challenged and possibly eroded and delays are often introduced which make the final decision irrelevant, especially in the case of planning. It is notable too that these kinds of participation are not necessarily a means of achieving concensus. On the contrary, they can and do establish conflicting views. Whilst this may produce a better definition of issues, decisions have still to be made and the legal authority for this purpose is vested in elected people. Participation can also develop into protest — an open door to the unscrupulous and a platform for the loudest voice, leading to minority rule and coming near at times to naked force.

It is evident that government based upon elected representatives to whom authority is given to make decisions is under considerable strain. Can representation be given new vitality in new forms or do we seek other ways?

Professionalism and a Managed Society

Some of the issues thus briefly stated require further elaboration. The complexity of society and the rising standards of expectation now insisted upon, enhance the status of the professional people involved. This is true of the social services and of the teaching and medical professions. Social workers with recognised qualifications are consequently employed by Local Authorities and immediately there is potential conflict. There may be a clash between loyalty to clients, based on professional standards, and to the employing body. Where these differences are expressed to the employing body, leaving it to that body to make the final decisions, the present system works. However, when the employee insists upon the rightness of his expert judgement and organises resistance to the elected body, the system breaks down. Breakdown also ensues when the professional insists that he alone is competent to provide the necessary service. Volunteers and amateurs are regarded as dangerous both to the profession and to society and the facts that there are not enough professionals to carry the load — and never will be — and that this attitude weakens the sense of neighbourly responsibility, are either ignored or tolerated as interim concerns. Similar assumptions made by teachers in the educational field and by doctors and the medical profession where health is concerned, are discernible. A parallel trend would make the police alone responsible for law and order. Are we becoming a managed society? What is happening to the hopes and expectations of social democracy? Clearly, there are areas of operation in which the trained, skilled person alone should act. This however is far from leaving social work to the professional social worker, education to the trained teacher, health to doctors and surgeons, and the maintenance of order under the law, to the police. These areas of social life are public responsibilities to be carried by the organised public, and therefore by amateur bodies, advised and aided by professionals but not governed by them. The role of the professional person is that of servant. It is within such a concept that the distinctive and necessary specialist services of the skilled professional may find their proper and legitimate place.

It is perhaps not without significance that when Sir Keith Joseph was considering the re-organisation of the National Health Service, he called in a firm of industrial consultants to help him. Their report and his consequent action are excellent models for a managed society. As he was answerable to Parliament for the National Health Service, he devised means whereby those who administered it were of his choosing and responsible to him. Under him all power was given to a combination of appointed and professional people who were subject also to budgetary controls exercised by the Minister. The results were predictable. Emphasis shifted from preserving health to dealing with sickness; from seeking to create conditions of well-being for the many to hospitals with increasingly complicated, sophisticated and expensive machinery; to a vulnerable system in which a few determined and organised porters could prevent its working. In addition it divided the Health Service, detaching the social services, and leaving Local Authorities with responsibilities whilst depriving them of the financial means to discharge them. A good deal of ill health is collective in origin, involving housing, pollution and an unhealthy environment. These are largely matters of concern to Local Authorities. To separate them from the rest of the Health Service was a serious mistake. An opportunity to integrate the Health Service on a local basis was missed and the citizenry, whose interests are paramount, were left practically powerless. An attempt was made to redress the balance by setting up Community Health Councils, bodies with little power and few resources. These have worked well in some instances but their very success in a few areas is a criticism of the whole structure.

When to this management complex, which is relatively insensitive to public needs, is added the lack of common thinking between departments of government whose separate operations affect the health situation, it becomes virtually impossible to serve the needs of persons as whole beings. Health, education, housing, employment, environment, family income — and the rest — may each require a separate department of government, but people are not divisible in these ways nor are their best interests served. Few things are more difficult to achieve than the consultations between these departments which are necessary to ensure their acting in concert on behalf of people. This is the case both locally and nationally. The need is not met by cross-representation, a device often indulged in with false hopes. Nor does consultation require a vast bureaucratic structure. It is essentially a means of ensuring that government departments do their work differently because they take account of each other's contribution to the whole. It is when this wholeness becomes apparent that the expression of personal responsibility within it becomes a recognisable possibility.

Devolution — one way forward

Much has been written and said about the necessity for and the danger of the growing centralisation of government. The Keynes' White Paper (1944) introduced a change to a controlled economy designed, in part, to minimise the incidence of booms and slumps and to control inflation. This control could initially only be in the hands of central government. Political direction of the economy, or a command economy, ensued and on political grounds decisions were made concerning the proportion of the GNP to be allocated to public purposes, including welfare services, and what amount remained in private hands. In the earlier stages public expenditure was confined to the resources thus made available but later, for reasons of political strategy, the criteria changed. The establishment of a welfare society required increasing government control of the economy, and centralisation. It could be initiated in no other ways. The consequences are evident. It produced a welfare society which no right-minded person would wish to undermine. Whatever blemishes remain to be removed and whatever inequities still divide society — and these are substantial — life in our present welfare society is more human, more civilised and more desirable than in the period which preceded it. Our concern is not with changing back to laissez faire, to that sturdy independence of character which it was alleged to sustain, but with the extension of corporate provisions to meet personal needs within available resources, and with the growth of personal responsibility necessary for these purposes. It may be more blessed to give than to receive, but it is not always easy to receive responsibly. It is made more difficult when the donor is far removed from the receiver. It is not long before rights are insisted upon in isolation, unaccompanied by duties which are necessary to ensuring the means of satisfying them. 'They', the Government, are the providers, 'we' are the insatiable receivers. To think in terms of 'us' becomes difficult. As was observed at the beginning of this essay, self-interest grew in strength without the altruism necessary to sustain its proper satisfaction.

Such influence as the individual can bring to bear in a democratic society requires participation in politics — in party politics — at a national level, and consequently necessitates that local government be based upon political party allegiance. In no other way at present can local and national governments responsibly shape, or attempt to shape, social policy. Whilst this is not necessarily a bad thing it has its dangers. It can enhance and distort the status of political ideologies. These are good at giving general direction, but become both diabolical and contrary to our English political tradition if they are logically pursued. They are in this case a source of social discontinuity and can result in failing to recognise that, once elected, governments, both local and national, have to take account of those who did not vote for them as well as those who did. Rigid pursuit of ideologies can lead to dictatorship, and become a means of dividing society into conflicting groups unable to reach those compromises necessary both for living together and as a recognition of the limits of human wisdom and insight. Without a political ideology there is no sense of direction but to make absolute claims for it means that you cannot recover from mistakes. Compromise is a recognition of fallibility. The sense of powerlessness which recent political developments has enhanced, linked with these ideological trends, gives increased and undue power to the extreme left and extreme right as promising some sort of order in a confused situation, and they are helped by the centralisation of power. The individual, if he is to feel both effective and responsible, must either actively or tacitly share in the political decision-making process and, except for extremists, this is inhibited by ideological rigidity. A sense of direction, different in kind, is required.

Without at this stage seeking to specify what this sense of direction should be, it is possible to suggest some of its characteristics. There is a lot of experience in industry and elsewhere which indicates that centralisation must be followed by devolution if the original purpose is to be achieved. The central authority having set up and given general directions to its outlying parts continues to be useful only in serving these offshoots. The vigour and vitality of these parts is the principal concern of the central body. In political terms this implies that central government's concern is to enhance the significance and assist the enterprise of local government within a broad framework of social policy. Local Authorities are not agents of central government. They are elected bodies operating under statute law, and are responsible to their electors. They must be allowed the freedom of action necessary to fulfil their duties. The ways in which they finance their operations can be a determining factor and there is much to be said for enabling them, through local taxes, to raise a much higher proportion of their own funds locally. In any case central government resources, allocated to Local Authorities, are public funds and, in the interest of developing a sense of personal and, therefore, local responsibility, their use could increasingly be determined locally. The necessary safeguards can be provided by inspectorates and public audit. It is necessary both to cease eroding the powers and responsibilities of Local Authorities and to move in the opposite direction. It may be troublesome that some Local Authorities resist central government decisions but it is tragic to replace them by nationally appointed managers. Even Cromwell found this disastrous!

The Centrality of Voluntary bodies

The health and vitality of our society depends, in large measure, upon its voluntary associations and upon the proper exercise of their powers and regard for their duties.

It is evident that, beyond the area of immediate neighbourly help, personal responsibility for social measures requires joining together in voluntary associations. These range from political parties, trade unions, the Confederation of British Industry, the Stock Exchange and the churches to small groups providing a service for single parent families, battered wives and vagrants.

Within the area which is the concern of statutory social services the voluntary bodies have considerable resources of personnel and money. Far more man-hours are provided by volunteers than by those employed in the statutory sector and in 1978 around £2000 million were found from non-government sources. Clearly some services are better rendered by volunteers and their work can make them constructive critics of public social policy as well as innovators and initiators of new work. The more people are engaged in this work the more likely are small and minority groups to experience enfranchisement over and above the vote and to influence both bureaucracy and government; to acquire the social power necessary for the exercise of social responsibility.

It is evident that both national and local government authorities give a modicum of aid to voluntary bodies. This is a legitimate use of public funds and is to be welcomed. At the same time it is questionable whether the basis of this action is right. In the interests of politically healthy society it would appear that, even in meeting their statutory obligations, Local Authorities might first consider whether the allocation of funds could better be done by volunteers and voluntary organisations, reserving to themselves the right of inspection and that work which at that time no other body could undertake. There is also the need for a different kind of partnership between Local Authorities and voluntary agencies in determining priorities within clearly limited resources. This should become a joint enterprise as distinct from a purely consultative arrangement. It could be undertaken by a body which included both, and cross-representation is no substitute. Moving in these directions might also result in a more economical use of available financial resources without impairing the quality of the services rendered. After all, the funds involved are public funds and the distinction often made between grants from rates and taxes to voluntary bodies and the money they raise from other sources is basically questionable. It is also worthy of note that volunteers and voluntary bodies deal with whole persons whose needs do not neatly fall within government departments and they consequently have a role in promoting inter-departmental co-operation in meeting human needs. It might be alleged that the resulting structures are untidy and make control and public accountability difficult to ensure. This is likely to be the case but some administrative untidyness is a small price to pay if the results are the more effective meeting of human needs and the increase in the number of people who accept responsibility for social welfare. The rights and duties of elected people to govern, which it is important to maintain so long as we have representative government, would not be undermined in the area of social services by pursuing the lines indicated. They would be undertaken in new ways which might go some way towards remedying the defects of the system. Notably they would involve more ordinary people in making social judgements and could provide a training ground for potential councillors.

It is not easy, given limited resources, to meet the special and distinctive needs of run-down areas of cities and at the same time serve the total population. A balance has to be kept. At least an elected body has to keep a balance if it is to remain in power and there is some justice in this. Pressure groups arise in both run-down areas and elsewhere ranging from action groups in the former to 'ratepayers' associations in the latter. Clearly there is need for the provision of means whereby these groups can influence public policies and programmes, but these provisions must leave decisions to the elected government. They must not usurp this power nor make it impossible for it to be exercised. When Local Authorities are given duties beyond their means, these problems arise. Local action groups and 'ratepayers' associations are doubtless manifestations of personal responsibility for social welfare and need to be encouraged to make their case, but it must be made to a government whose responsibility it is to govern. To govern in these circumstances demands considerable integrity, quality of character and skill from councillors. Their quality, and that of their permanent staff, is decisive and should increasingly be our concern.

The new Barons

There are voluntary associations of a rather different character from those normally involved in social services. These include political parties, trade unions, employers' associations, professional bodies and the like. Their purposes and activities have a direct bearing upon the cultivation of personal responsibility for social welfare. Conflict between them, and between them and government, has often been regarded as a guarantee that social justice will be done. This assumption needs critical examination. The concept known as the balance of power has a poor history internationally and some form of united nations, with its appropriate laws under which a police force acts to sustain peace whilst justice is achieved, has been shown to be necessary however reluctant sovereign bodies seem to be to relinquish absolute sovereignty. Similar considerations are relevant to employers' associations and trade unions. Free collective bargaining can prove disastrous for the community as a whole and needs to be checked by government whose purpose it is to ensure the welfare of all the governed. This may require a framework of law devised in the context of a generally accepted view of the nature of society and the meaning, in value terms, of life together. This framework can be sketched only when there exists a common acceptance of the basis of social cohesion. Without this, all law-making in this area is regarded as a threat both to liberty and justice. It remains the business of government to govern under law and if this is impaired by over-powerful and conflicting organised sections of society, employers and unions, we need not a new Magna Carta but a bloodless constitutional revolution; not 1215, but 1688.

The necessity for powerful voluntary associations to function with the restraint which it is the function of government to ensure is underlined by the vulnerability of sophisticated society. Our methods of industrial production and the size and complexity of public services render them sensitive to the determined action of small groups, either of wreckers or of people who insist exclusively upon their own status and rewards. These conditions present problems to the voluntary bodies themselves. These bodies have grown in size to match the organisation of industries and services and, in so doing, their leaders and representatives have become withdrawn from the rank and file. At least this is what is often felt to be the case. Evidence of it is both the rise of the shop steward movement — which is now beginning to suffer the same fate — and the growth in the number of unofficial strikes. There is here a double problem for all concerned with social democracy and with personal responsibility for social welfare — the problem of vulnerability and the problem of scale and size. These are underlined by the fact that lorry drivers and coal miners can, for example, by unilateral action, both impoverish everybody and bring society to a standstill.

It is apparent that the larger the scale of organisation which social institutions, including industries, appear to find necessary for their purposes, the more it is necessary for those involved to have deep local roots, otherwise the whole operation becomes impersonal and seemingly insensitive to personal life. The question is raised[4] as to whether concentration plus specialisation really equals efficiency. The assumptions behind such a formula are certainly under threat. We have seen how it makes the total operation vulnerable or, to use Professor Handy's phrase, how it gives "hi-jack power" to a few. Size makes it difficult if not impossible to comprehend the whole. The individuals involved are therefore not committed to it. Accountants are far too dominant, yet mergers based upon their criteria continue to grow and ultimately to defeat the original intention and to demean those engaged in the enlarged operation. It is doubtful leadership and undermines the possibility of achieving sound welfare in the context of employment combined with personal responsibility for it. It certainly results in a hierarchical structure at a time when co-operation is both required by all sharing in the undertaking and is necessary to a responsible society. Of necessity it regards labour as a commodity, as a cost, and this leads to increasing alienation bought off by increasing wages. This increases the pressure to reduce the quality of the workers involved which is, in turn, unavailing because it creates an overall unemployment situation. As we observe in our childhood game Happy Families, the people involved have names as well as functions; they are persons as well as workers. Management must take full account of both and *the name* implies consultation in the performance of particular jobs. This scale of values carries with it the necessity to care for human assets, and attempts to do this are well exemplified in the co-ownership movement and in the shop stewards' detailed and imaginative proposals within Lucas Aerospace. The germs of the future of social democracy in the context of employment are to be found in some of these new ventures rather than in our traditional industrial and commercial mammoths. Like the mammoth they are out.

As Mr. Callaghan discerned, there is a tendency to strike first and consult later. This is not sheer perversity however much it may be used for perverse purposes by groups with other objectives in view. It is a reaction to depersonalisation, and the fact that it is a fairly fruitless and outdated reaction should not hide its motivation. After all, the professions, with all their skills in other respects, have been unable to devise better ways of making the same point. They resort to industrial action with all its damaging effects upon themselves, society and their cause. There is perhaps in all this an excessive emphasis on rights as over against obligations and duties. The balance must be restored but the main source of the imbalance is not difficult to discern.

The necessary new developments in this area of concern must be the embodiment in community life of "a sense of common ownership, of leadership as a service role, of shared responsibilities, and a personal style."[5]

Continuity and Discontinuity

The possibilities held out by the new electronic technology are in dispute. There are those who compare these with previous revolutionary changes: the introduction of agriculture to replace hunting and gathering; the invention of the plough to replace the spade; the use of water power and steam power and electrical power and nuclear power to drive new machines; the conquest of the air to unite the peoples of the world. They declare that in all these changes, whatever may have been their immediate impact upon social life and well-being, new opportunities for employment for increasing numbers of people were eventually provided. Every new development, however revolutionary, was an opportunity to rise to a better form of life. There is much to support this attitude especially if, linked with it, is the view emphatically expressed by Barbara Ward that poverty is something we cannot afford. This view has important implications for the distribution of the increased wealth created by these innovations and for the enrichment of the quality of personal life of all people in conditions of plenty.

Of course, these broad generalisations hide a multitude of differences between the reactions to the changes in each case. The simplest example is to be found in a comparison between the early reactions to agricultural change which used the newly released energies to create cities and to build the cathedrals which for centuries have been sources of spiritual and cultural strength, and the monstrosities which grew out of our most recent industrial revolution. The former draw admiring and reverential crowds from all parts of the world; the latter we are seeking belatedly to redeem. The former were created by men of undoubted faith in an ennobling God; the latter by 'idiots' if the word is used to denote absent-mindedness about the wholeness of life. The former embodied an all-embracing belief in God which unified life and endeavour in all their aspects; the latter the accummulation of material wealth at all costs ranging from child labour to slum dwellings. These differences are of the greatest importance as we reflect upon the essential needs of our own times as we move into a further, novel technology. This latest change may demand an entirely new attitude to work and employment which requires a very distinctive cultural, and spiritual outlook, distinctive that is from our nineteenth century inheritance.

This leads us into the alternative interpretation of the implications of the new technology, namely that it is not a part of the continuous development of industrial life to be compared with some earlier changes. It may be that the employment situation created by the new technology cannot be compensated for by new forms of employment, by work-sharing, shorter hours, sabbaticals, or longer holidays. The right to work hitherto considered as the right to be employed and thus achieve a recognised status in society, may no longer be understood in this way. If this be the case, what concept of work can now replace its direct association with being gainfully employed in industry, commerce or administration?

Self-respect is a by-product of being manifestly needed by society, but being needed may no longer mean being employed in industry, commerce and administration. William Temple, in his *Christianity and Social Order*[6] insists that whatever work a person undertakes, be this employment by others or self-employment, should and must be regarded as service, the dedication of skills, time and energy to the well-being of others in the family and in society. This is a manifestation of Jesus' description of himself, his lordship and majesty being expressed in service. He emptied himself, taking the form of a servant. It is possible to rethink work as service and thereby to enable work to include employment and, at the same time, not to be confined by it. Some extreme examples spring to mind. In London there are scores of streets and neighbourhood groups serviced by young men and women, many of them ex-students, who live on Social Security payments (of their own volition and with the cordial support of the authorities). Some are squatters and the services they render in their local communities are both considerable and publicly appreciated. Of course, there are drones amongst them but there are drones in employment too. The growth areas are in individual enterprise, service, leisure and Job Creation Schemes together with recurrent education.

Being and Doing — new options

But it is also necessary here to outline a whole range of considerations raised in an unpublished paper: "Man the Worker" by Andrew Morton of the British Council of Churches. If we are moving into an era when men are no longer under the necessity of spending most of their time keeping body and soul together, then the high valuation we still place upon employment may be obsolete, out-dated and biologically passé. The Westminster Catechism gives a bias which needs re-emphasis when it states that "man's chief end is to glorify God and to enjoy him forever". A state of 'being' as distinct from 'doing' is desired and desirable. We tend to stress the consequences of activity, its future product, rather than the intrinsic value of behaviour. We thus depreciate ourselves and the present time. We under-value sheer doxology, the praise and enjoyment of God, as good in itself, which may be what Christians mean by 'celebration'. Of course, this useless and playful activity, which is not reaching out to the future or to others, has important results or consequences. It may enhance and enrich the person; it may make him more efficient and effective; it may enrich others and the relationship between him and those others. But that is not its point, the source of its value. This 'being' is not to be equated with those intervals of leisure we all need in order to return to work refreshed. It is nearer to the old Indian tradition of the four stages of life: student, householder, forest dweller and mendicant, the last two being those more highly valued. Neither is it 'coma'. As A.C. Craig, the first General Secretary of the British Council of Churches once said, "every act of worship is a spiritually athletic occasion" and as anyone who has tried to tease out the intrinsic values of life in novel, essay or report form knows, it is hard work!

Whilst these considerations are by no means irrelevant to any ethic of work, it may be that we are jumping ahead too fast. The majority of the world's peoples are in need of the means of ordinary livelihood and, although it is by no means necessary that they tread the same paths to plenty as the so-called developed nations, their needs are our care. In helping to meet them, altruism and self-interest meet, a necessary condition for political and economic action. Perhaps an emphasis on 'being' developed in a Western context could usefully moderate our own material demands and thus serve our needy neighbours.

Any transition of this kind, even if desirable and necessary, cannot happen speedily, nor will it be easy to replace the compulsions, constraints and obligations of employment by discipline, service and creative reflection which, in the new situation, may characterise work. The habits of more than two centuries of economic life are deeply engrained in Western society and the necessary ingredients of change are often suspect. One example is the common attitude to Social Security payments and 'the dole'. We all live on these whether they be overt or disguised as wages, salaries, dividends or land and property ownership. They are social wealth, pretty unevenly distributed, and welfare provisions are attempts to return some of this to larger numbers. Similarly our aid to underdeveloped and poorer areas of the world is partly an attempt to achieve a more equitable distribution of resources and partly a recognition of the fact that we cannot afford poverty. It is bad for trade!

Transition may involve all these phenomena and motives, but do we know what it is we seek and desire? It is not enough to speak of personal fulfilment within society. This is not the "chief end of man" and by aiming at it we could destroy both the person and his society. There is no escaping — even if we might wish to do so — the glorifying and enjoying of God as social beings together in the combined act of communion and celebration. This necessity puts the Church in the centre of our social witness and being and raises the question of its fitness and ability humbly to be there. It cannot *claim* this position, for the danger of pride would threaten its essential virtue. It can only be the lively leaven which transforms the lump; but it cannot be this unless it is involved at all points with the lump. There is no substitute for worship, communion, celebration and liturgy but these are leaven to be inserted in society and in all social relationships and not merely enjoyed in detachment from the rest of the world.

It should, perhaps, not surprise us to recognise this tension between 'being' and 'doing' in newly emerging nations. Their contacts with the Westen World and their desire to raise their economic standards by more efficient methods of production, by better health and by trade, involve them in the activism of the West. Can this be accompanied by a preservation and development of their old traditions of 'being', education and missionary endeavour removing old crudities without destroying ancient arts? An excellent study of this is Neil Thompson's *Colour and Chaos* which examines the situation in Papau New Guinea.[7] The revival, development, and invention of native arts is as crucial for us in the West as it is for Tanganyikans, Indians and Papuans. Some are already appearing as dialect and folk poetry presented in clubs and pubs, as folk dancing, folk and children's art, gardening, drama, music and festivals. This is work as distinct from employment, giving a texture and quality to life. Its encouragement in increasingly skilful form is a necessary part of education, alongside the other arts essential to a technological age.

All these visions of a possible future, if valid, give a vastly enhanced responsibility to persons for the quality of social life. Welfare, assured in economic terms by the new technology, now needs a fresh insistence on values. Is this a freedom we can bear, a responsibility which we have the spiritual resources to carry? Assuredly it implies new emphases in education and in the Church's teaching.

Too many freedoms?

There are other less speculative ways in which people in contemporary society are experiencing new freedoms which carry with them the burden of responsible choice, where the choices made undermine or affirm human values other than freedom. The developing economic independence of women, divorce law reform, the Abortion Act 1967, changes in the law affecting suicide and homosexual conduct, the availability of choice in schools and education, the expansion of subsidised university education, freedom of movement over the surface of the earth, the varied ways of exploiting natural resources — these are but a few examples. Without these freedoms we are not challenged to accept full personal responsibility for social welfare. With them we may be strained and tested beyond our resources in faith and discipline. It is evident that these resources need to be greatly enriched. Progress is by no means inevitable. It is possible to become so wearied with making decisions that we come to welcome an external authority directing what we must do. Social democracy then leads to dictatorship. Adulthood, growing up as responsible people, is exchanged for dependent childhood.

There is, however, a strand in our tradition which militates against this possible development. It surfaces from time to time in our history. Peasants' revolts, and the civil wars of the seventeenth century are cases in point. More recently it showed itself in resistance both to a standing army and to the setting up of a police force. Pitt's Police Bill was rejected because, at that time, the only European police force was that set up in France. The French police were the forceful agents of autocratic rule, operating aggressively and ruthlessly as independent agents subject to no law other than the will of the rulers, separate and apart from the majority of the people. Such a police force could not be tolerated in England. It was not until the nineteenth century that a police force could be created here. By then it was clearly seen that the police should be a part of the total community with few powers which were not shared by every citizen, that they should operate under the law, every policeman being personally answerable for his own actions before the courts, and that they should be unarmed. In other words police became acceptable when they were seen as a service to the whole community and not as a separate elite with special power.[8]

After the experience of Stuart government similar criteria led to the toleration of a small standing army in peace time. Only enough force to restore a modicum of order was permissible and officers and men exceeding these limits were heavily punished. It is a peculiar quirk of language still to describe police as a 'force' and to change the designation of the Armed Forces to the Armed Services. Over the past 150 years the police have been accepted by the majority as a necessary and welcome service; over the same period, and markedly in recent years the standing armed forces have greatly distinguished themselves as a vital service to the civil community. Not only do they form an essential part of our defences — and this is their principal reason for existence — but they serve snow-bound farmers, rescue stranded mountaineers or shipwrecked sailors, take urgent cases to hospital, build vital roads and docks to serve outlying areas, construct cathedrals and churches, and serve people in all parts of the world who suffer from natural or manmade disasters. This strand in our tradition, whereby power in the long run is only tolerated as a means of service to the whole community and only when it is exercised by an integral part of the community, is a persistent and vital one. It is possible that it may surface once more thus enabling us to use our new freedoms in the service of the whole society and accept personal responsibility for social welfare.

The Mushroom Cloud

Perhaps the area of social life in which the individual citizen finds it most difficult to exercise social responsibility is in international affairs. He is aware of dark forces threatening the continuance of any acceptable form of society, with which his only contact is that of a helpless and powerless sufferer. To move intelligently and effectively in this area of concern appears to require an expertise and knowledge which are beyond his capacity to attain. Even if this were not so, where are the agencies through which he could exercise the power necessary for the acceptance of real responsibility?

Without presuming to give full and adequate answers to these questions there are rays of hope to be discerned. Here we call attention to three only. The late Dag Hammarskjöld succeeded in persuading the Security Council of the United Nations to establish on an ad hoc basis peace-keeping forces, for example in the Middle East and in the Congo. Other than his own bold spirit, his resources were slender indeed. They consisted of one military adviser and a secretary. With these he made a start but he was unable to persuade the UN to make provision for a continuing service of this kind and to accumulate the knowledge and experience for its development and improvement. Such measures were regarded as threats to national sovereignty. He could not even pass on his files and documentation to his successors. The hope of steadily creating an international peace-keeping and policing force along these lines was apparently wrecked. It was at this point that independent and voluntary initiative emerged to redeem the situation. Dag Hammarskjöld's military adviser, Major General Indar Jit-Rikhye, pulled out of the UN and, with Hugh Hanning (later Secretary of the International Affairs Committee of the Church of England Board for Social Responsibility) and others set up, as a voluntary body, the International Peace Academy[9]. This Academy invited governments to send service personnel and diplomats to courses of training in the arts of peace-keeping and peace-building and began to accumulate material based upon successive exercises in this field and to make it possible to learn from experience. At this date the value of this enterprise is evidenced by the fact that most of the member nations of the UN have sent people to Academy courses. Equally significant is the fact that peace-keeping operations have recently become an integral part of the syllabus in Defence Staff Training Colleges, using the material supplied by the Academy. Such developments patently require close consultations between governments and their departments, notably in this case those responsible for foreign affairs and defence respectively. In this country the external agency under whose auspices this could be achieved was the Church which functioned as an enabling body.

There is a long way to go before the world has an effective police force operating under international law but a start has been made entirely by voluntary effort including that of Church bodies. In this fact lies the guarantee that the ultimate outcome is *a service* and derives its power from this essential fact. Such a force can only operate by invitation.

The second ray of hope has a similar history. International provision for disaster relief, using the Armed Forces, owes its direction and vitality to the voluntary efforts of Hugh Hanning, Maurice Chandler and the late Bishop of Leicester (the Rt. Revd. R.R. Williams). Once again, under their leadership, the Church enabled governments to come together to create an ambulance service throughout the world. It is only a beginning, but it is already evident that in achieving international action of this kind, new possibilities for international understanding are provided; for example Warsaw Pact and NATO countries together helped in Jugoslavia. The individual citizen is not altogether helpless.

The third ray is associated with the name of Alec Dickson, the founder of Voluntary Service Overseas and similar enterprises. He has concentrated upon the use of the Armed Forces in works of civil reconstruction to which reference has already been made[10].

All these are examples of force and power being orientated towards service and human welfare under the impetus provided by volunteers and voluntary bodies — by ordinary citizens. The list could be greatly extended. The international operations stemming from Coventry Cathedral and the initiative of Christians in Northern Ireland are obvious examples. Whether these hand-sized clouds are promises of fruitful rain or whether they will be dispersed by the mushroom cloud of nuclear armoury remains to be seen. Perhaps, once again, holy fear linked with caring love and service will prevail. This is our faith.

Power, whatever its source, finds its finest outlet in service and the more powerful the corporate body or person is, the more they are required humbly to serve the whole community. This, which is a central element in the Christian revelation of God, is one of the hardest to embody in social policy. As Michael Ramsey put it, "we may seek to do justly and to practise mercy, but unless we walk humbly with our God justice is blind and mercy calculating and patronising."[11]

Faith not optimism

In many areas of social life: in local government; in relations between local and central government; in the status of the professional person; in industrial organisation including the functions of trade unions, employers and managers; in the police and the Armed Forces, amongst others, the Church's responsibility is not to provide solutions to the problems raised. It is to indicate the direction in which solutions may be found by people executively involved. In each case we have presented this is what we have sought to do.

There is, however, another important set of criteria to keep in mind. It is difficult, if not impossible, to assume personal responsibility for social welfare unless given the power to do so. This is basic to social democracy. The power to vote governments in or out of office is important but not enough. Other arrangements are clearly necessary if personal responsibility is to be expected of the ordinary citizen. This again has been demonstrated in the situations outlined in this essay. The acquisition of power is necessary and is, of course, a prerequisite of humbly exercising it.

It is patently essential that Christians must develop a social ethical stance. This is required of them by their faith which makes meaningful sense of experience. But ethics are derivative and secondary and become diabolical if placed on the throne of God. This can be occupied by God alone. Worship is the central act and, at the heart of Christian worship is tragedy: the fact of the crucifixion. We cannot therefore assume that enlightened people will see the direction in which to move to establish a responsible welfare society without experiencing tragic reverses. Progress is not inevitable. The way ahead is not smooth, but it is illuminated by the Gospel and tragedy which is not destructive of hope but the source of new life.

Notes

1. This essay is largely based upon records of discussions over the past seven years in the Bishop of Coventry's Council for Social Responsibility. This Council is appointed by the Bishop to advise him and the Church in the diocese on social issues. It is a consultative body, not executive. I am indebted to the Council for permission to use this material. The Council however is not responsible for the use I have made of it. That responsibility is mine alone.

2. Leakey, R. and Lewin, R., *People of the Lake,* London, Collins, 1979, pp.103-126.

3. Williams, R.R. in Barker, E., (ed.), *The Responsible Church,* London, SPCK, 1966, p.5.

4. Handy, C., "The Shape of Organisations to Come", *Personnel Management,* June 1979, pp.24-27.

5. Ibid.

6. Temple, W., *Christianity and Social Order,* London, Penguin Books, 1942.

7. Thompson, N., *Colour and Chaos,* 1976.

8. Ascoli, D., *The Queen's Peace,* London, Hamish Hamilton, 1979, pp.67ff.

9. See Rikhye, I.J., Harbottle, M. and Egge, B., *The Thin Blue Line,* Newhaven and London, Yale University Press, 1974.

10. *The Peaceful Uses of Military Forces,* Report of the Coventry Conference April 1978, London, International Committee of the Church of England Board for Social Responsibility, 1978.

11. Ramsey, A.M., *Introducing the Christian Faith,* London, SCM Press, 1970, p.29.

6

Sustainability — A New Dimension in Ecumenical Social Thought

Paul Abrecht

At the Oxford Conference on Church, Community and State in 1937, the churches of the world were urged to avoid a simple identification of the faith with any economic ideology or system. This argument was used to warn the churches of the dangers of taking sides in the ideological struggle between capitalism and socialism. In his recent book *Religion and the Persistence of Capitalism,* Ronald Preston maintains that there is still no easy resolution of the historical struggle between capitalism and socialism, nor is there likely to be one despite repeated and emphatic prophecies to the contrary. This conclusion is based on theological understanding as well as empirical observation and experience.

Preston holds that for a whole set of historical, social and ethical reasons neither the socialist command economies nor the capitalist market economies are entirely discredited, nor are they collapsing. He develops a type of convergence theory to explain his point of view. These two systems have actually evolved into a number of types of mixed economies which reveal the tendency and ability of each to discern and incorporate compatible elements of the other. As Preston says: "There is no inherent reason why elements of a command economy in the shape of planning cannot be mixed with elements of a market economy to make the market a better instrument for maximizing public benefit."[1] He also observes that "in fact there is no evolutionary tendency at work to produce either the collapse of capitalism or the advent or collapse of socialism. These grandiose theories of the progress of history are all discredited."[2]

The temptation to absolutize any social system or to endow it with absolute righteousness is contrary to the Gospel:

> Christianity is always in search of an economic order through which to express itself. It cannot simply say that socialism is the economic expression of Christianity . . . it (socialism) is an inspiring vision beyond empirical realization, and it is as impossible to move from it directly to immediate decisions in the economic order as it is to base them directly on the New Testament concept of the Kingdom of God. In so far as the term socialism refers to existing socialist economies, they exhibit ambiguities which cry out for theological as well as political and economic critiques. Still less can capitalism be said to

> be the economic expression of Christianity; only the belief in the 'divine hand' ever gave that view plausibility. Capitalism relies explicitly far too exclusively on self-interest, ignoring the necessity of other motives on which (as we have seen) it must implicitly rely in practice but does nothing to cultivate, and indeed actually undermines. On the other hand, socialist theorists, whether Christian or secular, have tended to work with an over-optimistic view of man which assumes that it is only because of capitalism that self-interest is so powerful; change to socialist structures and it will disappear, together with the conflicts of interest which go with it.[3]

This wisdom has been the basis of ecumenical social thinking about capitalism and socialism especially since the 1937 Oxford Conference. It is the kind of wisdom which underlay the well-known statement on the Responsible Society of the First Assembly of the World Council of Churches in Amsterdam in 1948, and which proposed that:

> The Christian churches should reject the ideologies of both Communism and *laissez-faire* capitalism, and should seek to draw men away from the false assumption that these extremes are the only alternatives. Each has made promises which it could not redeem. Communist ideology puts the emphasis upon economic justice, and promises that freedom will come automatically after the completion of the revolution. Capitalism puts the emphasis upon freedom, and promises that justice will follow as a by-product of free enterprise; that, too, is an ideology which has been proved false. It is the responsibility of Christians to seek new, creative solutions which never allow either justice or freedom to destroy the other.[4]

But where does this analysis lead us today as we look at our economic future? Do the resulting mixed economies offer a viable solution to the world's urgent economic problems? Some observers say that the socialist economies, measured by their productivity and efficiency, are turning into second-rate capitalist systems, bailed out by the technical know-how and efficiency of some of the greatest transnational corporations of the world; others say that the USA and the nations of the European Economic Community are rapidly becoming second-rate planned societies which make selective use of the least offensive of the socialist principles of state planning and income distribution. There is a growing sentiment that the end results of these kinds of concessions, forced upon both systems by political and other circumstances, are not producing answers to such critical problems as inflation and poverty and people's participation which beset all countries, including the technologically advanced ones.

Moreover, all these contemporary economic systems are based on the constantly expanding use of science-based technology not only involving the continued intensive exploitation of non-renewable resources, but adding to the economic and social problems we now associate with highly developed technological systems. To use a word which has been added to ecumenical social jargon in recent years, all these industrial systems appear to be increasingly 'unsustainable'.

While Preston does refer to this growing concern about sustainability in the ecumenical debate he clearly does not regard it as of primary importance. He acknowledges that there is need for new attitudes to affluence and to nature, and he examines sympathetically the ecumenical efforts which have been made to develop criteria for sustainability. But in the final analysis he believes that the issue of sustainability and possible limits to growth has been overstated:

> The likely scenario is still economic growth. Indeed it is possible that the vastly greater productivity from technical resources, which is more and more characteristic of our time, may enable us to make a serious inroad into the apalling poverty which still cripples so many parts of the world. The danger is that we shall not do this, but use our wealth to live in a wealthy ghetto in a global slum.[5]

At another point he states:

> My estimate is that at any rate another hundred years of *disciplined* growth will be needed to break the primordial global poverty barrier, and it is on this that we should set our sights.[6]

And in two further passages he makes clear his reservations about the whole growth-sustainability debate:

> What is basically overlooked is an exponential increase in technical innovation which is matching the other exponential increases (of population and resource use) . . .[7]

> The problem is not so much that of a sustainable society as of a just one — nationally and internationally — . . . technical possibilities are increasing so fast that there is the possibility that within a century the burden of crippling hunger and toil which has afflicted most of humanity most of the time can be lifted.[8]

Preston's reservations challenge me to try to clarify the new ecumenical emphasis on the 'sustainable society', and its significance for the further development of Christian thought about economic life. It seems to me that we cannot begin to comprehend the real dilemmas of modern society, capitalist or socialist or any mix of the two, without some new study of the technological assumptions on which they are based and the difficulties now confronting all technologically based systems. Nor can we confidently tackle the problems of world economic development until we have some clear understanding of what constitutes a sustainable economy and socially appropriate technology. Far from being issues of secondary importance these seem to be fundamental and decisive for further thinking about social justice, economic theory and the needed changes in the international economic order.

When we begin to explore this problem we rapidly discover that capitalism and socialism, especially in its Marxist forms, have one thing in common — both are the children of the scientific-technological world-view which came to power in the eighteenth and nineteenth centuries and still flourishes. This world-view encompasses the triumphalistic, optimistic, essentially materialistic, often reductionist and secularizing faith in a constantly expanding and progressing human control over the forces of nature. The faith-like quality of this world-view has not diminished in our times despite the growing disillusionment produced by the disparity between its promises and present realities. Many millions more people have come to believe in the unlimited possibilities of science and technology to solve problems and indeed all of us, rightly, acclaim the leaders of the new scientific-technological revolution in electronics, in communications, in medicine and in nuclear physics. It is on the promises of this view that these modern economic systems built their understanding and their hopes for human welfare, happiness, justice and freedom. However, this world-view seems increasingly to be based in part on illusions — illusions which are in large measure responsible for the practical economic and social difficulties we now face. An examination of this world-view and of the challenge to it posed by the concern for sustainability would, I believe, do much to explain the growing lack of credibility of both systems and of the various mixes their encounter has produced.

Effects of the Challenge to the Technological World-View

The industrial revolution of the nineteenth century and the societies to which it gave rise cannot be adequately explained in strictly economic terms: the accumulation of capital, new trade networks, etc. The critical element was science, "especially physical science, which has opened up such seemingly illimitable prospects for industry."[9] "The impact of science, stimulating the technicians, developing new sources of power, using power to create more than human accuracy, reducing the cost of machines until they were available for a multitude of purposes; this surely is the essential novelty, the essential revolution working so vast a transformation . . .".[10]

It has become increasingly clear that this science and technology were not merely a neutral package of new facts about the physical world and new techniques for bringing it under human control. They involved also new ideas about the role of humanity in relation to nature and embodied new hopes of releasing it from age-old insecurities. As Whitehead says, the technological revolution of the nineteenth century opened up the vision and the possibility of completely changing the conditions of human life:

> the full self-conscious realisation of the power of professionalism in knowledge in all its departments, and of the way to produce the professionals, and of the importance of knowledge to the advance of technology, and of the methods by which abstract knowledge can be connected with technology, and of the boundless possibilities of technological advance, — the realisation of all these things was first completely attained in the 19th century.[11]

The philosophical and practical basis of all modern economic systems has been this belief and hope in the promises and unlimited possibilities of the scientific, technological, industrial world-view. Since both capitalism and socialism, in ways which are remarkably similar, have founded their vision of human possibilities now and in the future on this world-view, any substantial challenge to it is bound to have serious repercussions on the self-confidence of these economic systems and their accompanying ideologies. It is my thesis that the contemporary uncertainty about the outcome of these technological systems and the concern for economic and resource sustainability represents such a challenge.

As the ecumenical discussion of sustainability has developed especially at the World Council of Churches' Conference on Faith, Science and the

Future at the Massachusetts Institute of Technology in 1979, it has focussed on three concerns:

i The heavy burden of modern industrial systems, and their related affluent consumer societies, on non-renewable resources, on the physical environment, and on people and their communities. Ronald Preston accepts the importance of this concern but he, like many other observers and thinkers is confident that new technological breakthroughs will come in the future as they have in the past, enabling us to use new resources and making it unnecessary to limit economic growth. This is not a simplistic faith in technology but it is fairly optimistic about the possibility of technological breakthroughs in areas like energy and agricultural land use which many scientists and technologists are now rejecting.

ii The ethical and social problems posed by further rapid development of science and technology and the question of the morality of such development beyond certain limits. Increasingly forms of technical power are emerging which seem intrinsically to be beyond human control, to be morally dangerous and perhaps inherently evil, and to pose urgent ethical and social questions. Such ethical issues have become acute especially in relation to various nuclear and genetic techniques. The possibility of limits to scientific enquiry is now being raised by scientists and technologists themselves. This has added a new quality to the discussion of earlier periods when the question of limits was raised by religious leaders on the basis of traditional and static understanding of human morality and nature.

iii The need to clarify the essential vision underlying human activity in science and technology, the vision to which the scientist and technician consider themselves accountable, and its relation to and interaction with the vision of faith. In the words of the Report of Section I at the MIT Conference on Faith, Science and the Future, the fidelity of scientists and technologists to their essential vision is basic to their internal integrity. Hence all depends on their understanding of that vision and their faithfulness to it. Historically the vision of science emphasized the values of objective, rational and impersonal analysis of the phenomena of the natural world. The aim was to serve human need through the prediction and control of nature. But the emphasis on reason produced also a self-sufficient rationalism which seemed to suggest that human reason could resolve all human problems. And the search for power over nature resulted often in a manipulative, mechanistic and materialistic view of the natural world. As the Report of Section I points out the world has come to distrust the faithfulness of science, and faith, to their respective visions.

> Our culture today insists that both faith and science allow themselves to be enlightened by the actual impact which they have on the world about them. Both faith and science are disturbed by what this . . . reveals. The community of faith and the community of science see that the inner visions to which they hold themselves accountable have implications for the affairs of this world, some of which they themselves abhor. Both have become in some sense captive to ideology, with the result that the essential vision of each is used in a

distorted manner for purposes that it recognizes are alien to its integrity . . . Many would insist that in recent times science has become so wedded to the technological-industrial manipulation of nature and human beings that it has, in fact, become in many places the dynamic centre of materialistic and destructive exploitation that threatens our entire planetary ecosystem.[12]

Hence the concern for sustainability involves nothing less than "faithful correction" of faith and science in order that "their praxis may promote the just, participatory and sustainable society" by liberating the truth and power of the essential visions.[13]

All three concerns have to be included in the further discussion of sustainability. How they are related is still very ambiguous, and a source of conflict most especially between the developing and developed countries. Yet it is clear that the three concerns *are* integrally related and it is not possible to concentrate on any one without seeing it in the context of the other two. It is this complex of concerns which forms the basis of the new discussion of the scientifically and technologically sustainable society so fundamentally important to the further development of our ecumenical vision of the future of humanity.

The Crisis of the Technological World-View as Revealed in Capitalism

With the development of capitalism, the technological exploitation of the world and of its resources for profit (and indirectly for human welfare) became the motor of all economic activity. Industrial capitalism is the embodiment of unceasing technological innovation and expansion. The industrial technologist became the colleague of the businessman, and together they were the great revolutionaries producing nearly two centuries of stupendous social transformation, unleashing the creative force of modern science and technology and setting off an explosion of economic activity whose material benefits, especially to the industrialized countries, were immense and obvious. They carried their revolutionary praxis to every corner of the globe with the zeal of missionaries determined to save the soul of world humanity by technological-economic change and uplift. Even today the leaders of the transnational corporations still exemplify some of that primitive conviction about the saving power of revolutinary technique, applied especially to the developing countries. And they have made converts of many of the technologically 'unsaved': some of the strongest support for the technological world-view today comes from the Third World countries, determined to get their share of the marvels of technological ingenuity before the economically and technologically satiated peoples of the developed countries decide that the limits to the exploitation of non-renewable resources, and therefore the limits to industrial technological growth, have been reached.

The amazing thing is that this capitalist industrialism took shape without any clear plan for technological development. It was created by a series of quite haphazard bursts of activity resulting from fortuitous inventions and technological discoveries by a multitude of individuals and groups all striving to be first in the race to conquer new markets. These entrepreneur-capitalist-industrialist-technologists were revolutionaries, but blind revolutionaries — almost totally unaware of the upheaval they were creating in traditional societies and cultures. Will there ever again be a period in history so incredibly creative, so dynamic, unscheduled, unpredictable, destructive and wasteful! Even two world wars fought primarily between the greatest technological nations served merely to stimulate new technological capacity and productivity. A recent report summarizes the economic growth between 1948 and 1973 thus:

> Between 1948 and 1973 world production grew at an average of 5% per year, an all time record which allowed per capita income to increase at an annual rate of approximately 3% from 1950 to 1975 in the OECD countries and 3.1 in the developing countries . . . During the same period (1948-1973) world value added in industry, expressed in US dollars at 1970 prices increased from $234 billion to $1,023 billion, i.e. an annual rate of growth of more than 6%. Agricultural production doubled in the space of 25 years (1950-1975) in the developed market-economy countries and 130% in the developing countries (excluding China).[14]

Despite the stupendous achievements of capitalist-technological economies and societies the world-view on which they are based has now come under sharp radical, challenge, especially in the developed countries but also in some developing countries. The attack comes not from its chief ideological opponent, socialism, but from a growing group of dissenters and heretics in its own ranks. Accoding to them, its very success has made it unsustainable.

Their concerns may be summarized in part as follows:

i The new realization of the extent of the costs and risks (to man, society and nature) in technologically organized society. These have turned out to be much greater than expected and difficult to estimate in advance, for example, the present uncertainty about the exact costs of nuclear energy including the disposal of its wastes, and about the ultimate effect of pesticides and other pollutants on the human and natural environment.

ii The increasing complexity of the technically organized society and the fear that we are putting ourselves too unguarded into the hands of the experts and technicians who control the buttons and levers of technical power, and through them exercise power over people.

iii The uneasy feeling that few people know what the scientists and technologists are doing in their laboratories; and what may be the possible future implications of their work; in other words that science and technology are beyond social control.

iv The suspicion that the productive technological systems have accustomed the rich industrialized countries to standards of affluence and welfare which are impossible for the whole world to attain and impossible for the rich countries to sustain without robbing the poor countries of the resources necessary for their future development.

v The growing awareness that the present systems of research and development serve primarily the interests (political, military, economic) of the rich (capitalist and socialist) societies and that the bias in their favour will increase rather than decrease with further technological advance, unless a way is found radically to reverse the present trend.

The effect of these doubts and questions is to undermine what was once a general fundamental social consensus about our technological-economic goals. Even some scientists themselves are beginning to ask, "Should we not stop many of the things we are doing?" Without belittling the contribution of science and technology to human welfare, people today are beginning to question their further uncontrolled and unrestricted development. Popular enthusiasm for more spontaneous technical-economic growth in the developed countries is in decline. The 1979 Organisation for Economic Cooperation and Development (OECD) Study, *Facing the Future,* prepared for the governments of the developed countries, acknowledges the new situation. The report observes:

> The complex relationships between values, growth and structures now make any linear view of development untenable. Values are changing radically, even if the changes are slow and of the greatest possible variety. The legitimacy of growth as a goal in itself is questioned by some, and it is running foul of structural rigidities... The danger, therefore, is that of a long-term persistence of moderate growth scenarios . . . with aggravation of rigidities and consequent reduction of growth, and in prospect, political and social destabilization of the developed countries.[15]

The OECD report thinks that the capitalist and mixed economies of Western Europe, North America and Japan will be able to maintain the moderate growth scenario which it considers necessary. But this relatively optimistic view is based on some assumptions which are clearly being questioned in practically all developed countries. The confidence even in the moderate growth scenario is based on the assumption that "in the field of energy, strongly sustained policies for energy conservation and for the development of coal and nuclear power are necessary in order to limit the risk of a major energy crisis".[16] Yet since this report was written new doubts have been expressed about this assumption.[17]

The concern for sustainability and limits to growth are therefore not theoretical issues, not issues for the future; they are part of today's reality. They involve not primarily economic issues but a wide range of far deeper questions about the role of technology in society now and in the future.

It is also becoming evident that modern capitalist societies are ill-equipped to cope with the widespread loss of confidence in the scientific and technological system which up to now has been the source of their social and economic strength. No compelling vision of the future has appeared to harness once again the enthusiasm and interests of people for cooperation in the conquest of nature or the achievement of some technological goal. Even the contest with socialism in the international sphere has lost the quality of an ideological struggle and turned into a technological competition which no-one can win: to see who can build the most sophisticated, most devastating (and most expensive) nuclear missiles.

The OECD report recognizes (very inadequately) that the developed capitalist countries lack a viable vision for the future and that there is little prospect of discovering such a vision in the context of the emphasis on national self-preservation which now predominates.

> Behind the economic difficulties from which certain developed countries are suffering, there is the *absence of a grand design* that represents the consensus of society. The existence — implicit, of course — of such a design played a vital role in the success record of the quarter-century following World War II: whether it was the United States, custodian of world order and purveyor of an ideology in which the developed countries believed; or West Germany, France and Italy, determined to rebuild their future; or Japan, for which economic growth was the means of recovering its sense of identity and its role on the world scene. These schemes no longer have any significance — partly because they have been achieved.
>
> Can a new scheme come into being? At all events it will not be brought into existence by legislation, nor by a political party's programme, but by the complex alchemy which governs the evolution of societies. It will have to be sufficiently broad to be the rallying point of widely differing beliefs as to how society should be organized. It cannot be confined to purely national objectives since, in these days of interdependence, the advanced industrial societies can no longer plan their futures in isolation and independently of the rest of the world's development.[18]

Does Marxist Socialism Provide the Needed Vision?

We are perhaps not too astonished that capitalism is deeply wedded to an untenable and unsustainable ideology of technical-economic growth and that it will have difficulty in adjusting to the crisis of this ideology. Are the socialist societies better able to respond to the challenge?

There is little evidence that this might be so. There is little in the Marxist tradition which responds to the contemporary doubts about the technologically organized society. In his own writings, Marx strongly supported a positivistic and optimistic view of technology and its power. He shared in the prevalent nineteenth century glorification of science and technology as power over nature, and over the ignorance and superstition of pre-scientific humanity. *The Communist Manifesto* speaks eloquently in praise of the bourgeois conquest of nature through science and technology:

> The bourgeoisie, during its rule of scarcely one hundred years, has created more massive and more colossal productive forces than have all preceding generations together. Subjection of nature's forces to man, machinery, application of chemistry to industry and agriculture, steam-navigation, railways, electric telegraphs, clearing of whole continents for cultivation, canalization of rivers, whole populations conjured out of the ground — what earlier century had even a presentiment that such productive forces slumbered in the lap of social labour?[19]

And Marx sharply rejects any sentimentalism about the advantages of rural over urban-industrial life:

> The bourgeoisie has subjected the country to the rule of the towns. It has created enormous cities, has greatly increased the urban population as compared with the rural and has thus rescued a considerable part of the population from the idiocy of rural life.[20]

And similarly bourgeois industrialism has provided for the betterment of non-European peoples whom Marx did not hesitate to call "barbarians":

Just as it has made the country dependent on the towns, so it has made barbarian and semi-barbarian countries dependent on the civilized ones, nations of peasants on nations of bourgeois, the East on the West.[21]

The key to all this historic "advance of civilization" is the power of science, a power which the bourgeoisie have been so instrumental in liberating. Marx hints at a kind of Faustian element at work: the bourgeois class which has "conjured up such gigantic means of production and exchange, is like the sorcerer who is no longer able to control the powers of the nether world whom he has called up by his spell."[22] The real problem however is that the bourgeoisie having created and developed all this industrial wealth are unable to create a society which would ensure that it will be usefully employed for the benefit of humanity. Fortunately they have also called into existence "the working class — the proletarians" who will be able to give full freedom to the scientific-technological potential.

Marx's optimistic assumptions about science and technology — his concept of nature as something to be manipulated, his attitude concerning the absolute inevitability and desirability of the technological civilisation — are in fact very similar to those held by his bourgeois capitalist contemporaries. The assumption is that science and technology are neutral forces; the wave of technological advance is good and cannot and should not be held back; the main problem is to utilize and distribute its output justly among the true producers — the workers. Despite its recognized alienating characteristics (acknowledged by Marx in both his early and late writings) there is for humanity no way other than the technological way.

By all criteria Marx was utopian in his view of the liberating character of industrial technology. He believed that automated industry under the control of communism would eventually lead to the complete abolition of the division of labour. He wrote:

What characterizes the division of labour in the automatic workshop is that labour has there completely lost its specialized character. But the moment every special development stops, the need for universality, the tendency towards an integral development of the individual, begins to be felt. The automatic workshop wipes out specialists and craft-idiocy.[23]

. . . in communist society (in contrast to earlier patterns of division of labour) where nobody has one exclusive sphere of activity, but each can become accomplished in any branch he wishes, society regulates the general production and thus makes it possible for me to do one thing today and another tomorrow, to hunt in the morning, fish in the afternoon, rear cattle in the evening, criticize after dinner, just as I have in mind without ever becoming hunter, fisherman, shepherd or critic.[24]

Even contemporary Marxist philosophers and theorists agree that the problem of alienation in technological systems has not been solved in socialist societies and that it is much more intractable than Marx perceived. Adam Schaff, a Polish Marxist philosopher, says:

Marx analyzed the crippled human nature of . . . alienation under capitalism. Unfortunately, the technical aspects of the problem cut across all systems — for example, work on an assembly-line is inherently the same regardless of government . . . To make matters worse, technical progress since Marx's days has only aggravated the situation . . .[25]

And he adds:

> And so alienation can be found in socialist society, not only as a relic of the past, but also as something more durable and more organically linked with the new social conditions. At any rate the problem is real . . .[26]

Among Marxists today there is, therefore, much rethinking about Marx's view of technology and his hopeful and uncritical acceptance of it. Contemporary Marxist philosophers like Bloch, Marcuse and Habermas, all in their own way seek to escape from Marx's too easy acceptance of the premises of the scientific and technological world-view. Their dissatisfaction is well summed up by Alfred Schmidt in his book, *The Concept of Nature in Marx.* Referring to the frustrations of Bloch, he writes:

> The great technology which arose with the bourgeoisie remains in its main aspects relatively independent of the no-longer bourgeois form of social organization. It is therefore not just the interest of the capitalists which thwarts the 'broader physics' considered possible by Bloch. Not only will men continue to try to outwit nature, an endeavour which Bloch criticized, but also, in view of the immense growth of the forces of production, a non-mathematical and qualitative relation to the Object, such as he had in mind, will hardly be capable of realization.[27]

And Schmidt concludes with these words:

> Today, when men's technical possibilities have outstripped the dreams of the old Utopians many times over, it appears rather that these possibilities, negatively realized, have changed into forces of destruction, and therefore, instead of bringing about an albeit always humanly limited salvation, lead to total destruction, a grim parody of the transformation intended by Marx, in which Subject and Object are not reconciled, but annihilated.[28]

These problems in Marxist socialist theory help, I believe, to explain the great difficulty which contemporary socialist action has in facing up to newly recognized problems of technological and ecological sustainability. Socialist tradition has so glorified the possibilities of technological power when controlled by the principles of socialism that it is unable to attack the heart of the problem: the ideology of technology, its social assumptions and consquences.[29] Socialist practice still conforms to that theory. Hence socialist societies based on that theory have difficulty for example in recognizing the legitimacy of popular resistance to such technological developments as nuclear energy.[30]

These societies do not find it any easier than do the capitalist ones to accept the inevitability of lower rates of economic growth forced by the new concern for the human and natural environment.[31]

This situation also helps to explain why contemporary theories of social justice (based as they so often are on socialist theory) are so frustrated by the whole ecological and technological debate. This is true not least of traditional Christian theories of social justice. Clearly there is need for new definitions of social change and justice which take into account the wide range of issues which have arisen in the context of the concern for sustainability.

The Response of the Third World

The Third World countries have the greatest difficulty with the concept of the sustainable society. They have expressed, often very sharply, their disagreement with its presuppositions.

Some of their objections are based on misunderstanding. The concern for 'limits to growth' and 'appropriate technology' has sometimes been presented in a way which suggests that the Third World would not be enabled to develop further or have access to modern sophisticated technology. These countries fear that in an all-out effort to ensure a sustainable world society they would be kept in a state of technological and economic servitude to the developed countries. This has never been part of the ecumenical understanding of sustainability. On the contrary, it has been argued that the rich countries must stop growing *in order that* the poor countries may have greater prospects of growing. 'The rich world must learn to live simply in order that the poor nations may simply live.'

Given the low per capita income in the poorer countries of the world it may seem that the latter do not need to give much attention for years to come to limits on technological and economic development. But in reality many of them are facing decisions about their technological future which involve the criteria of sustainability (for example, in their choice of energy systems, communications, and transport). Some of the developing countries are also beginning to recognize the spiritual and cultural dimension of the struggle for a sustainable society, as they try to cope with secularism characteristic of most technologically developed societies. Events in Iran, Indonesia, Malaysia and in many other countries reveal the nervousness of traditional societies subject to the onslaught of rapid technological change, especially when this is accompanied by a secularist philosophy of life. Hence the growing interest in finding ways to make technology serve traditional values rather than seeing their communities increasingly subjected to technological values imported from the industrialized countries. The reactionary religious spirit in which this feeling often finds expression is most unhelpful, but it reveals the vitality of the spiritual resistance to technological takeovers.

The issue of sustainability as it appears in the Third World is more critical than in many developed countries. The problem is not just that they, like us, are enamoured of the new technological gadgets. It is that they are becoming locked into an interdependent world economic system where the prizes still go to the technologically advanced. No country, especially the larger Third World countries, can realistically plan its economic future without looking at these larger political consequences. The spread of nuclear energy technology is a case in point. Nations which have few resources to spare are tempted to engage in the highly intensive and costly nuclear development either because they lack indigenous energy resources or because they cannot afford to fall behind in the world technological competition whatever it may cost their people in terms of the necessities of life.

These problems may be overcome in part once the economic and social interests of Third World countries are given a larger place in the new international economic order.

It was interesting to note that at the MIT Conference the Third World participants were divided on this question. The younger participants were opposed to increasing dependence on Western technology and especially to the introduction of high technologies like nuclear energy. But they lacked any consistent theory of sustainable economic development. The older participants still expressed the desire for technological growth, primarily for reasons of national political and economic power. They were often the most outspoken opponents of the concern for sustainability. Part of the problem is that in these Third World countries there is so little discussion of these subjects between the government, the scientific community and the public. Clearly the churches in these countries could play a significant role in stimulating this discussion. But they are presently at a disadvantage since like the churches in the developed countries they have had little experience in relating Christian faith and ethics to scientific issues.

New Directions for Ecumenical Social Thought

For fifty years ecumenical social thought has been primarily concerned with the search for a just society. Justice was seen to involve the development of new economic and social systems as well as the increasing participation by people in the decision-making and community-building process. Today we appear to be at a turning-point. The concern for a Just, Participatory *and* Sustainable Society is not just a new slogan, nor is it a blueprint for a new society. It is an attempt to hold together three concepts that while in tension with each other express three realities of contemporary life. We are far from arriving at satisfactory answers to questions arising from this new constellation of issues.

i Are the criteria of a sustainable society reconcilable with those of a just society? In an earlier stage they seemed to be competing. Now they appear to converge: "A sustainable society which is unjust can hardly be worth sustaining. A just society that is unsustainable is self-defeating."[32]

ii Is there a conflict between the goal of a participatory society and the essential role of expertise and technical knowledge in defining a sustainable technological system? A WCC statement on the "Public Acceptance of Nuclear Power" says: "The decisions (on the use of nuclear energy) are too important to remain confined within the technical arena of the nuclear, scientific and engineering communities. However, without the full collaboration of these expert groups there can be no resolution of the questions . . ."[33]

iii What stand should the churches take when it appears that further scientific and technological advance in certain areas can be achieved only at the price of presently incalculable risks? An American scientist, who helped develop the technique of recombining the genes of one organism with those of another, an accomplishment which is regarded as significant as the splitting of the atom, now questions whether this technique should be used. He said:

> To impose any limit upon freedom of inquiry is especially bitter for the scientist whose life is one of inquiry; but science has become too potent. It is no longer enough to wave the flag of Galileo.[34]

The search for a sustainable society involves a re-examination of many cherished assumptions about the freedom of science and technology; the formulation of new criteria for limiting that freedom; and the development of social institutions capable of exercising the necessary control.

Notes

1. Preston, R.H., *Religion and the Persistence of Capitalism,* London, SCM Press, 1979, p.40.

2. Ibid., p.38.

3. Ibid., p.47.

4. Visser 't Hooft, W.A., (ed.), *The First Assembly of the world Council of Churches: The Official Report,* London, SCM Press, 1949, p.80.

5. Preston, op.cit., p.35.

6. Ibid., p.64.

7. Ibid., p.34.

8. Ibid., p.125.

9. Hicks, J.R., *Theory of Economic History,* London, Oxford University Press, 1969, p.45.

10. Ibid., p.148.

11. Whitehead, A.N., *Science and the Modern World,* Cambridge, Cambridge University Press, 1927, p.122.

12. Abrecht, P., (ed.), *Faith and Science in an Unjust World,* 2, Reports and Recommendations, Geneva, World Council of Churches, p.13.

13. Ibid., p.14.

14. *Interfutures: Facing the Future,* Paris, OECD, 1979.

15. Ibid., p.187.

16. Ibid., p.417.

17. See for example Lantzke, U., "Expanding World Use of Coal", *Foreign Affairs,* Winter 1979-1980, pp.351-373.

18. *Interfutures,* op.cit.,

19. Marx, K. and Engels, F., *The Communist Manifesto,* New York, International Publishers, 1948, p.13ff.

20. Ibid., p.13.

21. Ibid.

22. Ibid., p.14.

23. Quoted in Schmidt, A., *The Concept of Nature in Marx,* London, New Left Books, 1971, p.146.

24. Ibid.

25. Schaff, A., *Marxism and the Human Individual,* New York, McGraw-Hill, 1970, p.135.

26. Ibid., p.137.

27. Schmidt, op.cit., p.158.

28. Ibid., p.163.

29. See Habermas, J., *Toward a Rational Society,* Boston, Beacon Press, especially the essay "Technology and Science as Ideology", p.111.

30. For example, Yemelyanov, V.A., "Atoms for Peace, Science for Man", International Institute for Peace, Vienna, 1980, where the anti-nuclear campaign is attributed to the capitalist oil companies.

31. A contemporary East German Marxist philosopher who accepts limits to growth maintains that the socialist dictatorship of the proletariat is best able to achieve it because only through dictatorship can the necessary large changes be accomplished. See Harich, W., *Kommunismus ohne Wachtsum?,* Reinbek bei Hamburg, Rowohlt-Verlag, 1975.

32. Report of the Glion Meeting of Church and Society, 1976, *Anticipation,* 23, November 1976.

33. "Public Acceptance of Nuclear Power", *Anticipation,* 24, November 1977, p.17.

34. Robert Sinsheimer, formerly Chairman of the Biology Division at California Institute of Technology.

7

Fraternity and The Fraternal Society: The Problem of Governability in Britain

Kenneth Medhurst

The importance of Ronald Preston's *Religion and the Persistence of Capitalism* partly lies in its willingness to confront, without undue simplification, complex contemporary political issues. The problems posed by capitalism are seen as political as well as economic. This contribution to the present volume is most certainly inspired by such political preoccupations. It is not the contribution of a theologian, nor even of a political philosopher, but of a political scientist. It seeks, albeit summarily, to draw on empirical investigations of political realities. On the other hand the discussion clearly strays into territory occupied by theologians and philosophers. The ensuing discussion of 'fraternity' is related to empirical issues but it necessarily raises normative questions. It is not claimed that questions of fact can be wholly divorced from questions of value. Rather scope is seen for fruitful contact between the political analyst, on the one hand, and the philosopher and theologian, on the other. 'Fraternity', not least, is seen as a theme lending itself to such contact.

This reflection on 'fraternity' was first inspired by A.H. Halsey's 1977 Reith Lectures, *Change in British Society*[1]. Underlying his analysis of contemporary Britain is a commitment to the British social democratic tradition and a plea for the redeployment of resources that he (and this author) see as being latent within that tradition. In particular he argues for a new emphasis upon the idea of 'fraternity' and the quest for a 'fraternal' society. This essay seeks to think aloud about these themes as part of a continuing reflection upon contemporary British affairs. In principle the subject could be handled on a comparative footing, and the experience of other polities is certainly drawn upon, but the focus here is necessarily more limited.

Of the great French revolutionary triad of liberty, equality and fraternity, the latter has perhaps received least systematic attention from political thinkers and practitioners. On the subject of liberty and equality, and the tension or potential conflict between them, there has been extensive debate. The liberal tradition, obviously, has placed its stress on the first of these coveted values. From Locke, through Mill down to Rawls or Dahrendorf, the accent has tended to be on maximising individual freedom of choice and minimising the danger of arbitrary governmental intervention in personal lives. The emphasis has been on the primacy of society over the state and of the individual over and against society. Indeed, society tends to be viewed as an aggregate of substantially autonomous individuals each seeking, through a rational calculation of self-interest, to promote their personal welfare.[2]

One obvious difficulty about this position arises from the need to resolve clashes of individual interests, for this presupposes the recognition of some limited measure of inter-dependence and some generally agreed procedures or understandings concerning conflict resolution. Rawls, for example, is one of the latest of a distinguished line which has wrestled with the theoretical problem of establishing criteria in terms of which limits to individual freedom may be legitimately and justly established. Despite the undoubted intellectual power of such theorectical constructs it cannot safely be assumed that, within the framework of their essentially individualistic philosophy, liberals have wholly succeeded in holding the balance between individual and collective interests.[3]

Social democrats and, still more, Marxists would clearly argue that liberal individualism tends to the perpetuation of unacceptable inequalities. For the liberal inequalities of wealth, opportunity and power may, subject to some limitations, be a necessary price for the fostering of liberty. Recently, for example, Dahrendorf persuasively argued that the central political issue of modern industrial societies, like Britain, is the quest for greater liberty and the enrichment of individual lives to be expected from more diversified opportunities for the exercise of personal choice, responsibility and creativity.[4] He relegated the quest for greater equality to the realm of secondary concerns on the ground that the battle against more extreme forms of poverty had been largely won. Other 'neo-liberals', such as Friedman or Hayek argue, far more strenuously, that the deliberate pursuit of further equality necessarily leads to such a strengthening of bureaucratic state power that we would find ourselves on "the Road to Serfdom."[5] The requisite economic management would decisively shift us toward a positively illiberal command economy. Indeed, this case significantly hangs on the assumption that the classical liberal freedoms largely depend on the preservation of relatively untrammelled free market capitalist relationships.

Radical critics would take issue with these viewpoints on a number of grounds. Firstly, it seems clear enough that there is no necessary link between capitalist economies and liberal political institutions or values. Chile's military dictatorship, for example, indicates that a capitalist pathway to development is compatible with or may even, in certain circumstances, presuppose, authoritarianism.[6] Secondly, within liberal democracies of the already industrialised world it could be argued that the liberal case does not view with sufficient seriousness the extent and possible significance of remaining inequalities. For example, Peter Townsend's work (and the comments in this volume by John Atherton) point to poverty as a more crippling and deeply embedded phenomenon than the more optimistic commentators would allow.[7] Equally, the latter seem unduly sanguine concerning the capacity of existing economic and political arrangements to resolve the problem. For the victims of this situation serious questions arise about the extent and nature of the liberty that they can enjoy.

This latter point raises the further possibility that, not least in Britain, liberal democracy may have tended historically to operate to the general advantage of already favoured interests and to have excluded truly radical questioning from the political agenda.[8] Thus, it can be maintained that the consensus which has underlain modern Britain's relative political stability has embodied a substantial conservative bias. On the one hand, it could be asserted, that liberal democratic freedom and the extension of formal liberal democratic rights have, in practice, afforded ample opportunity for the economically advantaged to organise in self-defence. On the other hand, it can be claimed, the economically disadvantaged are correspondingly constrained by a complex combination of structural and cultural factors. Structurally it may be a question of seeking to operate liberal democratic institutions within the context of a hierarchically ordered society characterised by persistent and patterned inequalities of a largely class based kind. Substantial inter-class mobility and increasingly complex occupational structures may have considerably complicated the picture but have apparently failed radically to alter the underlying realities.[9] It seems true, for example, that, since 1945, there has been some marked reduction of overall income inequalities (and on this count Britain comes out better than, for instance, France) but striking differentials clearly remain.[10] Moreover, it is evident that inequalities in the work place are far from being just matters of very unequal remuneration.[11] Hierarchical patterns of authority coexist with discriminatory patterns of recruitment into leadership positions. Likewise, working conditions, job security, pension rights and fringe benefits are unevenly distributed as between classes. Finally, when distinctions are drawn between accumulated wealth and current income it is apparent that traditional inequalities remain deeply entrenched.[12] The net result is still very unequal access to our society's material and cultural rewards. Equally, it means, *de facto,* an unequal competition for positions of power and influence within the society. Though, particularly, in the 1950s and 1960s, the industrial working class frequently experienced rises in material living standards it became apparent that this section of society was not, on the whole, experiencing 'embourgoisement' and that established class divisions remained stubbornly resistant to change. Similarly, new opportunities for upward social mobility and for access to the benefits attendant upon secondary or higher education have been essentially meritocratic in nature and have not substantially transformed the class divided nature of British society.[13]

In this situation the chief source of leverage, on the part of the relatively disadvantaged, has been their capacity to show some solidarity and to capitalise upon the relative weight of their numbers. The Labour movement, in its broadest sense, might seem to provide the organisation needed to press home such potential advantages. In Britain, however, it can be argued that the movement's radical potential has been inhibited by the established political context within which it has felt constrained to function. Thus, from its inception (and beyond the time when it supplanted the Liberals) Britain's Labour Party, and its trade union allies, have been up against an already entrenched Conservative party representative of traditionally dominant social groups. Such groups, moreover, espoused values to which other sections of society quite readily subscribed.[14]

These values point to the cultural factors which may have inhibited radical questioning of the status quo. There is reason to suppose that traditionally dominant groups espoused and were legitimised in terms of a loose knit but widely diffused value system — a system that could be characterised as the dominant one within Britain's relatively homogeneous political culture. This system has incorporated liberal values supportive of liberal democratic institutions. Not least these have perhaps facilitated a substantial degree of civility and restraint in pursuing political conflicts. But the same political culture also seems to have been characterised by a stress on patriotic values frequently associated with widespread belief in the legitimacy of traditional hierarchies. Deference has commonly been accorded to institutions or groups perceived to be at or near the apex of such hierarchies. The monarchy and traditional upper class groups have fallen into this category. Traditionally the established Church also tended to be an integral part of the same pattern. By the same token hierarchically defined status or prestige distinctions have traditionally tended to legitimise established socio-economic inequalities and so to make them to some extent acceptable to the relatively disadvantaged. Unwillingness radically to challenge inequalities may have been, as Runciman persuasively argued, significantly due to the narrow horizons of the disadvantaged and their tendency only to compare themselves with those closest to them in existing stratification systems.[15] But such understandings of relative deprivation have also to be viewed in the context of a society which has shown widespread willingness (at all levels) to accept or, at the least, acquiesce in hierarchical arrangements and uneven distributions of power, wealth and prestige. Thus, from the outset, a political movement in some degree dedicated to challenging such inequalities is placed at some disadvantage and faced with awkward dilemmas.

One facet of this situation has been a persistent tendency of substantial portions of the working class to vote Conservative.[16] The 'deference vote' apparently has helped substantially to account for this phenomenon.[17] Deferential attitudes, however, seem by no means confined to the working class nor, perhaps more significantly, to habitual Conservative Party supporters. They appear to have been widely disseminated throughout much of the British electorate and to have extended to many working class Labour supporters. These supporters, at shop floor level, may be frequently engaged in continuing conflicts with management. Equally, such conflictual relationships are both cause and effect of a situation in which many workers have aligned themselves with trade unions and the wider Labour movement. Nevertheless, industrial conflicts have rarely threatened to be transformed into generalised class warfare aimed at the promotion of radical political change. Imprecise and fluctuating yet real boundaries have traditionally been maintained between the polity and the realm of industrial conflict. Likewise, British trade unions have not, in the main, given hospitality to syndicalist ideas of engineering radical political change through industrial action. They have generally subscribed instead to a social democratic or reformist position which accepts the limitations set by existing institutional arrangements and the prevailing value system with which those arrangements have traditionally, in significant measure, been associated.[18]

To radical critics of social democracy these limitations suggest that, at best, social democrats consent to fight with one arm tied behind their back. At worse (and this might be a general Marxist interpretation) they confirm that liberal democracy exists, by definition, to defend bourgeois interests and so must almost inevitably doom to failure efforts to achieve substantially new forms of political or socio-economic organisation on the basis of established forms of consent.[19] According to this view the real choice lies between reformism which effectively perpetuates the status quo and some decisive breach with the established order.

Such critics might and do point to some post-1945 developments as evidence for their case. Thus they cite the disappointing end to the post-1945 Labour experiment and the failure of subsequent Labour governments substantially to add to what was achieved under the auspices of Attlee's administrations. Similarly it is argued that substantial extensions of public ownership and the machinery of the Welfare State did not combine radically to transform Britain's socio-economic structures. The same line of reasoning also tends to assume that the capacity of post-1945 Conservative governments (at least until very recently) significantly to adapt to the new realities of the mixed economy and Welfare State was not just a tribute to Conservative pragmatism but also a measure of the relatively limited nature of change.[20]

Simultaneously critics can point to long term trends possibly subjecting existing liberal democratic institutions to growing strain and putting question marks against the stability of the compromises and understandings which have traditionally undergirded these institutions. Two developments, in particular, could be isolated under this heading. Firstly, commentators point to a decline in the power of traditional patterns of status to command respect. Established patterns of socio-economic stratification may (despite substantial modifications) remain entrenched but the resulting inequalities can perhaps be less readily legitimised by reference to traditional notions of hierarchy than once was the case.[21] More complex social structures, increased mobility and enhanced educational opportunities may not have radically altered the class based nature of British society but together they may have contributed to some erosion of earlier concepts of status and prestige. This, of course, does not necessarily mean a major shift toward egalitarian values. Rather, there may well be a spreading of the competitive, acquisitive consumer and achievement orientated values of the capitalist market place. Trade union wage demands, additionally fuelled by inflation, seem to be due at least as much to this type of dynamic as to any essentially egalitarian thrust. The maximisation of individual or group advantage, the protection of differentials and (as with white collar unions) reactions against perceived threats to earlier positions of relative privilege all, in significant measure, could be construed as comprehensible concomitants of market economic relationships relatively unrestrained by traditional norms or a clearly articulated and commonly held social ethic.

In the political domain the same situation seems reflected in the propensity of many parts of the electorate, including very substantial working class elements, to favour the party currently perceived as the most likely to offer effective management of current economic arrangements and to maximise sectional or private economic rewards. The deferential Conservative voter perhaps more than ever now coexists or overlaps with working class voters who have opted for the Conservatives on prudential grounds. Equally, traditional working class loyalties to the Labour Party may in some measure ebb or flow along with shifting perceptions of the party's competence as an economic manager.

Such patterns of voting behaviour may partly explain recent fluctuations in British electoral fortunes. Not least they may help to explain the substantial support trade unionists evidently gave to the Conservatives in the 1979 general election.[22] That election, however, also pointed to other possibly related trends of apparent significance. In particular it seemed to underline the diminishing attractiveness of both major parties for significant portions of the British electorate. Such questioning has sometimes expressed itself in support for 'minor parties'. This was generally less true in May 1979. On the other hand the victorious Conservative Party was elected on the basis of a relatively small proportion of the possible electorate and the Labour Party's share of the vote was the smallest in post-war years. By the same token there has been a falling off in the mass memberships of political parties.[23] There are, in other words, signs of decreasing confidence in the parties responsible for managing British political institutions and this seems substantially related to the apparent inability of the institutions to resolve underlying economic problems. After a lengthy post-war period in which the state's role (to some extent irrespective of the party in power) has tended to increase and during which it has been increasingly viewed as the necessary instrument for satisfying individual or group aspirations it now seems as if its credibility has correspondingly diminished.[24] Demand for state action has grown but disappointment with the effects of such action has simultaneously tended to create some scepticism concerning the viability and even the integrity of the political system. In some measure a vicious circle has been set up, for failures of state policy (especially in the economic realm) have eaten away at that very basis of support for the system which seems necessary for its long term stable evolution. It appears, in other words, as if contemporary governments can less readily assume the electorate's willingness to accord them the benefit of the doubt and, to that extent, they have diminished room for manoeuvre. Conventionally, as A.H. Birch has indicated, our representative institutions have coexisted with governmental conventions that concede much latitude to the executive.[25] Our governments still seek substantially to operate on the basis of such conventions and assume the degree of trust that this habitually presupposed. In reality, however, there are grounds for thinking that the past frustration of many popular expectations has contributed to a diminution of such trust.

The problem can, of course, be grossly overstated. Talk of an immediate or major crisis of Britain's political system seems exaggerated. Perhaps such talk unduly stresses the processes of change within Britain's polity and underestimates elements making for continuity. Nevertheless, there is a logic inhering in certain trends or developments which, if unacknowledged, inappropriately handled or left without countervailing measures, could make for serious difficulties. Three issues, in particular, could be considered under this heading. Two of them, the question of race or British citizenship and the question of the unity of the United Kingdom, are not of an obviously or overtly economic kind. Nevertheless, a solution to these problems would seem linked to the general question of economic welfare the fostering of which constitutes the third and arguably most fundamental question. Thus the diminution of potentially destructive racial tensions partly depends on reducing conflicts over scarce jobs and resources.[26] It also partly depends on significantly reducing the disproportionate share of the collective burden of unemployment which ethnic minorities currently assume. Similarly, the implementation of a durable modus vivendi amongst the United Kingdom's constituent elements seems to hinge significantly on widespread belief in the willingness and capacity of the British state sensitively to handle local economic grievances and to oversee an equitable regional distribution of the benefits of national economic activity.[27] More universally, the long term stabilisation of a viable form of government, by some form of consent, would seem to depend significantly on the perceived efficacy and legitimacy of that economic activity.

Certainly the economic issue has been the central one in modern British political debate and it is the sense of collective failure in this domain which most threatens to place our political institutions under strain. The relevant factors are many and complex and cannot here be adequately analysed. Three relatively recent trends do, however, warrant brief mention because of their particular impact upon the state and its position within Britain's polity. Firstly, allusion should be made to the tentative experiments in 'indicative' economic planning which were first launched, in the early 1960s, by a Conservative government and were, for a while, developed by a Labour administration.[28] Initially they were presented as a means of facilitating guaranteed, controlled and rationally ordered economic expansion. They were viewed as an instrument for overseeing that economic growth required for the fulfilling of the mass consumer society's material promises. As such they were received amongst portions of Britain's economic and political elites as one possible key to the effective management of our mixed but still largely capitalist economy. In practice, however, the initial expectations were soon frustrated and there was a retreat back to less ambitious and considerably more piecemeal forms of state economic intervention. Such forms of intervention, in face of international economic troubles and domestic political constraints, have clearly not got to grips with perennial problems of sustained productivity, industrial reorganisation and, still less, of industrial relations. Problems of industrial relations have gone into the making of a second noteworthy trend. Thus, in the past two decades trade union leaders have appeared increasingly to articulate their wage claims on the basis of more far reaching and less parochial comparisons than once was the case.[29] Consequently it seems likely that, amongst many of their constituents, the sense of relative deprivation has been intensified. This has revealed itself in additional pressures upon national union leaders. But it has also manifested itself in localised demands by workers over whom official unions have, at best, very limited influence. The whole process is perhaps both cause and effect of previously mentioned changes in traditional status distinctions. It has also perhaps been facilitated by growing awareness on the part of some workers of an increasing capacity, within the setting of complex and inter-dependent economic institutions, to exert unusual leverage. Not least the process has been additionally encouraged by the competitive scramble for scarce resources characteristic of inflationary periods.

Finally, as a consequence of the above development, recent governments have felt constrained, sometimes in new ways, to attempt to regulate trade union behaviour and/or to implement incomes policies. Consequently matters conventionally perceived as non-political have become patently politicised. Equally, conflicts which traditionally tended to be confined to the quasi-autonomous sphere of industrial relations have spilled over more obviously into the political arena. To that extent pressures upon the political system may have mounted and the potentially destabilising consequences of class conflict have somewhat increased. One governmental response has been a series of efforts to introduce elements of order into the contentious sphere of wage bargaining and distribution. So far, however, the chief long term practical result seems to have been to highlight what Goldthorpe has described as the essentially unprincipled nature of the national economic reward system.[30] It is a system which cannot be readily legitimised through reference to moral principles or customary usages but which has tended to be the outcome of interactions between structured inequalities, market forces and the uneven bargaining power of competing groups of workers. Workers, in other words, have been locked into economic relationships which, despite the union movement's crucially important intervention, are substantially characterised by the unstable and, in principle, unceasing competitiveness of the market place. Their collective efforts have, in general, not been geared to significant overall income redistribution. Moreover, state intervention has tended to take the form of relatively short term measures not designed to command that sustained and extensive support which is probably needed if greater long term elements of rationality or equity are to be introduced into income distribution. Recent policies have not, it may be argued, seriously addressed themselves to the questions of justice and legitimacy which have to be addressed if a more obviously justifiable and acceptable reward system is to be fashioned.

In this discussion such ethical issues necessarily bulk large. As Fred Hirsch observed, and Ronald Preston subsequently indicated, the motive power behind capitalism may, in significant measure, be competitiveness and acquisitiveness yet its smooth functioning depends, perhaps paradoxically, upon minimal levels of trust and some shared moral understandings.[31] For example, there seems a need to cooperate in the fulfilling of contracts and to exercise some discipline or restraint in pursuing sectional advantage. On the other hand, as Hirsch further comments, the underlying materialist, individualist, competitive and acquisitive dynamic may work, in the longer run, to erode this original moral base. Similarly, as Daniel Bell has argued in the North American context, the disciplined but essentially individual acquisitiveness required for capital accumulation can turn into the individualistic hedonism of a mass consumer society.[32] In such a society, as both Hirsch and Bell indicate, economic growth has been linked to the continuing stimulation of private wants. But it is a further part of Hirsch's important argument that there are necessary limits to the satisfying of such wants. The appetite for some material goods may, in principle, be quite readily met. On the other hand, the demand for some non-material benefits and what Hirsch identified as 'positional goods' cannot be universally satisfied for they are necessarily scarce commodities. For example, enjoyment of countryside may diminish in proportion to the numbers of people securing access to it. Traffic jams on bank holidays might symbolise this situation of diminishing returns. Still more are there limits to the numbers of people able to obtain posts now conventionally defined as 'top jobs'. Thus, within the context of current socio-economic relationships, it seems as if the consumer society's promise of ever increasing rewards must always, in key respects, have been illusory and liable to generate frustration.

In Hirsch's view only such non-economic factors as shared religious or cultural values and commonly exercised citizenship rights can act to restrain the potentially destructive forces at work in this situation. He does not, however, much elaborate this aspect of his work nor explore at length the possibly realistic alternative options open to our society in confronting such dilemmas. In the remainder of this essay the intention is very briefly to suggest four such options and to commit the author to one of them. In doing so questions of religion, culture and citizenship, albeit very succinctly, will be taken up. These four options, it should be added, are presented as analytically quite distinct models. In reality, however, it must be acknowledged that elements of all of them are liable to coexist in any foreseeable empirical situation. By the same token this writer's plea for 'a fraternal option' is not to be viewed as an all or nothing commitment to a nebulous utopian vision. Rather, it is a plea for strategies and policies, at a variety of levels, that might tend to take us a few steps toward a more obviously 'fraternal society' and emphasise certain types of socio-economic relationships at the expense of others.

The Free Market Model

The first perhaps theoretically available option is the one which implicitly and to a certain extent explicitly may underlie the thinking of elements within Britain's current Conservative government. Such elements wish substantially to re-draw or push back the boundary dividing the polity from the economy. They seek a marked reduction in the role of the state and a correspondingly renewed emphasis on the values or practices of the open market place. The challenges and disciplines of the market, it seems to be assumed, will ultimately foster energy and initiative on the scale needed to regenerate our economy and to create new wealth. Stress is laid on individual effort and self-improvement rather than the collective endeavours of trade unions or the state. Clearly, in this scheme of things, the quest for greater equality is abandoned in favour of the quest for greater individual freedom.

In the very short term it seems just possible that such an approach could have some very limited successes. For example, in a harsh economic climate characterised by fear of unemployment there may be some temporary lowering of material expectations and some acquiescence in the perpetuation if not accentuation of entrenched inequalities. In the longer run, however, it seems likely that the stress on competitiveness, acquisitiveness and self-help, underlying such an approach, will exacerbate existing conflicts and so further question the viability or legitimacy of existing socio-economic and even political arrangements. Moreover, the free market model envisaged appears to pay little heed to the asymetrical nature of power relations within the market place. In particular it does not confront the problems faced by the existence of large scale national or multi-national business corporations which, to some extent, can insulate themselves against the disciplines of the market place and whose activities impinge so massively upon society that only the state has any possibility at all of rendering them accountable.

The logic of this approach would therefore seem ultimately to lead to increased inequality, competitiveness and social tension, on the one hand, and to substantially unregulated concentrations of private economic power on the other. The latter trend, moreover (which has characterised much of modern British economic development) seems liable to exacerbate another range of attendant problems. These would include the tendency for economic resources and power to be concentrated in particular regions, for existing communities to be disrupted and for workforces to feel increasingly powerless, alienated and remote from the decision making processes governing their lives.

Faced with such developments, and the possible absence of those extra material rewards initially promised, there may be an additional temptation to resort to populist and even quasi-authoritarian measures as a means of diverting attention from underlying difficulties. Such responses would clearly be at odds with the avowedly liberal objectives at stake. Nevertheless, as C.B. Macpherson argued in his comments upon Hobbes, the self-interested strivings inherent in market economic relationships might logically point to such levels of conflict that, in the absence of other restraining factors, only a powerful sovereign could keep the conflict within acceptable bounds.[33]

The Command Economy

A second possible option might be moves, in an opposing direction towards something more obviously resembling a command economy. Certainly there are those left wing groups whose frustration, in face of persisting inequalities, points them in this direction and sometimes inclines them to despair of existing political institutions. Their strategy supposes large scale extensions of public ownership, more detailed economic planning, a diminished role for private enterprise, an enhanced policy making role for trade unions, substantial redistributions of wealth and, as a necessary corollary of all the above, a strengthening of the state apparatus.

In this connection at least three possible difficulties suggest themselves. Firstly, if greater equality is viewed as the overriding aim, and as an aim to be pursued for its own sake, then it seems likely that such strategies could lead to disappointments and the creation of some new patterns of inequality to complement or supplant existing ones. Thus, studies of East European societies indicate that though traditional inequalities may diminish they do not vanish or else they give way to new patterns of stratification based on relative degrees of access to state bureaucracies.[34] Secondly, and by the same token, serious thought has to be given to the overall consequences of the strengthening of state power on the scale envisaged. In the absence of sustained efforts to render the state accountable, to establish viable participatory mechanisms and of the cultural values needed successfully to sustain such mechanisms there is a serious possibility of simply reinforcing the remote, potentially self-regarding and insensitive bureaucratic apparatus which arguably lies behind some of the contemporary disenchantment with political activity. Certainly there are some grounds for thinking that tensions arising from the remote impersonality of centralised bureaucratic machines and the centralising tendencies observable in both the economic and political life of modern industrial societies (both capitalist and communist) in part underlie the appeal of centrifugal nationalist forces and the populist postures alluded to above. This model of political change, in other words, seems, of and by itself, unlikely to acquire a high degree of legitimacy or, in the long term, to command popular affections. Finally, in the absence of accompanying and widespread cultural changes it seems likely that the vested interests opposing such changes could rally much support and so contribute to a process of political polarisation. The consequence might be to erode those habits of restraint and tolerance which provide government by consent with some of its necessary cultural underpinning. Comparisons with Chile are generally unhelpful but they could point to the more extreme dangers of such a situation. Strategies for radical political change have realistically to assess the forces mobilisable in support of innovation and the strength of likely resistance. Not least, the possibility must be considered that radicals may more readily provoke mobilisation of their adversaries than the potential beneficiaries of their changes.

Corporatist Tendencies

A third option, seen by some as the likeliest medium term possibility, is the persistence of already significant corporatist tendencies within the British polity. Proponents of this view perceive a long term tendency for decision making to be increasingly a matter of inter-play between the state and major interest groups (notably business and labour) with the former tending toward a position of *primus inter pares.* Group leaders are seen as being incorporated into a network of decision making processes co-ordinated under state auspices. To employ terms used by Ghita Lonescu processes of 'concertation' take place implicating, at national level, all major sectional groupings and involving the implementation of bargains struck by governments with the most salient economic interests.[35]

This model does appear to explain much recent political history. Two queries, however, need raising. Firstly, the state of British industrial relations and the inability of official union leaders consistently to retain authority over their constituents indicates the highly imperfect nature of the incorporation process. Secondly, and by the same token, the ostensibly balanced nature of centralised tri-partite bargaining relationships between state, employers, and employees are not effectively underpinned by truly balanced bargaining relationships in the realm of work where high level decisions have eventually to be implemented. The trade union movement may, to varying degrees, be incorporated into national policy making processes (though even this must currently be in doubt) but in the industrial domain distrustful hierarchical relations, frequently characterised by poor communications, still generally prevail. Such a situation seems likely to compromise the stability or legitimacy of centralised industrial policy decisions.

Fraternity

The fourth option, for which this chapter pleads, is the attempt to build on or foster 'fraternal' values and practices within British society and so to promote a substantial shift in general perceptions of contemporary political dilemmas and of their possible outcomes.[36] The argument is for a fresh emphasis on the fraternal dimension of the French revolutionary triad and for renewed emphasis upon the abiding significance of individual and group relationships which this seems to imply. In making the argument it is suggested that the notion of fraternity can perhaps supply a framework within which some sort of balance or accommodation can be reached between the conflicting demands of liberty and equality. As experience of the other options indicates the tension between these two latter concepts cannot readily be resolved. Nevertheless, it is maintained that a way forward could perhaps be found by relating them both to a third and overarching notion of fraternity! By seeing the problem of equality as not just a somewhat abstract question of distributive justice, to be pursued for its own sake, but as an objective to be pursued in the interests of non-divisive or co-operative human relationships, it is hoped to suggest strategies that will point away from the remote bureaucratic authoritarianism of the command economy and of the positively illiberal society. Equally, it is hoped to point toward potentially liberating patterns of political participation and accountability that are not readily afforded by technocratic or corporatist models of political management.

Further clarification clearly involves additional attention to the meaning of 'fraternity'. Obviously it is a metaphor derived from experience of family life. It particularly relates to those family relationships characterised by some, at least, rough equality of treatment and by relatively substantial degrees of reciprocity. It contrasts with paternal relationships of a substantially hierarchical, subordinate-superordinate nature. As against the latter, 'fraternal' relationships might seem to imply divisions of labour and responsibility based on an underlying equality and on some shared decision making rights. They also apparently imply a capacity and willingness explicitly to acknowledge social inter-dependence, to engage in co-operative endeavours, to assume an equitably shared responsibility for the common welfare, to eschew clearly disproportionate portions of the collectively engendered rewards and to find some practical expression for such notions as communal solidarity or service. Equally, they suggest or point to networks of relationships capable of commanding the sustained affections of those concerned and conducive to the development of their social (or political) skills. Not least, they assume some potentiality for relationships in which the competitive, conflictual, individualistic, manipulative and authoritarian elements have some tendency to give way to more co-operative, voluntary, participant and democratic elements. Notions of 'fellowship' of the sort to be found, implicitly or explicitly, in the works William Morris and R.H. Tawney, might provide alternative ways of grappling with the same range of ideas.[37] Some understandings of the term 'community' would be in the same category.[38] They both seem to share with 'fraternity' a stress on the importance of symmetrical and co-operative relationships in determining a modern society's justice, legitimacy, cohesion and capacity for non-destructive conflict resolution. Equally, they may share with 'fraternity' a stress on the solidarity, the forging of stable identities and the establishment of personal (and group) significance which arguably derive from active experience of shared understandings, values and goals.[39] Such thinking is clearly at odds with classic liberal views of society as an aggregate of largely atomised individuals intent upon the maximisation of a rationally calculated self-interest. It is also somewhat at variance with those pluralist models (which are so potent in political science) which see politics as a constant and perhaps beneficient competition amongst a diversity of groups with roughly equal bargaining power. Rather there is an implication that viable polities ultimately suppose some avowed recognition of inter-dependence and some capacity for commanding loyalties that extend beyond the simply prudential.

The model of community here envisaged, it must be underlined, is not of a traditional circumscribed and perhaps parochial kind presupposing fixed hierarchies, rigid status distinctions and deference to traditionally ascribed authority. Actual or potential liberation from the constraints of this latter model has been represented as one of the historic achievements of modern, liberal bourgeois and urban society. Not least a theologian like Harvey Cox, in his *Secular City,* has pointed in this direction.[40] Nevertheless a hugely influential European sociological tradition extending from de Tocqueville through Tonnies to Durkheim has emphasised the collective and personal insecurity, disorientation and destructiveness resulting from the erosion of such communities within industrial society.[41] Spokesmen for the tradition assume the need for reforged communal ties for psychological health (both individual and corporate), social cohesion and if widely acceptable political institutions are to be sustained. They tend to see the impersonal functional relationships of modern industrial society as frequently inimical to the minimal levels of trust and shared belief arguably necessary for preserving social cohesion.

Such views have had an essentially conservative thrust, but it would be here maintained that those on the left would be unwise to reject such insights into possibly relevant non-material factors. As J. Osmond persuasively argues in his book, *The Politics of Welsh Devolution,* centralised state power, abstracted from substantially shared cultural understandings, may result in apparently remote, insensitive and seemingly non-accountable rulers.[42] The consequent alienation of the ruled may manifest itself in nothing more sinister than apathy but this may, in itself, register a decline in the legitimacy of the governors. By the same token writers like Osmond imply that the institutions most likely to elicit long term popular allegiance are those according at least some recognition to the importance of the quest for fresh forms of community. In special cases, like Wales, this may particularly involve building upon well established cultural identities. In all cases, however, a premium would seem to be put upon institutions (political and perhaps also economic) which are comprehensible to the governed, within which they may sustain some sense of personal political efficacy and which offer some incentive to participation. Not least, if the requisite 'fraternal' trust is to be nurtured there is a problem of maximising both vertical and horizontal communication — a problem perhaps only capable of resolution in organisational units of modest scale.[43] Thus, it could be argued, 'fraternal' skills and values may, initially at least, be best fostered, acquired and disseminated within relatively decentralised organisational frameworks which minimise obstacles to involvement and maximise the possibilities of constructive dialogue between governing elites and their constituents.

Participation may be too glibly invoked as a panacea for modern industrial society's ills. Its propensity for engendering fresh forms of conflict may be ignored. Likewise, as, for example, in Yugoslavia, there may be highly uneven rates of participation and a tendency for restricted elites still to retain quite disproportionate degrees of control.[44] Nevertheless, it should be observed that this particular example relates to a political culture largely devoid of precedents for effective participation. It also relates to a polity within which one political movement (albeit relatively decentralised) exercises hegemonic control. It seems conceivable that in Britain, with a somewhat more participant political culture and with the incentives of institutionalised political conflict, modified patterns of participation might just be forthcoming. There could be grounds for hoping that, in the long term, sufficient 'fraternal' skills and values could be fostered to engender some shift within Britain's prevailing political culture. The countervailing pressures of inertia and vested interest are not underestimated but it would be maintained that thought needs to be given to mechanisms likely to facilitate appropriate cultural modifications.

A very brief look at Sweden may confirm the importance of such cultural factors.[45] This is particularly the case given the success of Swedish social democrats in engineering changes which, though far from utopian, have arguably been of more widespread and abiding significance than those attributable to their British counterparts. Thus Sweden's institutional development, by contrast with that of Britain, has associated with the emergence of a political culture relatively supportive of egalitarian social democratic values and relatively unhospitable to traditional hierarchical norms. Sweden's prevailing consensus owes far more to the imprint of social democratic images of society than has, so far, been the case in Britain. In the latter country, therefore, radical reformers should perhaps pay particular heed to fostering deep seated cultural changes. Relatively modest institutional changes of the type alluded to above might be one modest but positive contribution to a strategy for nurturing such change.

Some radicals will object that their objectives presuppose a strong state whose effectiveness would be reduced by the diffusions of power proposed above. Likewise, it could be argued that the idea of community already articulated cuts across and weakens socialist ideas of class solidarity. It could even be maintained that communitarian ideas risk becoming an anarchistic rejection of necessary state authorities. Here, however, it is being tentatively argued that state authority, capable of promoting significant change, may need to be grounded on the popular consent and legitimating power which decentralised institutions, relatively close to the governed, might best engender. Naturally a careful balance has to be struck between central and peripheral authorities, and careful attention needs to be paid to their appropriate spheres of competence. Likewise, imagination and skill needs to be exercised in the containing of potentially centrifugal forces.[46] Nevertheless, a case is here being made for the diffusion of decision making responsibilities as an appropriate step toward more acceptable and 'fraternal' forms of state authority.

This effectively challenges those thinkers who regard 'fraternity' as such a generalised and abstract concept that it overrides or precludes loyalty to small scale humanising institutions and points realistically toward the aggressively intolerant solidarities of French revolutionary Jacobinism.[47] Here, rather than 'fraternity' precluding diversity and dissent, it is being hinted that the 'fraternal' society might best be promoted within a plurality of overlapping, interlocking and mutually reinforcing agencies, or 'schools', for the fostering of appropriate skills and values.

Naturally local or group loyalties constantly threaten to become of such mutually exclusive kinds that 'fraternity' turns to 'fratricide'. (Indeed, the destructiveness of intra-family feuds may incline some to abandon 'fraternity' as an appropriate metaphor.) Certainly, some understandings of 'fraternity' or 'brotherhood' do imply introverted exclusivity. A Masonic 'fraternity' could fall into this category. The challenge is to fashion an over-arching framework of democratic values, practices and institutions which may, to some extent, harness the self-interest of sectoral groups for communal purposes and set limits to the more destructive of sectional ambitions.

In constructing such a society it is suggested, following on from T.H. Marshall, that systematic attention be paid to the continuing extension of commonly shared citizenship rights.[48] The equalising tendencies arguably inherent in the deepened understanding and extension of such rights would seem to cut across and place potential restraints upon the destructively competitive forces operative in our society. Existing legal, political and welfare rights provide some restraining counter-weight to the divisive effects of otherwise unregulated market relationships. Part of the strategy for nurturing national political relationships of a somewhat more 'fraternal' kind seem to require imaginative building upon this legacy. Not least, there seems a need to interpret or spell out citizenship rights in ways that foster sentiments of reciprocity and shared responsibility for social welfare.

It is the relative absence of such sentiments from the individualism of middle class liberalism that, in Hobsbawm's view, helps to explain the low priority given to 'fraternity' in much radical political thought.[49] He further explains this low priority by referring to the relative ease with which liberty and equality can be translated into the small change of mundane political programmes and the relative difficulty of giving some substantive content to the apparently less defined notion of 'fraternity'. Finally, he asserts that it is those less privileged social segments, most likely to benefit from the articulation of 'fraternal' values, who are least capable of finding a distinctive political voice and putting their needs on the political agenda. Rather, as earlier observed, they may be constrained by other and dominant political values or institutions.

If Hobsbawm is correct, this seems to confirm that those preoccupied with 'fraternity' have not only to pay heed to institutional but also to cultural factors. In the midst of the complex interplay between cultural patterns and institutional frameworks efforts have to be made to shift prevailing perceptions of political realities and prevailing assumptions about the aims of legitimate political activity. Institutions which embody shape and reinforce prevailing values may require change if the values are to be modified. But, by the same token, viable institutional change may, to a significant extent, presuppose cultural change.

It is perhaps at this level that exponents of the Judaeo-Christian tradition (in co-operation with relevant secular groupings) can make a particular contribution. Certainly 'fraternity' as understood above seems compatible with at least some Biblical understandings of man and his destiny. It seems, to some extent, to square with Israelite ideas of a covenanting community and the importance of communal bonds for shaping personal identities. Equally, it seems readily compatible with the more universalist New Testament Christian ethic and Gospel insights into the abiding significance of reciprocal human relationships. New Testament emphasis on fellowship, service, non-coercive or non-manipulative relationships and the lowering of barriers between individuals or groups certainly could be seen in this way. Likewise, some understandings or versions of liberation theology could point in the direction of a society relatively free of instrumental or exploitative relationships. The development of such themes cannot be part of this writer's present remit. At this point it is simply being suggested that there are Old and New Testament clues pointing toward the vision of a more 'fraternal' society in which the personal and corporate aspects of man's being are held in some sort of balance and find more adequate forms of expression.

Thus, in the light of this, there seems the possibility of theological reflection and committed activity contributing to that shifting of perceptions which has been mentioned. This may entail efforts to influence the general thrust of particular public policies or the content of specific policy decisions. But it would also seem to entail a more general prophetic or educational role aimed at opening minds to new political possibilities, the promotion of radical questioning, the fostering of new forms of dialogue between ideologically divergent groups, and some reordering of priorities on the national political agenda. Religious institutions and groups, it is being suggested, could still find ways of contributing to some modification of our national political culture. Hopeful signs of commitment already exist but many unmet challenges remain.[50] Even in this allegedly secularised epoch churches can still command a hearing and retain not wholly insubstantial mass bases. There is even some reason for believing that they contain disproportionate numbers of political activists with access to positions of influence.[51] What may be needed are more energetic and carefully thought out strategies for capitalising on such resources. Not least, religious bodies, in their own lives, could perhaps be more self-conscious about the appropriateness of their institutions and the use or misuse of power entailed in such arrangements. That might give their witness, in this realm, extra credibility and perhaps generate fresh models of social or political involvement.[52] Such thinking could well pay attention to the problem of articulating and managing conflict rather than seeking to minimise or deny its significance.

Some Possible Policy Implications

In such a discussion it is clearly legitimate to request some indication of the practical policy implications of the line being pursued. The argument has deliberately been couched in largely theoretical terms. Moreover, the space is not available for proper treatment of the vast array of issues that could appropriately be raised. Nevertheless, a few simple and very brief discussion points can be presented if only to provoke the disagreement of those who have thought more deeply about the matters in hand.

Some of the policy implications have, in fact, already been hinted at. At the heart of the matter seems to be the legitimacy, viability and responsiveness of state institutions. The search after greater equality, on a basis of consent, suggested as a characteristic of the 'fraternal society', presupposes strong state machinery but machinery that derives much of its strength from the reserves of general popular support or trust upon which it can call. That, as already indicated, might imply radical thinking about the proper balance between centralised and decentralised governmental agencies, the appropriate scale of governmental operations and the opportunities for authentic consultation or participation made available to the general citizenry. Equally, it might imply reforms supportive of changed perceptions amongst established governing elites.[53] Thus, a higher degree of openness and accountability in the processes of government seems appropriate if still strong paternalistic notions of public service (characteristic of the best in the British civil service tradition) are to give way to more co-operative and clearly democratic attitudes.

Part of the same process might be a more general willingness on the part of official bureaucracies or servants to nurture and capitalise upon and, where necessary, institutionalise altruistic impulses within the polity. Richard Titmuss' classic study of Blood Doning Services, *The Gift Relationship,*[54] here provides valuable clues. As he showed, the British service, based on a purely voluntary and non-cash basis, contrasted markedly with those services characterised by commercial considerations. Not only could ample reserves of goodwill be voluntarily mobilised by the British system but that system also emerged as more efficient and more generally supportive of co-operative social relationships than, for example, its North American counterpart. As Richard Crossman indicated when meditating upon his ministerial experience, there seem ample opportunities for extending similar 'fraternal' principles to other areas.[55] He, for example, cited the more systematic involvement of council home dwellers in the management of publicly owned housing. Such enterprises might have a long term part to play in rendering official agencies more accountable and responsive to popular needs. They might also contribute to the sense of solidarity and political efficacy, particularly among the economically or culturally disadvantaged, which a 'fraternal society' presupposes.

The questions of legitimacy, accountability and participation also seem to be of central significance in the correspondingly vital realms of economic management and industrial relations. Here there are two particularly important but closely linked issues at stake. On the one hand there is the question of groping after more rational and equitable criteria for distributing the rewards of our economic system.[56] On the other hand there is the question of asymetrical power relationships within the industrial domain. The two are linked, not least, because economic planning endeavours, including incomes policies, have failed to command stable support from a trade union movement generally lacking the incentives needed for fuller co-operation in communal wealth creating enterprises. Thus, it can be argued, far more extensive industrial democracy, in both public and private sectors, is required if workers are to accord a higher degree of legitimacy to economic institutions and to state attempts to oversee their management. Indeed, this writer sides with those who tend to see radically reformed industrial relations as one necessary prelude to greater long term economic productivity. This link if correctly perceived, is particularly important because the wealth redistribution and greater communal welfare provision associated with a 'fraternal society' seem more readily obtainable, on the basis of some form of consent, within an expanding economy.

Clearly educational provision is one particularly relevant feature of the situation and appropriate educational policies are particularly important in the constructing of a more 'fraternal society'. Whether or not such policies need involve the complete abolition of private education is debatable. (This writer sees room for valuable experimentation within a specialised private sector). It does seem clear, however, that Britain's entrenched inequalities are associated with unequal educational opportunities and that any attempt to reduce inequalities must involve marked changes of emphasis in the educational sphere.[57] Indeed, nothing short of positive discrimination in favour of the disadvantaged seems likely to suffice. This is partly a question of evening out currently very uneven life chances. It is also a question of nurturing and widely disseminating the values and skills appropriate to a 'fraternal society'.

Finally, but most problematically, this discussion has to be set in its proper international context. The discussion has deliberately focussed on the British polity but in an era characterised by increasing (if still highly inadequate) awareness of international inter-dependence or of international patterns of exploitation it seems evident that 'fraternity' cannot be adequately understood in a purely parochial fashion. The vast complexities of this international dimension necessarily lie beyond the scope of the present discussion. It could be suggested, however, that the quest for a 'fraternal society' in Britain cannot be pursued in isolation. The image of 'fraternity' is borrowed from the narrow and bounded context of family relationships. Equally, as argued above, 'fraternal' values and skills may initially be best learnt within a relatively parochial context. Families, however, cannot live by and for themselves. The values and skills they nurture find expression within a wider context. Thus, in the international domain, the practicalities of world politics, as well as the imperatives of the Christian Gospel, suggest that our limited quest for 'fraternity' would have to be seen as part of a much more far reaching endeavour.

Notes

1. Halsey, A.H., *Change in British Society,* London, Oxford University Press, 1978.

2. Cf. Rawls, J., *A Theory of Justice,* London, Oxford University Press 1972, and Dahrendorf, R., *The New Liberty,* London, Routledge and Kegan Paul, 1975; cf. also Berlin, I., *Four Essays on Liberty,* London, Oxford University Press, 1969. A brief discussion of equality and relevant literature is in Rees, J., *Equality,* London, Macmillan, 1972.

3. For a sensitive criticism of Rawls' work cf. Barry, B., *The Liberal Theory of Justice,* Oxford, Clarendon Press, 1975.

4. Cf. Dahrendorf, op.cit.

5. Cf. Friedman, M., *Capitalism and Freedom,* Chicago, University of Chicago Press, 1962, and Hayek, F., *The Road to Serfdom,* London, George Routledge and Sons, 1944.

6. On the Latin American context, see Collier, D., (ed.), *The New Authoritarianism in Latin America,* Princeton, Princeton University Press, 1979.

7. Cf. Townsend, P., *Poverty in the United Kingdom,* London, Penguin Books, 1979.

8. For a statement of this general view, see Parkin, F., *Class Inequality and Political Order,* London, MacGibbon and Kee, 1971; also Lukes, S., *Power: A Radical View,* London, Macmillan, 1974.

9. Cf. Halsey, op.cit., also Goldthorpe, J.H., *Social Mobility and Class Structure,* Oxford, Clarendon Press, 1980, and Halsey, A.H., Heath, A.F., and Ridge, J.M., *Origins and Destinations,* Oxford, Clarendon Press, 1980.

10. Griffiths, R.T., *Government, Business and Labour in European Capitalism,* London, Europotentials, 1977.

11. Cf. Fox, A., *Beyond Contract: Work, Power and Trust Relations,* London, Faber, 1974.

12. Cf. Atkinson, A.B., *The Economies of Inequality,* Oxford, Clarendon Press, 1974; Wedderburn, D., (ed.), *Poverty, Inequality and Class Structure,* London, Cambridge University Press, 1974.

13. Goldthorpe, J.H., et. al., *The Affluent Worker,* 3 volumes, London, Cambridge, University Press, 1968-9. On 'meritocracy' cf. Young, M., *The Rise of the Meritocracy,* London, Penguin Books, 1958.

14. Cf. Jessop, B., *Traditionalism, Conservatism and British Political Culture,* London, Allen and Unwin, 1974.

15. Runciman, W.G., *Relative Deprivation and Social Justice,* London, Routledge and Kegan Paul, 1966.

16. Cf. Jessop, op.cit.

17. On the subject of deference see apart from the work of Jessop, McKenzie, R.T., and Silver, A., *Angels in Marble,* London, Heinemann, 1968; Kavanagh, D., "The Deferential English: A Comparative Critique", *Government and Opposition,* 6: 7, 1971, pp.333-360, and Newby, H., *The Deferential Worker,* Allen Lane, London, 1977.

18. On the Labour Party, see Howell, D., *British Social Democracy*, London, Croom Helm, 1976, and Minkin, L., *The Labour Party Conference*, London, Allen Lane, 1978.

19. One must of course be extremely careful about unduly general presentations of a Marxist viewpoint because of the many Marxist 'schools' or tendencies. For example, some would say that, in reality, present 'Euro-Communist' tendencies point in reformist directions not unreminiscent of once bitterly criticised social democratic positions.

20. Cf. Parkin, op.cit.

21. This theme is taken up in Halsey, op.cit., especially chapter 3.

22. Butler, D., and Kavanagh, D., *The British General Election of May 1979*, London, Macmillan, 1980.

23. For one, perhaps not very typical example of this decline as it affects the Labour Party, see Hindess, B., *The Decline of the Working Class Politics*, London, MacGibbon and Kee, 1971.

24. Cf. King, A., "The Problem of Overload" in King, A. (ed.), *Why is Britain Becoming Harder to Govern?*, London, BBC, 1976.

25. Birch, A.H., *Representative and Responsible Government*, London, Allen and Unwin, 1964.

26. Cf. Rose, E.J.B., *Colour and Citizenship: A Report on British Race Relations*, London, Oxford University Press, 1969.

27. On the regional issue cf., Osmond, J., *Creative Conflict. The Politics of Welsh Devolution*, Llandysul, Somer Press, 1978; Nairn, T., *The Breakup of Britain*, London, New Left Books, 1977, and Harvie, C., *Scotland and Nationalism*, London, Allen and Unwin, 1977.

28. Cf. Schonfield, A., *Modern Capitalism*, London, Oxford University Press, 1965; Smith, T., *The Politics of the Corporate Economy*, Oxford, Martin Robertson, 1979, and Hayward, J. and Watson, M. (eds.), *Planning Politics and Public Policy*, London, Cambridge University Press, 1975.

29. Cf. Halsey, op.cit., and Crouch, C., *Class Conflict and the Industrial Relations Crisis*, New York, Humanities Press, 1977.

30. Cf. Goldthorpe, J.H., in Wedderburn, op.cit.

31. Cf. Hirsch, F., *The Social Limits to Growth*, Routledge and Kegan Paul, London, 1976, and Ronald Preston's comments in *Religion and the Persistence of Capitalism*, London, SCM Press, 1979.

32. Bell, D., *The Cultural Contradictions of Capitalism*, London, Heinemann, 1976.

33. Macpherson, C.B., *The Political Theory of Possesive Individualism*, London, Oxford University Press, 1962, chapter 2.

34. Lane, D., *The Socialist Industrial State*, London, Allen and Unwin, 1976.

35. Ionescu, G., *Centripetal Politics*, London, 1975; also Middlemas, K., *Politics in Industrial Society*, London, Andre Deutsch, 1979; Harrison, R.J., *Pluralism and Corporatism*,

London, George Allen and Unwin, 1980; Winkler, J.T., "Corporatism", *Archives Européenes de Sociologie,* XVII: 1, 1976; and Winkler, J.T., and Pahl, R., "The Coming Corporatism", *Challenge,* March-April, 1975.

36. As will be evident such thinking draws very much on the legacy of R.A. Tawney particularly as expressed in *Equality,* London, George Allen and Unwin, 1952, and *The Acquisitive Society,* London, Bell and Sons, 1921; also cf. Illich, I., *Tools for Conviviality,* Harper and Row, 1973.

37. Cf. note above for reference to Tawney. On William Morris cf. *Three Works by William Morris* (with an introduction by A.L. Morton), London, Lawrence and Wishart, 1977.

38. On the idea of community, see Plant, R., *Community and Ideology. An Essay in Applied Social Philosophy,* Routledge and Kegan Paul, 1974; also Williams, R., *Culture and Society,* London, Chatto and Windus, 1961; and *The Country and the City,* London, Chatto and Windus, 1973.

39. On the subject of identity in a political context, see MacKenzie, W.J.M., *Political Identity,* London, Penguin Books, 1978.

40. Cox, H., *The Secular City,* London, SCM Press, 1965.

41. This tradition is surveyed in Nisbet, R.A., *The Sociological Tradition,* London, Heinemann, 1967, especially chapter 3.

42. Cf. Osmond, op.cit.

43. The problem of size is discussed in Dahl, R. and Tufte, E., *Size and Democracy,* Stanford, Stanford University Press, 1974.

44. On the general theme of participation, see Pateman, C., *Participation and Democratic Theory,* London, Cambridge University Press, 1970. On the particular case of Yugoslavia, see Denitch, B.D., *The Legitimation of a Revolution: The Yugoslav Case,* New Haven, Yale University Press, 1976; also Zukin, S., *Beyond Marx and Tito. Theory and Practice in Yugoslav Socialism,* New Haven, Yale University Press, 1976.

45. On the subject of Sweden, see Castles, F., *The Social Democratic Image of Society,* London, Routledge and Kegan Paul, 1978. His argument is summarised in *West European Polities,* 1: 1, February 1978.

46. For an interesting discussion by a political scientist of ways of managing powerful centrifugal forces in sharply divided societies, see Lijphart, A., *Democracy in Plural Societies,* New Haven, Yale University Press, 1977.

47. This is the burden of the article by Mount, F., "The Dilution of Fraternity", *Encounter,* October, 1976.

48. Cf. Marshall, T.H., *Class, Citizenship and Social Development,* Westport, Conn., Greenwood Press, 1964.

49. Hobsbawm, E., *New Society,* Vol. 34, November 1975.

50. For a survey of political involvement as it affects the Church of England cf. *The Church of England and Politics. Reflections on Christian Social Engagement,* Report by the Church of England Board for Social Responsibility, 1980.

51. For evidence of this as, again, it affects the Church of England, see Moyser, G., and Medhurst, K., "Political Participation and Attitudes in the Church of England", *Government and Opposition,* 13: 1, Winter 1978.

52. This point is discussed by Medhurst, K., and Moyser, G., in their contribution to Jones, K., (ed.), *Living the Faith,* London, Oxford University Press, 1980.

53. On the British elites of Stanworth, P., and Giddens, A., *Elites and Power in British Society,* London, Cambridge University Press, 1974, and Guttsman, W., *the British Political Elite,* London, MacGibbon and Kee, 1963.

54. Titmus, R., *The Gift Relationship,* London, George Allen and Unwin, 1970.

55. Crossman, R.H.S., in Halsey, A.H., (ed.), *Traditions of Social Policy,* Oxford, Blackwell, 1976.

56. On the subject of income distribution cf. Wootton, B., *Social Foundations of Wages Policy* London, Allen and Unwin, 1953, and Goldthorpe, J.H., in Wedderburn, op.cit.

57. Cf. Goldthorpe, op.cit. and Halsey, Heath and Ridge, op.cit.

8

Religion and The Persistence of Poverty — A Challenge To British Social Democracy And The Churches

John R. Atherton

The challenge of poverty for many Christians and social democrats is not only associated with its enervating effect on contemporary society. It is also connected with the effect of its persistence over generations on the moral credibility of a nation through its disruptive implications for the practice of caring politics and compassionate religion. It should come as no surprise that throughout the long history of industrialisation in Britain the issue of poverty and its treatment has cast its shadow over social policy-making in general and over the lives of politicians and churchmen in particular.

It was in 1903 that Edward Caird, the great Master of Balliol, urged Beveridge, the author of the modern Welfare State, and Tawney, the philosopher of social democracy, to go "to Poplar to discover why with so much wealth, there was also so much poverty in London."[1] In presenting the two young students with the challenge of poverty Caird was, of course, only repeating an imperative which had disturbed previous generations, for example in the question put to the House of Commons by the radical MP, Bright, in 1869 when he declared "Why is there so much poverty in this country? This is the great problem in comparison with which many of these piddling questions which sometimes occupy us are nothing."[2] That question regarding poverty and its persistence in the midst of plenty has been revived for our generation particularly through the publication by Peter Townsend, the last of "the three Ts" (the others being Tawney and Titmuss), of his magisterial survey, *Poverty in the United Kingdom,*[3] and through the reports of the Royal Commission on the Distribution of Income and Wealth. The latter has particularly reminded us of the persistence of poverty as inequality even in a period of rapid change.[4] It is through the writings of such men and the reports of such commissions that the issue of poverty in a modern industrial society is so vividly illustrated. Yet many of their insights also suggest that the question of the persistence of poverty can never be faced up to effectively if it is divorced from the question of the persistence of capitalism. Tawney's skill in particular was to understand the connection between poverty, capitalism, social democracy and religion. It is that relationship which warrants further exploration, particularly from the perspective of Christian social thought.

Concern for the poor and underprivileged, as Professor Preston has rightly reminded us,[5] is one of the great moral imperatives emerging out of the Judaeo-Christian tradition. Reflecting not simply a concern for the individual but also for society, it became transfused into a wider tradition which tested the moral adequacy of a social order by the quality of its treatment of the poor. It came to reflect the belief that there is "no touchstone, except the treatment of childhood, which reveals the true character of a social philosophy more clearly than the spirit in which it regards the misfortunes of those of its members who fall by the way."[6]

With the existence of poverty, Christians are therefore rightly concerned. With the question of its persistence, and particularly of its contrived persistence, they are less easily at home. Answers to this question could well have most awkward implications for current Christian thought and practice, and for the credibility of social democracy itself. The two are, of course, closely connected. Both have the avowed aim of being concerned with the pursuit of a more just society, and with the removal of poverty as gross inequality. It is not surprising, therefore, that between them there has grown an alliance based on mutual interest. Both are understandably threatened by the charge of at best condoning and at worst contriving the persistence of poverty as grave inequality. To examine the issue of religion and the persistence of poverty is consequently of some importance not only because it enables Christians to express their traditional concern for the poor. It also provides them with an opportunity to examine the future of social democracy in Britain, and in the light of this, to explore the Church's future contribution to society. The persistence of poverty is one of those issues which forces men and women back to the drawing board in order to recast basic political philosophy and theology, and to reconsider the role of the Church within society and its relationship to other social movements.[7]

With such an overall aim, it seemed best to begin this exploration in Part 1 with an examination of the nature, extent and explanation of poverty in contemporary Britain, paying particular attention to its continued existence in the form of gross inequality. It is to the question of the persistence of poverty as endemic in British social democracy that attention can then be addressed. By accepting the failure of social democracy to seriously erode inequalities, it becomes possible in Part 2 to begin the task of rethinking the moral imperatives and political strategies necessary for overcoming the persistence of poverty. Such an exercise should be connected with the ecumenical movement's concern to pursue a more just, participatory and sustainable society. It is therefore a task which has significant implications not only for the practice of politics, but also for the life and thought of the Christian Church. The latter may have much to learn from these wider considerations regarding the form and practice of its faith. Indeed it is hoped to show how secular insights emerging from the experience of Christians involved in the struggle to remove contrived poverty and inequality can be used to develop Christian social thought and practice beyond so many of its traditional limitations in this field.

Part 1: The Nature, Extent and Explanations of Poverty and its Persistence in British Society

Anyone who is aware of the great and recurring volume of evidence regarding the persistence and extent of poverty and inequality in British society[8] is forced to conclude that the building of a more just society, like the Kingdom of Heaven, "cometh not by observation". As Tawney wisely noted in his Preface to the 1938 edition of *Equality,* "what prevents effective action is, in the main, neither ignorance nor lack of resources but the absence of political will."[9] Despite Tawney's warning, however, there is a case for re-presenting the evidence regarding the state of the poor in British society today. After a generation of increasing and widely spread affluence,[10] and the election in 1979 of a Government committed to inequality,[11] the case for a more just and consequently more equal society has to be made once again. Unlike in 1938, 'the burden of proof' now rests on the critics of the economic and social inequalities examined in the next few pages, rather than on their defenders.[12]

Any brief survey of the nature, extent and explanations of poverty must inevitably be selective; it will always represent more an interpretation of a complex reality than a simple statement of fact. Despite such a limitation, compounded for example by current arguments over the measurement of personal wealth, it is possible to build up a picture of some of the main features of the poverty scene. Their presentation in the form of connecting the definition, explanation, and implications of poverty for policy-making represents an argument reflecting the complex inter-relationship between these three stages of analysis and practice. It confirms Townsend's careful judgment that "too commonly in the social sciences, we assume that the definition and measurement of the problem is independent of the conclusions for policy. In fact, they are embodied in each other".[13]

Definition: the nature and extent of poverty

There has been a growing awareness among Government officials and academics that poverty is more extensive than generally believed. In Townsend's major survey conducted in 1968-69, even measuring poverty by the state's standard with its limited definition of needs,[14] there were approximately 4,950,000 people (9.1% of the population) living in poverty.[15] A further 12,600,000 (23.2%) were living on the margins of poverty.[16]

There is an increasing recognition however, that poverty cannot simply be described and measured in relation to the more 'objective' view of hardship as developed by Beveridge in the inter-war years and relating to the physical efficiency of manual workers. Alongside the understanding of poverty as "hearing the babies cry because they are hungry or cold",[17] there, therefore, needs to be placed a view of poverty as relative deprivation. For so many families and individuals the problem is not as much being poor, as being poor in relation to others. In the words of a manual worker interviewed by Townsend's team, poverty is also 'when you can't enjoy life like everyone else".[18] Relative deprivation can therefore be understood as having "inadequate resources to make possible the style of living required or expected in the society to which one belongs, and as a result being excluded from normal living."[19] According to this definition, 14,000,000 (25.9%) were in poverty.

Regarding the defining of poverty, two further matters need to be carefully noted. First, an adequate analysis of poverty should be based on more than the concept of relative deprivation. Unless this happens, it will be open to the criticism that there will always be some people relatively poor in relation to others unless the aim of policies is a state of complete equality. Understandings of poverty as inequality should always therefore be complemented by understandings of poverty in itself. General labourers in the North West are poor in relation to other occupational groupings because of their vastly greater vulnerability to unemployment; they are also poor because that vulnerability can be measured in terms of the low income received from the state.[20] Secondly, it is important to note that the adoption of either the state or relative deprivation definition of poverty has major implications for the kind of social policy promoted by society. "What is at stake is whether a society adopts a starvation standard, destitution standard, subsistence minimum standard or a more generous and broader cultural minimum standard in legitimating part of its management of income distribution".[21]

Irrespective of the criterion chosen, perhaps poverty's most striking and disturbing characteristic is its all-embracing nature. There is a most marked correlation between poverty and the great arenas of employment, income, health, education and welfare. This characteristic of deprivation is in turn complemented by the concentration of poverty in certain social groups. It particularly affects the retired, one-parent households, families with three or more children, the sick and the disabled. To survey these different contours of deprivation obviously suggests a number of common strands, but the most disturbing and powerful is that of social class. The selection of class as the key fulcrum for understanding poverty emerges by virtue of its cumulative impact. For example, Townsend's survey reveals that there is a "steep increase in poverty in relation to descending occupational class".[22] It is the unskilled manual worker who bears the disproportionate burden of poor housing, bad health, and defective education. This concentration of the features of deprivation in social class V is particularly evident in the great shaping force of employment. Whether in the form of poor working conditions, low pay and the absence of fringe benefits, or in the form of a greater vulnerability to unemployment, it is the unskilled manual worker who bears and has borne the brunt of industrial poverty.

Faced with the cumulative evidence of deprivation as a persisting class phenomenon, there appears to be no way of avoiding the sad but disturbing conclusion that British society at least condones the existence of a substantial underclass of citizens. It is not simply that those living off unearned state benefits — the sick, the disabled, the children, the unemployed and the elderly — are thereby condemned, in the words of the Chairman of the Supplementary Benefits Commission, to "a miserable way of life".[23] It is also that even those with access to more resources through earned income include a sizeable minority (18.0%) who are paid wages at or only marginally above the poverty line.[24] To put such benefit and wage recipients together produces nothing less than an underclass in relation to the standard of life enjoyed by the majority of the population.

Poverty as inequality: the persistence of injustice

The perpetuating of myths unrelated to reality is not the monopoly of Christianity. One of the most disturbing examples of the contemporary dependence on illusions is the commonly held view that poverty as inequality either no longer exists,[25] or if it does, then it represents the remnant of a process which has witnessed the major erosion of inequalities over the last generation. That poverty still does exist on a large scale, has already been indicated. It is equally important, because poverty and inequality are so closely inter-related, to also explode the myth of a Britain moving towards any serious equality with regard to income and wealth distribution. To undertake this second piece of demythologising is necessary because the problem of the poor is not simply that they are poor, but that they are poor in relation to the rich. If Townsend is right when he declares that "the single most notable feature of social conditions in the UK" is the concentration of wealth in the hands of a small percentage of the population, then the premise has to be postulated and examined that "exclusion from access to weath, and especially from property", is perhaps the single most notable feature of the poor.[26] To do so is both to recognise the link between the definition and explanation of poverty, and to follow the acid advice of Tawney that the student of poverty "will be wise to start much higher up the stream than the point he wishes to reach; that what thoughtful rich people call the problem of poverty, thoughtful poor people call with equal justice the problem of riches."[27] The issue of the persistence of poverty, particularly in a capitalist society, cannot, without impunity, be handled separately from the issue of the persistence of wealth.

The perception of a growing equality of income and wealth in British society arose out of the limited redistribution of resources which occurred in the years from 1938 to 1949. That perception becomes a myth if we examine the longer period from the Second World War to the mid-1970s. It can then be seen that the picture, in the midst of great change, is rather one of "short-run fluctuations in a more stable and continuing inequality."[28] To be reminded of the shape and content of that inequality can be a salutary if not devastating experience. It reveals, with regard to the distribution of wealth, that the top 10% of the total population of this country in 1975, aged 18 and over, owned 60% of estimated personal wealth, whereas the bottom 80% owned only 23.8%.[29] The distribution of income statistics reveal a similar picture. In 1975, the top 10% of income recipients commanded 26.6% of all incomes, before tax, while the poorest 10% received 2.6%.[30] Perhaps most disturbing of all is the fact that the earnings of the bottom 10% of adult male manual workers have remained at 68% of average earnings not simply, as Professor Preston rightly notes, from 1953-73, but *from 1868* to 1970.[31] (Indeed, it was 1% less in 1970 compared with 1868!). If the figures from the definition and extent of poverty, and its disproportionate concentration in social class V, are used to reinforce and give content to these figures relating to the bottom 10% of adult male manual workers, then the persistence of poverty as inequality becomes one of British society's most oustanding characteristics. It confirms Routh's conclusion, after a detailed study of occupational and pay structures between 1906 and 1960, that "the most *impressive* finding was the rigidity of the inter-class and inter-occupational relationships".[32]

Explanations of Poverty

The existence of poverty demands far more than description; it requires of moral men explanations. The challenge presented by poverty to people of goodwill is surely to produce, in the light of accurate definitions and explanations, policies to remove it.[33] The search for adequate explanations of poverty is an essential part of any attempt by individuals, groups or society to attack the problem of poverty at its roots.

To explain the presence of poverty is not as much to identify its causes as to give an account of some of the factors which appear to underlie its existence. For instance, it means acknowledging that the nature, extent and persistence of poverty in a heavily stratified and highly unequal society cannot be regarded primarily as a matter of individual misfortune. When the proportion of the retired at or marginally above the poverty level reaches 64% their plight cannot be attributed to personal fecklessness.[34] To extend the personal defect explanation of poverty to the defective local community is similarly inadequate.[35] There are invariably more poor people outside the defined area than within it. The search for explanations has therefore to move beyond the personal and communal dimension into a wider societal one. As Tawney noted even in 1912, "there is a unity underlying the individual cases of poverty; . . . they are connected with social institutions, specimens of a type, pieces of a system. . ."[36] When two in every 10 is in poverty, then their predicament cannot be accounted for by personal or communal defect. One is forced to accept that "the very structure of opportunities has collapsed". "Both the correct statement of the problem and the range of possible solutions require us to consider the economic and political institutions of the society and not merely the personal situation and character of a scatter of individuals".[37]

It is to this relationship between poverty and social system that the attention of those who seek to account for the nature of poverty in Britain today should be directed. At least four factors substantiate such a conclusion:

i The power and rigidity of social and occupational hierarchies

Having already indicated the persistence of a pattern of inequality, it is important to recognise the inflexibility of that ordering in relation to the myth of class mobility. The latter is exploded by the persistence of an elite, and the failure to achieve mobility through educational means.

The economic and political dominance of a "tiny class" of individuals which attracted Tawney's reluctant admiration in 1938,[38] is as strongly entrenched today as it was 50 years ago. Although only 4% of the population receive a public school education, there is no "major institutional sector where less than half of those in top positions are from public school backgrounds".[39] 86% of army officers of the rank of major-general or above, 81% of principal judges, 73% of the directors of the largest industrial corporations, and 85% of Anglican bishops, are all from public school backgrounds.[40]

It is not simply that the dominant class contents itself, in Kautsky's words, "with ruling the government"; the disease of plutocracy has been compounded by the failure of the post-war educational system to generate any significant mobility between classes. In a recent study of social mobility in relation to education, Halsey and his team concluded that 30 years after the Welfare State there had been no significant reductions in class inequalities.[41] The structure of society is such that the chance of birth is still the principal passport to wealth or poverty.

ii The denial of access to resources to the poor

Of course, an inflexible social stratification implies not simply that a small percentage of the population has easy access to resources; the obverse side of the same coin suggests that others are denied such access. With regard to health in general, or infant mortality rates in particular,[42] and especially in relation to education, certain social groups have a disproportionately large share of available resources. Given an understanding of economics as the allocation of scarce resources,[43] this inordinate claim on limited resources by the few inevitably diminishes the share available to others.[44] Consequently, the denial of access to resources has to be given the most serious attention as a part-explanation of inequality and poverty.[45] It necessarily includes a recognition that the self-interest of the rich requires that they actively defend as well as promote their hold on resources.[46]

iii The influence of social stratification on public attitudes detrimental to the poor

The unskilled manual worker, although only a minority in the population, is part of a society which explains social position significantly in terms of individual motivation, skill and qualification.[47] It is precisely these work ethic virtues which result in the unskilled worker being categorised relative to the more established ordering in society; he has no status in his own right, but is always described as the *un*qualified, the *un*skilled and the *dis*advantaged. The obverse side of a society whose cardinal values are skill, thrift and self-reliance, is one which treats with suspicion those who fall out of work and are not able to practise the majority virtues. British attitudes to the poor clearly reflect in particular the negative side of this dichotomy. Their hostility to the poor should not be considered separately from a rigid social stratification. It is disturbing to note that in a recent EEC survey, 43% of the British interviewed thought the main cause of poverty was laziness or lack of willpower compared with only 25% of those interviewed in the remaining member states.[48]

iv The influence of politics in the perpetuation of poverty

The cumulative command over resources and the dominant life styles of key occupational groupings cannot be dissociated from the political impotence of the poor. The persistence of poverty as gross inequality through the denial to the poor of access to the generally accepted standards of living in health, education, work, housing, income and wealth, suggests at best the grave limitations of civil and political rights divorced from economic rights. At worst, it suggests the use of civil and political rights to perpetuate the denial of economic rights to a significant proportion of the population.[49]

In each of these explanations of poverty, certain strong characteristics begin to emerge. First, it becomes apparent that poverty is not simply a problem to do with the poor themselves. It is significantly concerned with the very ordering of society. Secondly, the ordering is both relatively inflexible and does appear to enable some groups and individuals to have an easier access to resources and to deny it to others. It is the latter groups which primarily constitute the poor, and it is such an explanation of poverty which constitutes such a challenge to social democracy. It is this understanding which leads naturally and necessarily to a critical consideration of social democracy's role in the pursuit of a just, participatory and sustainable society.

Since social democracy in Britain has always been concerned to constrain privilege in order to increase the access of the poor to the resources of the good life, the above definition and explanations of poverty clearly raise grave questions regarding its past and present practice. Indeed, it does far more, since it also questions its theory. By its emphasis on an equality of civil and political rights and its corresponding neglect of an equality of economic rights, and by its support of majorities and rejection of dispossessed minorities, it may well preclude any serious attempt being made to remove grave inequalities and poverty.[50] A forceful statement of this argument has been formulated by Frank Parkin. He argues that

> a political system which guarantees constitutional rights for groups to organise in defence of their interests is almost bound to favour the privileged at the expense of the disprivileged. The former will always have greater organising capacities and facilities than the latter, such that the competition for rewards between different classes is never an equal contest. This is not merely because the dominant class can more easily be mobilised in defence of its interests, but also because it has access to the all-important means of social control, both coercive and normative. Given this fundamental class inequality in the social and economic order, a pluralist or democratic political structure works to the advantage of the dominant class.[51]

If this critique of existing political systems is accepted, and if the concern is to promote a more just, participatory and sustainable society, then thinking and practice has to face up to a challenge not simply to the future of social democracy. It is also driven to examine most critically the social thought and practice of a British Christianity inextricably bound up with the current thought and practice of social democracy. At the heart of this whole argument is a recognition that the implications for social democracy and Christianity of the persistence of poverty are so far-reaching as to require the most careful consideration of both political theorists and theologians.

Part 2: What Can Be Done With Social Democracy and Christianity?

A commitment to the poor expressed through definitions and explanations of relative deprivation has serious and critical implications for the British experience of social democracy. Besides highlighting the latter's grave limitations, the commitment can suggest an outline way forward for social democracy. To that way, Christians should be able to make a useful contribution, given their traditional concern for the poor and for the practice of social democratic politics. The following outline is a first tentative sketch of some of the main features such a Christian contribution could take. It uses material from major British Christian social theologians, including Professor Preston, and from key socialist politicians and philosophers. Like any other contemporary model of a good society sensitive to the plight of the poor, it should be tested by the hard criteria of justice, participation and sustainability

A The Development of Social Democracy into a Just, Participative and Sustainable Society

In the face of persisting gross inequalities, any return to the drawing board with social democracy needs to take account of the importance of emphasising both vision and the implementation of vision. Without vision and its associated moral imperatives, no political programme can be sustained with purposive vigour either for any length of time or through any radical reshaping of the social order. Equally vision cannot be translated into the particularities of society except through the vehicle of a political programme and strategy. The test of whether a social democracy seriously concerned for the poor can be developed into a more just society will be significantly dependent upon recognising its potential for a radical refurbishing of its vision and programmes. That potential can be identified by examining how proposals relating to vision and programmes confirm the radical elements in the social democratic tradition and contradict its inegalitarian features.

The moral imperatives of vision

Any adequate political theory needs to include glimpses of the society it wishes to work towards. The promotion of a 'just, participatory and sustainable society' is no exception to this rule. What kind of society does this World Council of Churches' slogan suggest? The answer can be sought in the imperatives required to sustain such a vision, since they provide not simply a motivation for change but also suggest key features of what the change wishes to achieve. Tawney perceptively noted this significance of imperatives with regard to the third Labour Government's pursuit of egalitarian policies. He acknowledged that by 1950 it had run out of steam. Its visionary demand of equality had failed "to seize the imagination of our fellow countrymen", so that although the Labour Government had enlarged the range of alternatives open to ordinary men and women, it had done "little to remove from wage-earners (the) sense that they belong to a subordinate class". The failure to develop a "fire at the centre"[52] able to begin to achieve such a transformation is precisely why the question of moral imperatives, and the search of a "new moral standard" has to be addressed and attempted.[53] To do this today requires, as Professor Preston rightly notes,[54] a collaborative way of working which brings together secular and theological skills.

There are three particular reasons for advocating this procedure. First, the increasingly plural and secular nature of British society ensures that no one ideology, theology or discipline can ever represent accurately the truth of a situation. Secondly, the growing complexity of an advanced industrial society can only be engaged by a consortium of skills. Thirdly, the development of moral imperatives in relation to societal changes has normally emerged out of a fusion of preferences and value systems. This has been especially so, for example, in the case of equality, a principle central to both the Christian and socialist interpretations of a just society.[55] Deriving from at least Stoic, Christian and Rationalist origins, equality is one of those moral imperatives most obviously relevant to any political attempt to move beyond a society still so much shaped by poverty and inequality. It offers the opportunity to collaborate with a number of faiths and ideologies in translating a principle so closely associated with "a religious accent" into a secular society.[56]

There are obviously a number of moral imperatives which could be selected to illustrate what could be meant by the development of social democracy into a just, participatory and sustainable society. However, there are two which particularly emerge out of Christian-humanist-socialist perspectives and warrant further attention. Together they suggest a basis for a person-centred political anthropology, from which principles like equality could be derived. The first is the imperative of recognising the importance of a person as a person, and not a person as defined simply by his or her occupational role or place in the social order. It is what Tawney referred to when he wrote of an egalitarian society as one in which "money and position count for less, and the quality of human personalities for more."[57]

The second is the imperative which asserts that a person does not live by bread alone, and which continually seeks to develop and promote new values. "What we require are not always higher wages . . . or new and more refined luxuries. What we need is a kind of secular puritanism, simplicity, humility, daily service in communities of all kinds".[58]

Such human-centred imperatives, by rejecting "the tedious vulgarities of income and social position"[59], and by stretching beyond, although leading to, a concern for the poor, are probably essential for any sustained attempt to significantly erode the persistence of poverty in British society. They represent the belief that the fundamental values in society are in the end not to be evaluated by their economic advantage, but by "the type of individual character and the style of social existence" fostered by them.[60]

The four pillars of a political programme

As Tawney and the Fabians recognised, the key to political success depends as much on the ability "to make ideas viable" as on the skill of generating vision.[61] It is this pragmatism of British socialism which is reflected in the tradition of selecting four central pillars of policy; together they suggest the priorities of socialism and the means for attaining them.[62] It is precisely in this area of an "organisational programmatic coherence"[63] geared to the eradication of poverty as gross inequality that Townsend has least to offer; yet without it, there can be no achieving of the political power necessary for the creation of a more just and equal society. In the light of these pressures, four main policy areas particularly warrant careful attention. They relate to an industrial economy, the state, participation, and the collective provision of basic human needs. Within each, certain social democratic traditions as developed by men like Tawney and Preston can be questioned in the light of their failure to remove poverty from Britain. It is also possible to suggest ways forward out of these limitations by including within each main strategy area both short-term as well as long-term policy guidelines. Clearly, all four are closely interconnected. The first two are concerned more with the realities of running a modern industrial society sensitive to the concern for justice as well as viability. The remaining ones are more obviously derived from the two moral imperatives identified above. In each case, however, the imperatives are brought to bear on realities in strategic ways so that the economic and social arenas are engaged with a social purpose related to person-centred values sensitive to the poor. This means, for example, that the reality and power of the state, so denounced by many radicals, is not avoided but is appropriated as an instrument for achieving the radical social change necessary to reduce inequality.[64]

The first pillar is the recognition that the industrial economy is the most significant of the central determining realities of a modern urban society. This recognition is particularly necessary since it is so associated with the occupational stratification of British society with all its related inequalities and poverty. Clearly, the problem of maintaining the viability of a modern economy is highly complex, particularly if it is proposed to subject it to powerful social constraints. In this limited space, it is only possible to suggest that if the reduction of poverty and the creation of a more egalitarian society are social priorities, then certain key traditional practices of social democracy in maintaining that social and industrial viability need to be challenged. They can be described as the myths of the market and growth.

First, regarding the myth of the market system as being compatible with the pursuit of a just society, it is essential to ask how much reliance in a just, participatory and sustainable society, can be placed on "the market as an instrument for maximising public benefit."[65] To what extent, even in a command economy, can the market mechanism ever be considered as a neutral, value-free mechanism since nominally equal economic and social rights are unequally operative because of "unequal but equalizable conditions and opportunities"?[66] In a heavily stratified, welfare capitalist society like Great Britain, to perpetuate the myth of individual choice through a market economy by divorcing it from the determinative influence of occupational class is inevitably to perpetuate the persistence of poverty as inequality.

Secondly, in response to the argument that economic growth must be an integral part of any anti-poverty strategy, it needs to be recognised that there is little evidence to support the belief that growth is productive of equality. During the post-war Conservative and Labour Governments, a period characterised by considerable economic growth, the remarkable fact is the relative stability of gross inequalities and the actual growth of poverty. The social democracy of Crosland, with its emphasis on achieving equality "by making a go of the mixed economy", has not generated the greater equality to which he aspired.[67]

The pursuit of a just society therefore questions a too-uncritical reliance on policies most obviously associated with capitalism, whether they are considered in their own right or against the background of a mixed economy. An additional and more damaging criticism of the latter can be found in the writings of Preston and Demant.[68] Both suggest that capitalism's reliance on a questionable self-interest was successful because it was essentially able to live off the moral capital of a previous age which emphasised more social and altruistic virtues. On the basis of this argument how can the development of an effective social democracy be expected if it has to depend on the 'virtues' of a pre-war capitalist society about which it has been so critical? Indeed, how can social justice even be significantly achieved if that dubious legacy so dominates the present mixed economy? Against the backcloth of these arguments, the pressure from the considerations of poverty suggested in this paper is inevitably for a more critical consideration of a demand economy and a more careful understanding of a command economy. Indeed that pressure is accentuated by the current rapid deindustrialisation of Britain,[69] a process begun in the golden age of capitalism, and suggests a greater and more sophisticated public control of the economy in general and of capital and investment programmes in particular, if it is to be countered effectively.

The second pillar is the recognition that the state has to occupy the centre of any contemporary concern for politics and people. To engage the modern industrial state requires a prior liberation from the constraints of nineteenth century views of and arguments about the state.[70] It means recognising that the modern state is composed not only of a government and state apparatus but also of a wide range of institutions with a corporate bias.[71] In response to this collective reality, Preston is surely right to emphasise, in contrast to Demant, the need for a "high doctrine" of the state.[72] If Preston's position is accepted, then it is clear that the state cannot perform a neutral role in society; it must be seen to occupy a key role in the achievement of a just, participatory and sustainable society. By expecting the state to require bad people to do good things, as distinct from making good people do bad,[73] Preston rightly projects it into the centre of any struggle to reduce poverty as inequality. Such a perspective on the state has important implications for any consideration of the future of social democracy in general, but particularly when the latter is examined in relation to the challenge of the persistence of poverty. On the one hand, by asserting a strong view of the state, it rejects a recent tendency of social democratic thinkers like Marquand and Luard[74] to assume that the omnicompetence of the modern state can be counterbalanced by asserting the importance of community or locality-based decision-making.

On the other hand, two consequences flow from the approach to poverty adopted in this paper; each suggests a view of the state at variance with Marquand and Luard's, and supportive of Preston's. First, the claim to a disproportionate share of resources by key social and occupational groups achieved partly at the expense of the unskilled and semi-skilled drives those with a concern for the poor to resort to the state to hold the acquisitiveness of the privileged firmly in check. Secondly, the gradual reduction of the proportion of the population in social class V (and therefore of its voting power) similarly suggests a highly interventionist doctrine of the state if the self-interest of classes I and II is to be constrained in favour of the poor in social classes IV and V. Both pressures put flesh on Preston's hope for British Christianity of a more reforming and less conserving role by offering the means of a strong interventionist state for achieving it.[75] To do this however, is to move significantly beyond present social democratic theory and practice. Yet it is difficult to see how the stranglehold of inequality on the social order can be broken with anything other than the tool of the state used as the means to achieve, in Cole's words, a "constitutional revolution".[76] Such a step plainly breaks with the unqualified dependence by British social democracy on evolutionary gradualism. It also presumably calls for the practice of ruthlessness, a virtue which Cole detected in Tawney, and which contrasts with Preston's emphasis on Tawney's goodness.[77] Disturbing as such a conclusion must be for social democrats in general and British Christians in particular, it is difficult to see how either the social control of an advanced industrial economy or the serious reallocating of resources to the poor, can be achieved by anything less.

The third pillar is the recognition that the radical extension of democracy is of critical importance if an industrial economy and a modern state are to be in any way person-centred. The moral imperative of participation[78] has very significant implications for two key features of contemporary British society — for the running of an advanced industrial economy and for the directing of a modern state. Both have profound implications for the viability of social democracy. Regarding the first of these features, industrial participation, it is important to note that if people are to have a greater say over what happens to them at their place of employment, (always a critical test of the effectiveness of the extension of democracy beyond the political arena) then the development of forms of economic self-management becomes a matter of urgency. Yet the record of social democracy in this field in a mixed economy is at the best one of limited success. Under its control existing centres of industrial and economic power have been as reluctant to embark on genuine power-sharing as have the traditional holders of power in Northern Ireland. Public industry has been as 'managerial' in its resistance to experiments in power sharing as has private industry. Indeed, the latter, through the Confederation of British Industry, succeeded in the mid-1970s in resisting any major innovations in shared decision-making in British industry.

Regarding the relating of participation to the modern state, the previous analysis of poverty has revealed the importance of functional groupings for the ease of access to power. Any serious attempt to promote greater equality in decision-making will therefore need to take at least two steps. It will need to recognise the significance of functional groupings for man, and it will need to redistribute power from established and establishment associations to those denied access to positions of responsibility. Both policies stand in a well-established social democratic tradition of dispersing power to producer, consumer and community groups.[79] Yet both also challenge the aloof primacy of parliamentary democracy by reducing it to a position of *primus inter pares* with other functionally representative bodies.

The fourth pillar is the recognition that common humanity requires the collective provision of basic human needs, and that this needs to be radically dissociated from the social stratification prevalent in Britain today. In a complex urban-industrial situation, person-centred imperatives and the challenge of a just, participatory and sustainable society[80] suggest that society inevitably has a major contribution to make to meeting the basic human needs of housing, sanitation, health care and education. In the light of these analyses of poverty, and using the effectiveness of the treatment of poverty as a criterion of a just society, it becomes possible to see both the limitations of past and present social policies, and possible ways of remedying these defects.

First, a concern for justice and the poor confirms the value of Townsend's typology of social policy as a tool of social criticism. He rightly notes that previous welfare policies reflect the principle of conditional welfare for the few, and that present policies are based on the principle of maximum rights for the many.[81] The former emerged out of a capitalist society and the latter out of a mixed economy. With regard to the contemporary practice of maximum rights for the many, it is important to remember that Beveridge's intention as its main author was to strengthen and not weaken a market economy. Indeed, within the constraints of this framework, even his proposals particularly relating to the abolition of means-tested benefits, have not been implemented.[82] The initiators and administrators of the Welfare State have always been convinced that the existing social order required underpinning rather than radically recasting. It is not surprising, therefore, that the practice of social democracy has been to use Supplementary Benefits to meet more than needs; it has also been used to control behaviour in conformity with what is required in theory as socially desirable and in practice as confirming society's hostile attitude to the poor.

Secondly, given these criticisms of welfare policies, Townsend's preferred model of "distributional justice for all", if adopted, has three implications for any attempt to develop social democracy beyond its present stalemate. Each reflects a close connection with the previous three pillars of policy; each suggests that the common needs of a common humanity can only be met through the "destratification of society through economic, political and social reorganisation and equal distribution, and wider diffusion of all kinds of power and material resources."[83]

i Despite all the problems of cost and incentives, there are still very strong arguments for trying to reach in the longer term, Beveridge's goal of security against want without a means test.[84] The fact that children, the aged, and long-term unemployed seem to be particularly vulnerable to poverty suggests that in addition immediate effort needs to be concentrated on raising child benefits, occupational pensions, supplementary benefits, and earnings-related unemployment benefit.

ii The radical redistribution of income and wealth through a progressive taxation policy needs to be attempted, and particularly with reference to a carefully thought-out wealth tax;[85] and it needs to be acknowledged as only one tool in a strong egalitarian social policy. Unless, for example, private health and education are abolished or the public sector is made equal to them, there can be no serious movement forward in the reduction of grave inequalities.

iii There needs to be a massive re-education of public attitudes in order to develop a "less arduous attitude" to work and conversely a more sympathetic attitude to the poor.[86] Inevitably this would move society towards the yearly negotiation of all incomes with welfare benefits being accorded the same status as earned incomes.[87] As Lister wisely notes "progress towards eradicating poverty is likely to be limited so long as politicans sense a general hostility, or at best indifference, towards the poor."[88] This change of attitudes is an essential *complement* to all the proposed policy changes.

In each of these proposals the challenge of poverty is seen to be a recall to the importance of the practice of politics but now located within a wider strategy. Any explanation of poverty which points beyond the personal defects of the poor has to acknowledge the significance of politics within any attempt to counterbalance the persistence of poverty. Only through the collective action of politics can we achieve those "ends which cannot be attained with the same measure of success by individuals acting in isolation".[89] Yet the challenge of poverty is also a recognition that the politics of social democracy will always require more than a series of practical policies, indispensable though these are. It suggests that unless those policies are located within, and therefore shaped by, an overview of society, they will not sustain the kind of purposive activity needed to overcome poverty. One of the most telling charges against social democracy is that it has been guilty of a "philosophical indifference".[90] The construction of an ideology which moves significantly beyond current social democratic theory and practice because it recognises the realities of running a modern industrial economy but subordinates them to a people-centred society, is one of the most urgent tasks facing today's society.[91] Such a philosophy in an increasingly secular and plural Britain would represent a coalition of values and perspectives rather than an unbalanced concentration on one key to open all doors. It would work with federal and not unitary models, but would also develop a purposive coherence around its commitment to people-centred imperatives. Without such a coherence, pluralism would almost inevitably engender inequality in our kind of industrial society. Lastly, and most importantly, it would be judged by the quality of the society it produces, by its attitudes and policies relating for example, to those least able to care for themselves. The reconstituting of politics so that it carries forward the tradition of social democracy beyond social democracy can emerge out of a consideration of the persistence of poverty as inequality. Indeed, unless this is enabled to occur, there will be little moral future for social democracy because there will be little future for the poor.

B The Implications of Poverty for Christian Thought and Practice

There are a number of implications for the Churches which emerge out of the previous explanations of poverty and suggested ways forward for social democracy. They need to be taken seriously by Christians for three particular reasons:

First the Churches, given the Judaeo-Christian tradition and their incarnational faith, are rightly concerned with the quality of society in general and with the plight of the poor in particular.

Secondly the churches in Britain are inextricably enmeshed with society. Whether in the form of a close involvement with the growth of the Labour Movement and the Welfare State, or with the powerful remnants of a Christendom and establishment mentality, Christians have made major contributions to the emergence of welfare capitalism and social democracy. Since poverty, and therefore society's response to it, is so all-embracing, any consideration of that response has to recognise the nature of the churches' inevitable involvement in what has so far happened and in what could happen. The pressure to do so becomes even greater if it is suggested that the limitations of welfare capitalism and social democracy are both reflected in and reinforced by church thought and practice.

Thirdly in the light of a growing recognition of the value of inter-disciplinary work, insights arising from a consideration of poverty and social democracy need to be taken very seriously by the churches. Professor Preston's understanding of religion "as an independent variable, reacting reciprocally with economic and other factors",[92] clearly includes the valued influence of politics and economics on theology as well as the impact of Christianity on social policy.

The cumulative effect of these reasons suggests that it is both necessary and useful for the churches to be involved in the debate about poverty and social democracy. It also suggests that since the churches are part of a wider debate, they can only develop their policies and theology effectively if they are sensitive to the pressures emerging out of that debate. What therefore follows are tentative insights arising out of the William Temple Foundation's[93] work on poverty and social democracy which need to be taken seriously by the churches as they attempt to witness to their faith in contemporary society.

The Implications of Poverty for Christian Social Thought

The insularity of British life affects its theology as much as its politics. There is a Whig interpretation of the ways faith has been related to society which is as powerful as the Whig interpretation of history and particularly of social democracy. Both represent considerable achievement, but both also communicate a complacency based on the assumption that this sceptered isle has achieved "a natural equilibrium in society" which is proof against the shock of unemployment, poverty and relative industrial decline.[94] The achievements are seen, for example, in the gradual evolution of a balancing of apparent opposites as represented in the mixed economy, and in the British experience of social democracy. It is in relation to this unbroken socio-political history that Reinhold Niebuhr rightly identifies the contribution of a distinctive Christian ethic in Britain. But Niebuhr also noted the defect of this virtue. He rightly commented that Britain "may well maintain many forms of capitalistic injustice because of her inability to mitigate them more successfully than other nations."[95] It is to this same conclusion that the analysis of poverty in this paper moves towards. That conclusion suggests that the persistence of poverty as inequality is associated with the very ordering of society, including its expression as social democracy, and that British Christian social thought is inextricably bound up with both.

If this double-edged challenge of poverty to both social democracy and Christianity is to be faced up to, it is obviously necessary to examine ways of developing the latter's contribution to the serious erosion of poverty in relation to the suggestions made regarding the development of social democracy. One of the main problems for both is to see whether and how, in the face of great challenge, a tradition can be moved forward. By suggesting radical ways to so develop social democracy, the implication is clearly that a similar development of Christian social thought can likewise occur. For this to happen involves at least facing up to, and moving beyond, the two main problems of petrifaction and dilution which Tawney associated with the defective handling of any tradition.[96]

The *petrifaction* of British Christian social thought can occur, for example, when theologians are pressured to move beyond the limitations of a characteristically Anglican incarnational "theology of explanation"[97] and its close association with an evolutionary gradualism. Their development in its place, of a "theology of redemption" so often assumes the form of a Barthian either-or interpretation of doctrine and politics,[98] or an emphasis on eschatology. The former fails to take a serious enough account of Niebuhr's recognition of "the right and duty of the empirical and historical disciplines to subject religious symbols to scrutiny and criticism",[99] or of mediating structures of value (principles). The latter fails to face up to Stuart Hampshire's criticism of the emphasis in Christian and Marxist dogma on a "historical destiny, a path to salvation at the due time",[100] as a means of neglecting the significance of the contingent. Both, by avoiding secular skills and a commitment to the contemporary moment, are symptomatic of an unwillingness to take the modern context with the thorough seriousness it demands. By proclaiming what seems so often either an unchallengeable certainty or a confusing paradox, they preclude the development of a Christian social thought able to speak effectively through the kind of debate about poverty and social democracy noted in this paper.

The *dilution* of Christian social tradition can occur when, after avoiding the pitfalls of petrifaction, Christian thought then fails to develop an adequacy in any way commensurate to the complexity and achievements of secular thought and experience. Clearly, Professor Preston's advocacy of the development of theology through collaboration in multi-disciplinary and multi-experience work is a most valuable way forward. Yet equally clearly, it has rarely occurred with the attention to detail and continuity required for any really serious engagement with modern society. At its best it has been episodic, rarely getting to grips with the ongoing central determining realities of a contemporary industrial economy. It is interesting to note that even one of its most useful achievements, its emphasis on middle axioms, has too often been handled in ways divorced from a concern for vision, ideology and analysis. In this it has perhaps reflected social democracy's absorption with means rather than ends, with the state of the roads rather than where the roads are going.

In the face of these criticisms the growth of Christian social thought in relation to the poverty debate therefore appears to require certain key commitments. Through the process of collaboration they suggest, on the one hand, the development of all Christian theology in ways sensitive to the pressures from secular skills and insights. This would mean, for example, the rejection of unitary models and the reliance on any one key to open all doors. Instead, it would involve co-operating in identifying mutually-held moral imperatives and encouraging the emergence from them of a coherence which would provide purposive frameworks within which they could be located. On the other hand, it also suggests the development and organisation of Christian social thought in relation to the great shaping forces of contemporary society over a period of generations. Collaboration by theologians with others in debates over the economy, deindustrialisation, industrial relations, the Welfare State, and social democracy in relation to the Labour Movement is really so necessary and really so unlikely. Such a development would indeed be distinctive because it would endeavour to promote Christian traditions and beliefs within and through the realities of contemporary society. Involvement in the wider debate about poverty and social democracy offers precisely such an opportunity for precisely such a development.

The Implications of Poverty for Christian Practice

The emphasis on taking part in, and making a particular and distinctive contribution to, wider debates in society spells the end, as Professor Preston acknowledges, of any commitment to the Christendom ideal.[101]

Collaborative ways of working in an increasingly secular and plural society preclude any commitment to any unitary views of life. Given this pre-supposition, three implications for Christian practice of the preceding examination of poverty and social democracy seem particularly important.

i The need to re-examine the undue emphasis on what in the end can only be described as the philanthropy model of response to society.

From counselling schemes to community work, and from Manpower Services Commission unemployment schemes to 'drop-in centres' for the deprived, the churches' responses are deployed in a variety of activities which, among other things, are significantly supportive of a defective social order. In other words, they and we neglect Tawney's judgment that

> as a nation's industrial system is, so will its philanthropy be. Industry creates poverty by refusing to treat men as ends or respect their personalities. and when charitable people start relieving the poverty which an individual system of industry has produced, they show as great a contempt for the rights of personality as do the organisers of industry themselves. They seem to be alleviating distress while they really are the embodiment of the principles by which distress is produced.[102]

The examination of poverty and the limitations of social democracy, when used to critically survey most church activities, only confirms the disturbing wisdom of Tawney's words, written in Manchester in 1913.

ii The need radically to revise the exclusive emphasis on locality-based mission and ministry, whether of the parochial or chaplaincy kind.

Examination of the persistence of poverty clearly indicates the extreme inadequacy of any policy which fails to engage those causes and shaping forces which lie outside any locality whether the latter is in the form of a geographical area or an institution. These limitations of a locally-based ministry are only exacerbated by the experience that both parochial and chaplaincy models of ministry are inevitably more supportive of the established order than of any radical challenge to it.

iii The need to transform the churches' social alignments. All my experience suggests that the Church does not exemplify, in relation to the poor, "a sign of what the plural society should express in its structures."[103] It rather exemplifies a commitment to the people, values and institutions who are not unskilled, poor and marginal, but who are qualified, rich and establishment-oriented. Whether faced by industrial conflict or by poverty, the Church of England essentially represents a predominantly middle-class individualism looking from afar at predominantly working-class secularised values.[104] Nowhere is this better illustrated than in the attitudes of the members of the General Synod. Comfortably liberal on personal matters, they typify the self-interest of the middle-classes when faced with issues like nationalisation.[105] The traditional alignment of the churches with social classes I and II is equally clearly revealed in the class origins of church leaders (85% of bishops are still from public school backgrounds, even in 1979), and in the style of living adopted by most clergy and their families. Both perpetuate, if not accentuate, patterns of social stratification in Britain. When taken in conjunction with the persistence of a strong work ethic and vicious attitude to the poor, they all combine to confirm Townsend's disturbing observation regarding the strong relationship in his survey between occupational class and institutionalised religious practice in defective perceptions of and hostile attitudes to the poor.[106] It is difficult not to conclude that the life and witness of the Christian churches and their members in Britain are a significant contribution to the justification and preservation of poverty as inequality. They suggest a contrived relationship not simply between religion and the persistence of capitalism, but also between religion and the persistence of poverty.

What emerges out of these criticisms of church practice significantly confirms the implications arising out of the previous consideration of Christian thought. Both suggest the need for the churches to promote and organise a way of thought and practice able to engage the causes of great contemporary problems and not simply their symptoms. To do this effectively so that, for example, social thought and practice also recognise the distinctive contributions of the different levels of society, will require of the churches a greatly improved vision and commitment. If they are to do this in relation to poverty, then it will also demand a radical revision of their existing alignments,[107] patterns of ministry, and types of response. The values of the challenge of the persistence of poverty as inequality is that it both requires a radical re-formation and development of social democracy and Christianity, and also suggests some of the most important means for achieving them.

Notes

1. See unpublished Beveridge Papers, London School of Economics.

2. Quoted in "Society Today: Poverty", *New Society,* October 4th, 1979.

3. Townsend, P., *Poverty in the United Kingdom,* London, Penguin Books, 1979.

4. *Lower Incomes,* Report No. 6, The Royal Commission on the Distribution of Income and Wealth, London, HMSO, 1978, p.144.

5. Preston, R.H., *Religion and the Persistence of Capitalism,* London, SCM Press, 1979, p.48.

6. Tawney, R.H., *Religion and the Rise of Capitalism,* London, Murray, 1926, p.268.

7. Cf. David Donnison's advice to the poverty lobby in his review of Townsend, op.cit., in *Poverty,* 44, December 1979, p.28.

8. See Townsend, op.cit., and Tawney, R.H., *Equality,* London, Allen and Unwin, 1931, for catalogues of such evidence over the last 100 years.

9. Tawney, op.cit., p.29.

10. Preston, op.cit., p.15.

11. See the report of an interview with Mrs. Thatcher, *The Guardian,* January 29th, 1980.

12. Tawney, op.cit., p.27.

13. Townsend, op.cit., p.17.

14. This view leads to a limited definition of rights, and is based on basic supplementary benefit scales plus housing costs.

15. These figures represent 'income units' rather than households, since 71% of households consist of a single income. The Supplementary Benefits Commission also uses this criterion.

16. That is, with incomes up to 40% above the state poverty line. The choice of 40% was made because "the State observes a higher standard than the basic rates by disregarding . . . certain minor amounts of claimants' income and by adding, for certain claimants, small amounts to the basic benefits" (Townsend, op.cit., p.272).

17. Donnison, op.cit., p.24, quoting from Townsend's case studies.

18. Ibid.

19. I owe this wording to Andrew Morton of the British Council of Churches. W.G. Runciman's classic study, *Relative Deprivation and Social Justice,* London, Penguin Books, 1972, sees both relative deprivation and the concept of reference groups as reflecting the truism "that people's attitudes, aspirations and grievances largely depend on the frame of reference within which they are conceived" (p.10).

20. In the North West, in June 1980, there were 11,855 registered unemployed managerial and professional workers competing for 1,889 unfilled vacancies. At the same time and in the

same region there were 91,305 unemployed general labourers competing for 357 unfilled vacancies. We also know that in November 1979, the average Supplementary Benefit payment made to the long-term unemployed was £25.79p per week: *Department of Employment Gazette,* September 1980, and *Supplementary Benefits Commission Notes and News,* No. 18, September 1980.

21. *Poverty,* op.cit., p.12.

22. Townsend, op.cit., p.394. Over 50% of the manual unskilled are at or on the margins of the state's definition of poverty; see p.293.

23. *Poverty,* op.cit., p.25.

24. 1.7 million men, and 2.7 million women were paid at less than two-thirds average earnings: *New Society,* op.cit.

25. Over a third of Townsend's sample did not believe there was such a thing as real poverty today; see Townsend, op.cit., p.427. See also Golding, P., "Poverty — What Poverty?", *Poverty,* op.cit.

26. Townsend, op.cit., p.921.

27. Tawney, R.H., (Winter, J.M., ed.), *The American Labour Movement and Other Essays,* London, Harvester Press, 1979, p.112.

28. Townsend, op.cit., p.116.

29. Field, F., (ed.), *The Wealth Report,* London, Routledge and Kegan Paul, 1979, p.26.

30. Ibid., p.48f, cf. Preston, op.cit., p.31f.

31. Townsend, op.cit., p.139; Preston, op.cit., p.32. Inequality of access to resources includes far more than incomes and wealth; it also includes, for example, unequal access to welfare benefits; see Townsend, op.cit., p.156.

32. Routh, G., *Occupation and Pay in Great Britain,* London, Cambridge University Press, 1965. p.x.

33. Tawney, like Townsend, notes the important link between definition, explanation, and policy making; see Tawney, R.H., *Commonplace Book,* London, Cambridge University Press, 1972, p.45.

34. Townsend, op.cit., p.819.

35. For arguments against explaining poverty by reference to geographical areas, see *Understanding Inequality,* British Council of Churches, 1977.

36. Tawney, ibid.

37. Wright Mills, C., *The Sociological Imagination,* London, Penguin Books, 1970, p.15.

38. Tawney, R.H., *Equality,* London, Allen and Unwin, 1938 edition, Preface.

39. Giddens, A., "An Anatomy of the British Ruling class", *New Society,* October 4th, 1979.

40. A most useful and splendidly satirical description of the enclosed world of the ruling elite

can be found in Thomas, C., "Family and Kinship in Eaton Square", *The Wealth Report,* op.cit.

41. See Halsey, A.H., Heath, A.F., and Ridge, J.M., *Origins and Destinations, Family Class and Education in Modern Britain,* London, Clarendon Press, 1980. See also Goldthorpe, J.H., *Social Mobility and Class Structure in Modern Britain,* London, Oxford University Press, 1980.

42. See *The Report of the Working Group on Inequalities in Health,* London, D.H.S.S., 1980, (known as The Black Report).

43. Preston, op.cit., p.24.

44. Two consequences flow from this recognition. First, there is little need to fear that 'positional goods' will ever be other than scarce. The appropriation of resources by social classes I and II, and its persistence as a pattern, suggests there will never be a time when "everyone stands on tiptoe" (Fred Hirsch quoted in Preston, op.cit., p.34). Secondly, the recognition that the poor are denied access to resources to which others have easier access, adds a confusing dimension to Preston's otherwise useful recognition of the conflict between consumer and producer. The explanation of poverty suggested in these pages subsumes that conflict within a different and more powerful one. The poor as producer, in terms of the low paid worker, suffers from the same denial of access to resources as the poor as consumer (whether the latter be seen as style of life, pattern of consumption, or as access to the benefits of a Welfare State).

45. The argument regarding the denial of access to resources is equally relevant to explanations of Third World poverty.

46. Society contributes to this position by concealing the true nature of poverty and inequality, see Townsend, op.cit., p.18.

47. Townsend, op.cit., p.240f.

48. *The Perception of Poverty in Europe,* Brussels, Commission of the European Communities, 1977.

49. Miliband, R., "Poverty and Politics", in Wedderburn, D. (ed.), *Poverty, Inequality and Class Structure,* London, Cambridge University Press, 1974. Tawney was also particularly concerned with the persistence of a social cadre and described how Britain, in accepting political democracy, "changed her political garments, but not her heart", see unpublished Tawney Papers, London School of Economics.

50. On dispossessed minorities, see Townsend, op.cit., p.566.

51. Parkin, F., *Class, Inequality and Political Order,* London, MacGibbon and Kee, 1971, p.181f.

52. See unpublished Tawney Papers, London School of Economics.

53. Donnison, op.cit.

54. Preston, op.cit., p.23.

55. Preston, op.cit., pp.48 and 52.

56. Kolakowski, L., and Hampshire, S., (eds.), *The Socialist Idea*, London, Quartet Books, 1977, pp.74 and 76.

57. Tawney, *Equality*, 1952 edition, p.260.

58. Kolakowski and Hampshire, op.cit., p.73.

59. Tawney, op.cit., p.153.

60. Tawney, R.H., *The Radical Tradition*, London, Allen and Unwin, 1964, p.174.

61. Beveridge's comment on Sidney Webb, in Beveridge, W.H., *Power and Influence*, London, Hodder and Stoughton, 1953, p.167.

62. See, for example, Tawney, *The Radical Tradition*, op.cit., p.144, and MacBriar, A.M., *Fabian Socialism and English Politics, 1884-1918*, London, Cambridge University Press, 1962, p.343.

63. Kolakowski and Hampshire, op.cit., p.224.

64. The problem is not to avoid reality but to engage it. Tawney acknowledged this in his critique of the outright Christian condemnation of usury in the 16th century, see *Religion and the Rise of Capitalism*, op.cit., p.183f.

65. A myth accepted by Preston, op.cit., p.40.

66. Kolakowski and Hampshire, op.cit., p.80. Note that the introduction of 'market socialism' into Yugoslavia has resulted in the widening of incomes and life chances.

67. Jenkins, P., *The Guardian*, October 1st, 1979. (Jenkins is hardly a radical!) See Crosland, C.A.R., *The Future of Socialism*, London, Cape, 1956.

68. Preston, op.cit., p.34. V.A. Demant followed Tawney's *Religion and the Rise of Capitalism* with his *Religion and the Decline of Capitalism*, London, Faber, 1952.

69. For an increasing recognition of the deindustrialisation of Britain, with regard to the erosion of the manufacturing base and especially in relation to regional economies, see Roy Hattersley's review of Skeet, A., and Cook, C., *Post War Britain*, London, Penguin Books, 1979, in *The Guardian*, June 28th, 1979; and Hughes, J., *The British Economy: Deindustrialisation Gathers Pace*, Trade Union Research Unit Paper, Ruskin College, Oxford. Preston does not consider this vital factor in his economic analysis, op.cit., p.57f.

70. See Preston, op.cit., p.15, and Tawney, R.H., *The Attack*, London, Allen and Unwin, 1953, pp.93-5, on the Hayek controversy.

71. See Middlemas, K., *Politics in Industrial Society*, London, Deutsch, 1972.

72. Preston, op.cit., p.15.

73. Preston, op.cit., p.51.

74. See Marquand, D., *Rita Hinden Memorial Lecture, for 1980* (privately circulated), and Luard, E., *Socialism Without the State*, London, Macmillan, 1979.

75. Preston, op.cit., p.65.

76. Wright, A.W., *G.D.H. Cole and Socialist Democracy,* Oxford, Clarendon Press, 1979, p.215.

77. Both are mentioned in the Postscript by Hugh Gaitskell to Tawney, R.H., *The Radical Tradition,* London, Penguin Books, 1966, p.222f.

78. This imperative is particularly recognised by Preston, op.cit., p.48f.

79. From Guild Socialism to the current Institute of Workers Control. The idea of a social or industrial parliament standing alongside a political parliament is discussed, for example, in Barker, E., *Principles of Social and Political Theory,* London, Oxford University Press, 1951, pp.78-88.

80. As expounded by Preston, op.cit., p.51.

81. Townsend, op.cit., p.923.

82. *Poverty,* op.cit., p.18; see also Harris, J., *William Beveridge,* London, Oxford University Press, 1977.

83. Townsend, op.cit., p.64.

84. See Lister, R., "The Down and Outcasts", *The Guardian,* February 15th, 1980.

85. See *The Wealth Report,* op.cit., p.80f., for a powerful indictment of the last Labour Government's performance in this area.

86. Preston, op.cit., p.59.

87. The yearly review of welfare benefits and linking them either with average incomes or the rate of inflation suggests a move in this direction.

88. Lister, op.cit.

89. Tawney, *The Radical Tradition,* op.cit., p.89.

90. Kolakowski and Hampshire, op.cit., p.6.

91. This task is vastly different from the simple Christian association with neo-Marxist philosophy. This trend is revealed in Ambler, R., and Haslam, H., (eds.), *Agenda for Prophets,* London, Bowerdean Press, 1980.

92. Preston, op.cit., p.16f.

93. Founded in honour of Archbishop William Temple, based now in Manchester, concerned to relate Christian faith to contemporary urban society.

94. Holland, op.cit.

95. Niebuhr, Reinhold, *Christianity and Society,* 8: 3, 1943.

96. Preston refers to this well-known aphorism — "The fate of all great minds is dilution by the world and petrification by the elect" — op.cit., p.87.

97. See Ramsay, A.M., *From Gore to Temple,* London, Longmans, 1962, p.viii.

98. Donald MacKinnon is a classic exponent of this school, see his *Explorations in Theology, 5,* London, SCM Press, 1979.

99. Niebuhr, Reinhold, *Man's Nature and his Communities,* London, Bles, 1965, p.18.

100. Kolakowski and Hampshire op.cit., p.247.

101. Preston, op.cit., p.20. To remove all traces of the ideal obviously needs rigorous application over a period of years. If taken seriously, it would presumably lead to the disestablishment of the Church of England.

102. Tawney, *Commonplace Book,* op.cit., p.68.

103. This contrasts with Preston's view, op.cit., p.63.

104. I owe this phrase to John Hughes, Principal of Ruskin College, Oxford.

105. Preston, op.cit., p.60.

106. Townsend, op.cit., p.399.

107. Including the re-establishing of closer links with the Labour Movement.

Appendix
Prospects For Social Democracy In India

M.M. Thomas

The First World and the Fourth World

In this essay I examine the idea of social democracy as contrasted with the ideologies of capitalism and communism, and look at its approach to world poverty, especially to the task of liquidating the pockets of abject poverty in what is called the Fourth World, that is, the non-Western societies which are not oil-rich. India comes within this Fourth World. For an Indian Christian, therefore, it is more than an academic enquiry to ask whether there is a social democratic approach to the alleviation of the massive Indian poverty.

I take Ronald Preston's exposition of social democracy in *Religion and the Persistence of Capitalism*[1] as a starting point. As a Christian ethicist looking at the Fourth World, Preston affirms that their "crippling burden of poverty *must* be removed".[2] He is also sure that in a world which is interdependent, the rich societies *can* do a great deal towards it by creating an international order which makes possible not just the "'green revolution' (which in some ways has been a disappointment)", not only food reserves, but also "the kind of investment in Fourth World farming which builds up self-help and dignity and provides the basis for a growth in manufacture".[3] is no reason to doubt that this could be done within the framework of economic growth of the rich. "The likely scenario is still economic growth. Indeed it is possible that the vastly greater productivity from technical resources which is more and more characteristic of our time, may enable us to make a serious inroad into the appalling poverty which still cripples so many parts of the world".[4]

All this is at the level of moral idealism and technical possibility. But will the rich societies do it? Are there forces which necessarily compel them to do it? Here Preston strikes a rather pessimistic note. He makes three points in this connection.

i Christian realism demands the recognition that human history itself has no *inevitable* utopian direction. Preston rejects the belief that because the world is God's creation, and governed by laws of morality, any situation of injustice must create such inner contradictions which will compel it to correct itself in the direction of justice. "In my view", he says, "the rich nations, if they chose to take an economically isolationist stance, could organise themselves on an available resource base which they could sustain for generations. To assume that they could not is once again to assume that what is morally wrong will necessarily collapse. This is true in the long run, but the long run may be a long one indeed; and in the long run, as Lord Keynes said, we are all dead. It is hardly relevant to decision-making in the present".[5] He does not deny the Wrath of God in history. But none of "the theories of the inevitable collapse" of the affluent societies can be deduced from it. It is clearly possible for them to decide "to live in a wealthy ghetto in a global slum" and get away with it.[6] In fact his estimate is that "after the brief check to growth we are now experiencing, our Gross National Product will continue to grow in the next decade and after that, at an average rate of about 3% per annum".[7] He says, "In fact there is no evolutionary tendency at work to produce either the collapse of capitalism or the advent or collapse of socialism".[8] This is true not only nationally but also internationally. By this Preston does not want to let the rich off the hook. It means rather that Christian ethicists should not only educate the moral conscience of the West but also investigate the technical-political power levers which can reinforce the morally desirable goal of responsible world order. As he puts it: "There is much cogency in the prayer which ends with the words, 'Save us Lord by love, by prudence and by fear'. God needs to use all the means at his command to weld recalcitrant humanity into tolerable coexistence and co-operation".[9]

ii Arising from the above argument, Preston considers that the creation of an international economic order which does justice to the poor society of the Fourth World is primarily a political task. How is the wealthy West going to use its wealth? This, to Preston, is an absolutely crucial question but the answer should be translated into a power-morals combination to be effective. But what are the levers of power available in the situation? He suggests that the rich societies need to "be shown that their long-term interest is the same as that of the developing countries" and "must search for ways of showing the unpleasant political consequences to them in the kind of world that will result if they pay no attention to the needs of the poor".[10] Preston does not seem to accept the "over-dramatic" ecumenical study arguments that limiting, stabilising or reducing the growth rate of the West is absolutely necessary for increasing the quality of its life or for bringing material growth to the non-Western societies. "In fact both could grow together, as has been happening for some time including the years of 1973 to 1977". And its continuity "depends very much on the behaviour of the rich, whose priorities in the use of their wealth needs to change".[11] He says: "In the long term of humane and just world is a gain for all, but in the short term the wealthy are only too likely not to see beyond their immediate interests. Will they learn in time?".[12]

iii Preston asks whether the Fourth World itself has any power-levers to operate to change the policies of the richer societies. He sees none.

I should be happier if I thought the Fourth World could exercise some pressure on us, on the grounds that in the political realm it is those who can exercise pressure by their votes or by their economic policies that are likely to be attended to. I do not see the Fourth World being able to exercise that pressure to any great extent, even if it were united to a greater extent than it is. The case of oil seems an exception.[13]

It is doubtful if the tactics of the OPEC countries with respect to oil can be used in respect of any other commodity needed by the wealthy, whether copper or aluminium or phosphorous or uranium.[14]

He repeats this idea of the weakness of the Fourth World.

How can the Fourth World exert enough pressure on the other worlds to secure that the vast resources of these worlds are used towards a more just international economic and social order? It seems clear that the comfortable do not take seriously the burden of rectifying injustices until the under-privileged both become articulate and have enough strength to make a dint on them. The Fourth World has become articulate, but it is in a weak position against the other worlds whose economic and technological power gets relatively greater than theirs.[15]

If there are no effective political power-levers, what is left? Preston says:

Therefore if fear and prudence may not be very powerful motivators of the wealthy, we are left with love; or if that is too deep a term for what can be expected, we are left with an appeal to a sense of common humanity or the unity of mankind".[16]

Clearly a very ineffective weapon in Preston's social democratic philosophy. From these premises, Preston rightly contents himself by advocating the promotion of social justice in the area of the world where it is possible.

It seems to me that if we in the United Kingdom resolutely tackle our own problems in terms of a just and sustainable society we are much more likely to make the right contribution toward such a global society, and not merely one for the wealthy West.[17]

It is in a way refreshing to listen to a Christian philosophy of realistic calculation. It is clear however that Preston does not offer any hope to those of us who are of the Fourth World. His Christian realism seems to stand on the verge of, if not already turning into, an apocalyptic despair, not unlike that of the advocate of limits to growth, but in this case from the viewpoint of advocacy of international justice. And in fact Preston's "Reflection on Theologies of Social Change"[18] ends with this apocalyptic note. But an Indian Christian is bound to ask whether this is not giving up the battle before it is joined, and therefore creating rather than recognising a situation of moral powerlessness. Does Preston suspect it himself when he says that his approach might become a weapon for the rich; but that truth must be spoken even if it happens?[19] This raises the ideological question of the relation of academic truth to praxis in Christian ethics. But the more important questions are two. First, whether the inner contradictions, not only economic, but moral and spiritual, of the rich societies when they choose to live in a global slum, have been seen by Preston at depth? Equally have the factors in the Fourth World which could be translated into political pressures on the rich societies, been underestimated? Possibly it is only the drowning Fourth World man trying to catch at the straw. Second, is there not a resource of political power itself in a determined minority's spiritual commitment to a messianic enthusiasm with willingness to suffer the cost? Preston points to this truth in his comment on

Karl Mannheim's and early Reinhold Niebuhr's justification of Utopianism. But is it right to call utopian dreams, which are necessary to create a new reality beyond the existing reality, "illusory" or "misleading" as Preston has done?[20]

This is not unrelated to the question of faith, where does the power of the resurrection as a spiritual dynamic of history, through and beyond the cross, overcoming the forces of death, come into Preston's calculation? In this context, what is the difference between moral idealism and spiritual dynamic? Maybe Preston is conscious of this dimension when he says:

> At any rate in the West, governments are influenced by their electorates and respond to pressures. It is also in the West that Christians are strongest and still represent in most countries a significant element in the electorate. Is it possible that they could become more alert and informed and thus politically more effective![21]

Paths of Self-reliance in the Struggle Against Poverty

Devoid of support form any emerging international economic order, the paths open to the Fourth World in their struggle against their poverty are of self-reliance. Preston seems to look at the language of self-reliance with understanding but with some suspicion. He says:

> They are also beginning to talk the language of self-reliance and of detaching themselves from the economic giants. It is easy to see why. They want to be free from the ties of what they call neo-colonialism. However it is not yet clear from the study material how self-reliance is to relate to the necessary and proper interdependence of the people of the world. The wealthy could also begin to detach themselves, and self-reliance is no gospel for the richer parts of the world; it would be an invitation to selfishness.[22]

That is trying to have it both ways. If Preston is correct in his analysis and forecast already made that the wealthy will go the way only of neo-colonialism and selfishness, and not the way of "the necessary and proper interdependence" of a just international economic order, he cannot turn round and condemn the path of self-reliance, which the non-Western world takes in its desperation to free its economy from neo-colonial exploitation as far as possible.

Preston however is very conscious of the revolutionary ferment at work in the societies of Asia, Africa and Latin America as the following paragraph shows:

> Here the speed of change is even more traumatic, as traditional societies are hit by the effects of the technology of the West without the infrastructure of social and political institutions which developed in the latter in the last century. Tribalism and caste system are instances of additional complications. Half the population is under twenty-nine and it is set against authoritarian and bureaucratice structures and restlessly in search of a new future, broadly interpreted as a socialism of self-management. Awareness of growing economic disparities between their world and the rest has led to a growing demand for a greater share of affluence, and a more fundamental demand for liberation from oppressive power-structures, both neo-colonial and domestic, and by force if necessary ... Meanwhile the influx into the cities of the Fourth World is becoming a cascade. Driven from the villages where there is no work, people settle in the shanty towns on the edge of the cities where there is also no work, and where the restraints of village life no longer hold. This is perhaps the most potentially explosive social factor of all.[23]

Only China has attempted a radical economic and social transformation of the situation by giving political expression to the fundamental demand of which Preston speaks, "for liberation from oppressive power-structures both neo-colonial and domestic", and for a new pattern of "socialism of self-management". This was of course achieved by "force". Preston sees in the Chinese communist society a pattern of command economy which has largely solved the problem of poverty and unemployment and reduced the inequality to "the ration of eight to one". He recognises that the Chinese revolution has "clearly proved in many respects a creative change", and sees in Maoism "a kind of Marxism *semper reformanda*" which he hopes will continue to "leaven the Chinese lump and prevent undue fossilisation" of the revolution. This and their this-worldliness without the "secularised biblical undertones which are unmistakable in Soviet Marxism" makes Maoist China theologically significant for Preston.[24]

In fact it may be said without contradiction, that even if Preston's argument that Marxism is an error with respect to 'facts' and interpretation of economic history in the West, is true, Marxism in some form or another provides the framework within which many intellectuals of the non-Western societies have been able to interpret the oppressive power structures which produce mass impoverishment of their people. More especially the nature of the tie-up between the colonial/neo-colonial forces on the one hand and the domestic oppressive structures on the other, in which technological development and economic growth itself produce more poverty. At this point there is more 'scientific' truth in the Marxian analysis than Preston allows. This is the clue to the Fourth World radicalists' emphasis on liberation as a condition of proper development (understood as technological and economic development achieving liquidation of poverty) and on the self-awakening and the organised struggle of the poor for justice as the condition of eventual stability and modernisation of society. This is also the clue to the liberation theologies of Latin America, which Preston examines.[25]

At this point there is not much difference between the communists and the non-communist socialists of the Fourth World in their approach. And they both accept conflict as the path to social change. The difference lies in their different valuations of the role of the democratic checks on power in the framework within which conflict takes place and in the structure of the state in the new society. The socialists learning from Stalinism are more aware of the betrayal of the human ends of the revolutionary changes inherent in the means used in the struggle and in the one-party structure of the state in the new society. In this context some of them have become too afraid of conflict and power policy and have lost the nerve and therefore the leadership to the extreme Left or Right. Preston's discussion of the role of conflict and power policy in his critique of R.H. Tawney is enlightening in this respect. Socialists who tend "to ignore the inevitability of social conflict" are only leaving it to the communists "to stress it" or to the status quo monopoly capitalists and landlords who "stress it as a permanent condition of life".[26] This is where on the whole the ideology of communisim has so far scored over the ideology of democratic socialism or social democracy. One may add, this is probably where China scored over India in the struggle to liquidate poverty — at least in the first round. This is also the appeal of the Chinese path and Maoism for the Fourth World.

The Social Democratic Path of India

If China followed the communist path of revolution by force, India under Gandhi and Nehru has chosen the non-violent and democratic path towards social transformation.

Actually Chinese communists could succeed to revolutionise Chinese society by force, not only because of the ideological strength of the Communist Party of China under Mao but also because of the war situation and the absence of a strong central state power in that country. The political situation in India has been different. The Gandhian non-violent leadership in the struggle for national freedom and the peaceful transfer of power from Britain to India, the centralised state with its strong civil service and army, and the education into and experience of the structure of parliamentary democracy created a climate in which peaceful and democratic means of social change had their appeal. Nehru's commitment to the ideology of socialist democracy was very strong too. He consciously rejected Caesarism of any hue because, as he himself put it, it would prevent or prolong the self-awakening of the masses into a mature responsible people. And he, like Gandhi, believed in revolution from the bottom, which democractic struggle made possible. And they both believed that the cost of violent revolution would be too high. It is thus that the dominant ideology in India turned out to be democratic socialism broadly defined. It is a combination of Marxism, liberal socialism and Gandhism.

But the crucial question is, Can this democratic path succeed in liquidating abject poverty in India? Only history can answer that question. But even now some issues in the democratic struggle against mass poverty are becoming clear:

i Economists including Christian economists like S.L. Parmar and C.T. Kurien have shown that Indian poverty is not solved merely by emphasising technological development for economic growth. Kurien in his recent study *Poverty, Planning and Social Transformation*[27] has shown how accentuation of mass poverty is related historically to the change from a "need-based" traditional economy to a "want-based" modern economy; and how poverty for the masses and plenty for the upper 10% are parts of one system, each producing the other; and how development resources introduced into the system accentuate rather than relieve poverty. The 'green revolution' (which Preston speaks of having been disappointing in its results) is an illustration. It left the landless labour in the same old impoverished situation. Kurien's study emphasises the necessity to give institutional transformation number one priority in India's planning for development if it is to tackle poverty and unemployment.

And Parmar has constantly argued for making social justice the condition of economic growth. He and many other Indian economists have been arguing also for giving up the idea of India catching up with the West in economic development, and for going for a pattern of development through appropriate technology[28] which is both small scale and labour intensive, and able to utilise the indigenous resources. This is in fact a modified form of Gandhian decentralised economy meeting basic needs but curbing wants and consumerism; and at the same time making participation in decision making possible for people in matters affecting their economic life. In fact Gandhi also wanted the state structure to be decentralised as far as possible to make direct democracy real to the people. No doubt for a large country like India large scale centralised key industries and a centralised state are necessary; and their social control and people's participation in them have to be through some form of representative democracy. But direct democracy in decentralised economic and political units is the proper basis for representative democracy of centralised power, as Preston himself has indicated.[29]

ii As Ambedkar the leader of the Untouchables of India and Ram Manohar Lohia the Indian socialist used to say, India's poverty is not just economic in character, that there are three sources of oppressive power in Indian society which are interdependent: property, social status and religious culture. The landless labourer is also the outcaste oppressed by traditional religions. If there is to be a dent on poverty, there should be simultaneous fighting on economic, social and cultural fronts. Incidentally one may add that all development projects have this three-fold dimension in India, as perhaps elsewhere. The programme of population control which India has been promoting for many years vigorously[30] has not made sufficient headway precisely because of the difficulty of integrating the various dimensions of life it touches. Indeed, at this level reformed religion and secular ideologies have their role to play.

iii A democratic state can become the instrument of radical change in economic, social and cultural life of the people and promote measures for the social participation and welfare of the hitherto submerged sections of the people, for example: Untouchables, Tribals and women, only if they themselves put pressure and engage in organised struggle for their rights. At present the bureaucracy, the political parties, the legislative and other organs of public life tend to be controlled by people drawn from the upper castes and classes. Therefore democracy has tended to buttress the oppressive caste-class power-structures of India, though at the time of elections votes are bought from the poor with promise of liquidation of poverty. Even if some of the controllers have good intentions, they cannot implement radical policies of structural change unless there is political pressure from the bottom layer, through organised agitations and struggles. It is through such struggles that the people understand their situation and become the subjects of change, rather than objects of charity, or welfare, or even technically engineered revolution from the top. The mass must become the people exercising responsibility and participating in shaping their own future. In any Christian aproach to India's struggle against poverty, this aspect of social democracy needs special stress.

Indeed, Indira Gandhi's Emergency showed that when the people's demands for structural change, opportunities to participate, and welfare measures get strong, the ruling classes are likely to take the path of suppression of democracy and its human rights. On the other side, there is also the danger of religious communalism asserting traditionalism and destroying the secular democractic framework for religious and cultural pluralism. Against these trends, social democrats must build up with those communists practically committed to the democratic path, a left democratic front. At the same time social democracy must recognise also the political cost if it fails and has to give way to a more militant communism with totalitarian ideas as the instrument of India's social revolution to liquidate poverty.

Notes

1. London, SCM Press, 1979. With one exception in note 27 below, all references are to Preston's book.

2. p.30.

3. Ibid.

4. p.35.

5. p.56.

6. p.35.

7. p.57.

8. p.38.

9. p.122.

10. p.57.

11. p.56.

12. p.143.

13. p.123.

14. p.56.

15. p.143.

16. p.123.

17. p.58.

18. Chapter 7.

19. p.56.

20. p.155f.

21. p.143.

22. p.55.

23. p.142f.

24. See pp. 36, 117 and 142.

25. pp.151ff.

26. p.95.

27. Madras, Indian Council of Social Science Research, 1978.

28. Preston seems to advocate it too, cf. p.55.

29. pp.48 and 77-79.

30. Cf. Preston's impression of the Fourth World, p.55.